Getting Started with Secure Embedded Systems

Developing IoT Systems for micro:bit and Raspberry Pi Pico Using Rust and Tock

Alexandru Radovici
Ioana Culic

Apress®

Getting Started with Secure Embedded Systems: Developing IoT Systems for micro:bit and Raspberry Pi Pico Using Rust and Tock

Alexandru Radovici
Wyliodrin, Bucharest, Romania

Ioana Culic
Wyliodrin, Bucharest, Romania

ISBN-13 (pbk): 978-1-4842-7788-1
https://doi.org/10.1007/978-1-4842-7789-8

ISBN-13 (electronic): 978-1-4842-7789-8

Managing Director, Apress Media LLC: Welmoed Spahr
Acquisitions Editor: Aaron Black
Development Editor: James Markham
Coordinating Editor: Jessica Vakili

Distributed to the book trade worldwide by Springer Science+Business Media New York, 233 Spring Street, 6th Floor, New York, NY 10013. Phone 1-800-SPRINGER, fax (201) 348-4505, e-mail orders-ny@springer-sbm.com, or visit www.springeronline.com. Apress Media, LLC is a California LLC and the sole member (owner) is Springer Science + Business Media Finance Inc (SSBM Finance Inc). SSBM Finance Inc is a **Delaware** corporation.

For information on translations, please e-mail booktranslations@springernature.com; for reprint, paperback, or audio rights, please e-mail bookpermissions@springernature.com.

Apress titles may be purchased in bulk for academic, corporate, or promotional use. eBook versions and licenses are also available for most titles. For more information, reference our Print and eBook Bulk Sales web page at http://www.apress.com/bulk-sales.

Any source code or other supplementary material referenced by the author in this book is available to readers on GitHub via the book's product page, located at www.apress.com/ 978-1-4842-7788-1. For more detailed information, please visit http://www.apress.com/ source-code.

Printed on acid-free paper

Table of Contents

About the Authors

Alexandru Radovici has a PhD in the field of mobile computing and works as an Assistant Professor at the Politehnica University of Bucharest, teaching subjects related to operating systems, compilers, and Internet of Things. Alexandru believes in the power of education and teaching is his passion, so 14 years ago he founded an NGO that focuses on organizing IT educational events. Alexandru is also the co-founder and CEO of Wyliodrin, being in touch with the latest IoT technologies. Alexandru has been a contributor to Tock, adding boards such as the STM32 Discovery Kit and the micro:bit and adding support for screens and touch screens.

Ioana Culic is currently a PhD candidate in the field of Internet of Things and the co-founder of Wyliodrin, a company that offers educational and industrial IoT solutions. She is a Teaching Assistant at the Politehnica University of Bucharest and has also been teaching IoT technologies to high-school and university students at different events for the last five years. Despite the technical background, writing has always been Ioana's passion and she managed to mix the two. She has published several articles in magazines such as *MagPi* and *Make* and books on Internet of Things technologies. Ioana has been porting Tock to the RP2040 microcontroller.

About the Technical Reviewer

Sai Yamanoor is an embedded systems engineer working for an industrial gases company in Buffalo, NY. His interests, deeply rooted in DIY and open source hardware, include developing gadgets that aid behavior modification. He has published two books with his brother, and in his spare time, he likes to build things that improve quality of life. You can find his project portfolio at http://saiyamanoor.com.

Acknowledgments

We would like to thank the Tock Core Team for their support, especially to Leon Schürmann (University of Stuttgart) and Branden Ghena (Northwestern University). Their feedback has been very important and has helped us greatly improve the book's contents.

A special thank you goes to our colleagues Ștefan Dan Ciocîrlan and Jan Alexandru Văduva from the University Politehnica of Bucharest for their suggestions that helped us improve this book.

Thank you all for your support.

CHAPTER 1

Embedded Systems and Architectures

Computers have been around us for many years. Even though most of us think of computers as boxes attached to a keyboard, a mouse, and a display, most of the computers used today are nothing like that. They are machines that crunch numbers, and they are everywhere. All the home appliances or even our cars have a computer inside; some have even more than one (e.g., in the case of a car, there is a computer that is driving the engine and another one that displays a friendly interface inside your vehicle and allows you to listen to your favorite song while driving). The Cloud we often refer to consists of large computers that look like boxes with blinking lights stored in large cool-aired rooms. The personal computer that we use daily, a laptop or a phone, is just the tip of the iceberg. Like most icebergs, the great majority of computers are not *visible* as they are *embedded* into devices, performing computations needed for the devices' functioning. These are called *embedded computers* or *embedded systems*.

The Eagle Has Landed

The first time computers were embedded into physical systems takes us back to NASA's Apollo program. Due to the complexities involved in maneuvering the Apollo spacecraft, in the 1960s, NASA turned to MIT's Instrumentation Laboratory (nowadays a not-for-profit research institution

© Alexandru Radovici and Ioana Culic 2022
A. Radovici and I. Culic, *Getting Started with Secure Embedded Systems*,
https://doi.org/10.1007/978-1-4842-7789-8_1

called Draper Laboratory[1]) for building a computer that could help astronauts fly the space vehicle safely to the moon. This is how the Apollo Guidance Computer[2] (AGC), one of the first *embedded systems*, was built.

As we can notice in Figure 1-1, the AGC looked very different from the computers we are familiar with today. Having the capabilities of a small chip, the Apollo Guidance Computer was built as a big ruggedized box, shielded to withstand the harsh outer space environment. The computer did most of its work without any human intervention. Astronauts could interface with the AGC using the *display and keyboard* interface (DSKY), also called the *dis-kee*. As the primary purpose of the AGC was to control the spacecraft, it had dedicated interfaces capable of reading and controlling various subsystems like the RADAR, the Telemetry Link (link to NASA's control center), and the engines.

Now, let's take some time to analyze the main hardware parameters of the AGC. The core was a 16-bit (15 information + 1 error detection) silicon integrated circuit (what we usually call a CPU today) capable of running at a clock speed of 2.048 MHz, with about 4 KB of RAM and approximately 72 KB of Program Memory (what we call today a read-only storage system). This is the powerful computer that flew us to the moon. To put it in perspective, your social media profile picture is 10,000 times larger than the AGC's RAM, and the simplest *Hello World* program that you could write would not fit into the Program Memory.

---

[1] www.draper.com/

[2] Details at: ftp://ssh.esac.esa.int/pub/ekuulker/Apollo15/The-Apollo-Guidance-Computer-Architecture-and-Operation.pdf

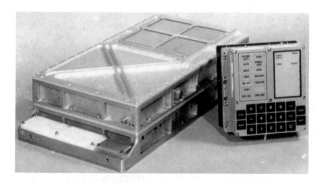

Figure 1-1. *The Apollo Guidance Computer (AGC, left) next to the display and keyboard (DSKY, right) interface*

Note   We will discuss the *Hello World* problem a little bit further. Just keep in mind that computers were much simpler at the time, and security was not a pressing issue as most of the things were not available for the public and were designed behind closed doors.

The user interface of the AGC, the DSKY, was specially designed for the Apollo spacecraft mission. Figure 1-2 shows the functions it provided. It is a little different from what we call today a display and a keyboard. It had several status lights like Altitude (ALT); Velocity (VEL); Tracker; a numbereh yrfd keyboard; some functional buttons like VERB, NOUN, or ENTER; a processing indicator; and some seven segment displays for displaying numbers.

If you think of it, this is very similar to today's buildings' alarm system interfaces that have a status display and a keypad for entering the alarm password and some functional buttons. In fact, both computers have more or less the same specific purpose, to control an extensive system according to particular needs. If we think further, this kind of interface is still used in many appliances, like an oven or a coffee machine.

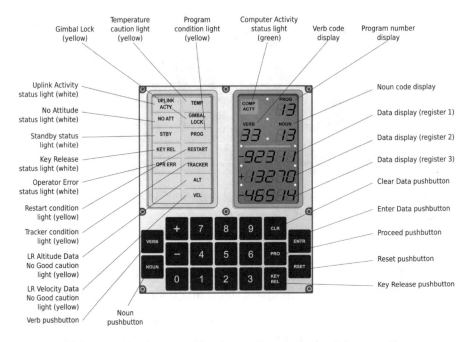

Figure 1-2. *The display and keyboard interface of the Apollo Guidance Computer*

The Architecture of a Generic Embedded System

The AGC was the first *embedded computer system*, as it was the first computer whose primary purpose was to take control of an extensive system, in this case, a spacecraft. Since then, embedded systems have become more and more complex and widely used. Nowadays, most of the electronic devices and appliances, cars, and other familiar objects that we use on a daily basis have an embedded computer inside.

Recently, following the expansion of the Internet, these embedded systems have started to be connected, creating what we call today the Internet of Things (IoT) field. Good or bad, all of the devices that we interact with will eventually be connected. While the advantages of this are pretty clear, we have smarter devices that can work with much more information and offer us faster access to information. The downside is still pretty much unknown. One of the significant issues the IoT field is facing is security.

As embedded systems were usually small computers with a specific purpose, software was written with functionality in mind rather than security. Most systems were not accessible from the outside, so there was no real danger of tampering. However, things are changing, and once these devices get connected to the Internet, a remote access path is opened. In this context, when building an IoT system, it has become the duty to assume that anyone with access to a computer or phone connected to the Internet may get access to the device. This brings changes to the way software for these devices has to be designed and built. With an increasing number of security attacks, the industry slowly acknowledges this problem and looks for more and more ways to deploy secure software.

Throughout this book, we will tackle the security issue related to the IoT field and focus on building and securing embedded systems. To this end, we will look into a new operating system for embedded devices, called Tock. The main characteristics of Tock are that it is one of the few operating systems written in a programming language different from C and that it has been built from the ground up with security in mind.

Now that we have a better idea of what an embedded system is and how these devices get integrated into our lives, let's look at the main components of a basic embedded system.

Note   Throughout this book, we will refer to an embedded system (or embedded platform) as the main component of an IoT system. It is important not to confuse the two, as we look upon the IoT system as a more extensive infrastructure that relies on sensors, gateways, and embedded platforms to create ambient intelligence. While smart home or crops monitoring solutions are considered IoT systems, the embedded platform is the component or components that control the whole platform.

A generic embedded platform consists of the following elements:

- A central processing unit (which might have several processing cores)

- A central bus

- A working memory unit, usually called RAM (random access memory)

- A program storage unit, usually improperly called ROM (read-only memory), EEPROM, or flash

- Several input/output interfaces

- An Interrupt Controller

- A debugging interface, usually JTAG or SWD

Figure 1-3 shows how these components interact with each other.

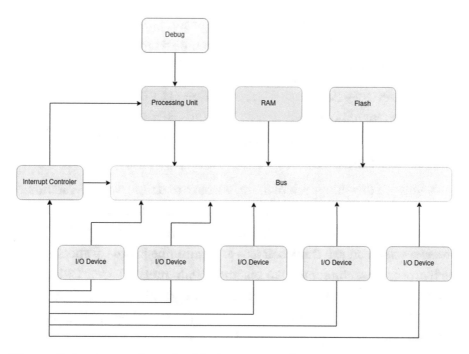

Figure 1-3. *A generic embedded system architecture*

Further on, let's get into the details about each of the components and take a look at some examples of actual existing devices.

Central Processing Unit

The central processing unit (CPU) lies at the heart of any embedded system. It is a microprocessor that performs mathematical computations, moves data around the system, and handles interrupts received from the Interrupt Controller (IC). While there are a lot of manufacturers that provide CPUs, almost all of them fall into one of the four architectures:

- **ARM** – Advanced RISC Machine, the CPU that we would usually find in a phone

- **MIPS** – Microprocessor without Interlocked Pipelined Stages

- **x86** – Intel and AMD's CPU architectures, in other words the CPUs that we find in our desktop and server computers

- **RISC-V** – Berkeley's fifth generation of CPU architecture (read as RISC Five), an open source standard that anyone may produce without the need to pay royalties

Before we dive into each of them, we have to define what ISA stands for. ISA, or Instruction Set Architecture, is an instruction definition, a standard. It defines what the instructions or commands known to a processor are. You can think of it as a programming language specific to each processor architecture. For instance, both Intel and AMD CPUs know how to process the sysenter instruction as they both implement the x86 ISA. ARM processors do not know this instruction as they implement a different ISA.

AVR

The AVR family of processors is probably one of the most used educational and prototyping embedded systems as it contains the *ATMega* and *ATtiny* chips that power the Arduino board. Designed in 1996 by Atmel, these chips are 8-bit microcontrollers capable of running at around 20 MHz. When they were created, these CPUs were more than enough for running alarm systems or automotive computers.

Tip   As a fun fact, the AVR chips, the ones that are the most popular in education, were themselves designed by two students, Alf-Egil Bogen and Vegard Wollan, at the Norwegian Institute of Technology in Trondheim. The name AVR is most probably an abbreviation for Alf and Vergard's RISC processor.

On the other hand, nowadays, most embedded systems require more processing power and more complex features, primarily due to their connection to the Internet, so AVR chips are slowly being replaced with more powerful architectures like ARM or RISC-V.

AVR chips are not powerful enough to run an embedded operating system, so we will not be focusing on them throughout this book.

PIC

The Programmable Interface Controller or PIC has been around for many years. It was designed in 1975 and was intended for the PDP general-purpose computers. PIC's popularity decreased as chips like the Intel 8080 or Apple's, IBM's, and Motorola's PowerPC became the standard for general-purpose computers. Finally, it was acquired by Microchip in 1985 and repurposed as an embedded systems' microprocessor.

PIC chips come in several flavors, ranging from 8-bit CPUs to 24-bit CPUs. With speeds up to a few MHz, PIC chips are frequently used in alarm systems and simple automation. Similar to AVRs, PIC CPUs are being replaced by more powerful architectures like ARM and RISC-V.

Until the appearance of Arduino, the PIC architecture was the most popular for embedded systems. Microchip, the manufacturer of PIC, has recently acquired Atmel and is now producing both PIC and AVR processors.

ARM

Formerly known as Acorn RISC Machine, now known as Advanced RISC Machine, ARM is the most commonly used ISA for embedded systems. Several producers like Apple, Samsung, Broadcom, NXP, Qualcomm, STMicroelectronics, or Nordic Semiconductor provide ARM CPUs. Of course, all of them have to pay royalties to Arm Holdings, the owner of the ARM ISA.

ARM has three CPU profile types:

- **Cortex-A** – Application, designed for running powerful computer systems, usually phones and tablets.

- **Cortex-M** – Microcontroller, designed to run low-power systems; most of the embedded systems will use this type of CPU.

- **Cortex-R** – Real time, designed for real-time and safety-critical embedded systems like the ones used in transportation.

Cortex-A processors, also called CPUs, are mostly used in powerful computer systems. They are very similar to the CPUs we know and use in our desktop computers. Operating systems like Windows, Linux, and macOS run perfectly on these CPUs. Unlike the ones we use in our desktop computers, Cortex-A CPUs are provided in the form of an SoC or System on a Chip. Manufacturers embed the CPU, the RAM, and sometimes the storage flash into a single chip, called an SoC. Speeds vary from a few MHz to a few GHz, and memory sizes range from a few MB to a few GB.

In this book, we will focus on the Cortex-M profile. These CPUs are also called MCUs or microcontroller units. Unlike Cortex-A CPUs, these SoC usually have only a few KB of RAM and a few MB of storage. The speeds may range up to a few hundred MHz. These chips are not capable of running full-fledged operating systems. Thus, they run simpler operating systems like FreeRTOS.

Cortex-R CPUs, also called MCUs, are very similar to Cortex-M but optimized for real-time applications.

MIPS

Designed in 1985 by MIPS Technologies, a Silicon Graphics spin-off, MIPS CPUs have been widely used in servers, home appliances, and automobiles. Sony's PlayStation and PlayStation 2 used MIPS, and Renault used it in their car infotainment systems. Nowadays, MIPS is used in most home network routers.

Interest in MIPS has been declining recently, with many of the CPUs being replaced by ARM.

x86/x64

The x86 ISA has been designed by Intel and licensed to AMD. This is what is commonly known as *a 32-bit system*. Desktop and server computers have been running based on these CPUs for many years. They are being used as high-end embedded systems, mostly where Windows is a prerequisite. In 2014, Intel designed an x86 processor series especially for embedded systems, named the Intel Curie. Arduino 101 was powered by this CPU.

The x64 ISA, officially known as AMD64, has been designed by AMD and licensed to Intel. Most CPUs in desktops and servers run using this architecture. These CPUs are a newer and more powerful version of the x86.

As these CPUs are designed for high-power embedded systems, we will not be discussing them in this book. We suggest reading an Embedded Linux[3] book for further details.

RISC-V

Probably the hottest topic in the field of embedded systems is RISC-V. Designed by the University of California, Berkeley, RISC-V represents Berkeley's fifth generation of ISA. Unlike the ISAs described earlier, RISC-V is an open ISA that does not require licensing or royalty fees. Any manufacturer can freely implement a CPU with the RISC-V ISA.

---

[3] Sally Gene, *Pro Linux Embedded Systems*, www.apress.com/gp/book/9781430272274

The ISA standard development is governed by RISC-V International, a not-for-profit organization based in Switzerland. The development process is very similar to one of open source software.

Unlike ARM, RISC-V does not provide a set of CPU profiles but provides several standards that can be combined. Some of them are still under development, so some changes might appear in the future. These standards are split into two categories: base and extensions. Table 1-1 shows the current base standards and their status.

Table 1-1. *RISC-V base standards version and status*

Name	Description	Version	Status
RVWMO	Weak Memory Ordering (the memory interface instructions)	2.0	Stable
RV32I	Base Integer Instruction Set, 32 bits	2.1	Stable
RV32E	Base Integer Instruction Set for embedded systems, 32 bits	1.9	Proposal
RV64I	Base Integer Instruction Set, 64 bits	2.1	Stable
RV128I	Base Integer Instruction Set, 128 bits	1.7	Open

The base standards are enough to have a fully functional CPU. A quick note here regarding the integer numbers instruction set: it contains only addition and subtractions. This has been specifically designed this way to support very low-end implementations. Several extensions have been discussed and adopted. Table 1-2 shows the extensions and their version and status.

Table 1-2. *RISC-V extension standards version and status*

Name	Description	Version	Status
M	Standard extension for integer multiplication and division	2.0	Stable
A	Standard extension for atomic instructions	2.1	Stable
F	Standard extension for single-precision floating point	2.2	Stable
D	Standard extension for double-precision floating point	2.2	Stable
G	Shorthand for the base I and extensions MAFD (general)	–	–
Q	Standard extension for quad-precision floating point	2.2	Stable
L	Standard extension for decimal floating point	0.0	Open
C	Standard extension for compressed instructions, useful for memory-constrained embedded systems	2.0	Stable
B	Standard extension for bit manipulation	0.92	Open
J	Standard extension for dynamically translated languages, useful for languages like Python or JavaScript	0.0	Open
T	Standard extension for transactional memory	0.0	Open
P	Standard extension for packed-SIMD instructions	0.2	Open
V	Standard extension for vector operations, useful for graphics acceleration and machine learning	0.9	Open
N	Standard extension for user-level interrupts	1.1	Open
H	Standard extension for hypervisor	0.4	Open
ZiCSR	Control and status register (CSR)	2.0	Stable
Zifencei	Instruction-fetch fence	2.0	Open
Zam	Misaligned atomics	0.1	Open
Ztso	Total store ordering	0.1	Frozen

The naming of a RISC-V CPU is in the following format: RV bits extensions. For instance, RV32IAM is a 32-bit integer instruction set with the A and M extensions.

The RVxG is the actual general-purpose CPU, having integer numbers with multiplication and division, both floating-point number precisions and atomic primitives. The x defines the word length as 32, 64, or 128.

While ARM, x86/64, and MIPS CPUs might have several processing units in one single chip, called *cores*, RISC-V processing units are called *harts*.

Several manufacturers are already providing RISC-V CPUs, the most popular being SiFive and lowRISC. Boards like the HiFive Rev B[4] and SparkFun Red-V[5] are already available for purchase.

While purchasing a RISC-V board might seem like a good idea, the RISC-V standard is still changing, and extensions are added. Most of the manufacturers offer free of charge their RISC-V CPU in the form of an FPGA bitstream. For research and development, we recommend using an FPGA board and loading a bitstream file.

The System Bus

All the components of an embedded system are linked together by the central data bus. This is composed out of the actual electrical links and the bus control unit (bus) that marshals the data transfers between components.

ARM CPUs use the Advanced Microcontroller Bus Architecture (AMBA) standard. It was designed by ARM and is now published as an open standard. Two of its essential components are

---

[4] www.sifive.com/boards/hifive1-rev-b
[5] www.sparkfun.com/products/15594

- **Advanced High-performance Bus (AHB)** – Used for interconnecting high-speed devices, similar to the North Bridge for x86 and x64

- **Advanced Peripheral Bus (APB)** – Used to connect lower-speed devices, devices that need less bandwidth, similar to the South Bridge for x86 and x64

Intel and AMD devices use the motherboard bus for communication. The bus is divided into two components: the North Bridge, used to interconnect the CPU to the memory and video adapter, and the South Bridge, used to interconnect the lower-speed devices, like hard drives, network cards, or keyboard and mouse.

RISC-V has defined its open standard bus named TileLink. It is simpler to implement than AMBA, has higher performance, and is a fully open standard. While it was designed for RISC-V, it can be used by other architectures.

The bus system also defines a device priority, allowing devices with higher priority to interrupt existing transfers, if needed.

The Memory

Running software means processing data through multiple operations. As this processing can be divided into several sequential phases, a lot of intermediary data is generated and has to be stored temporarily. As there is only a limited amount of storage space inside the CPU (in the form of registers and, optionally, CPU cache memory), the CPU requires a memory space where it can store and load data that is in process. This is the working memory unit (called RAM – random access memory). This memory communicates with the CPU using a high-speed bus component, usually having the highest bus access priority. Except for some very specialized systems, all embedded platforms have RAM.

Depending on the selected SoC, RAM sizes may vary. High-end embedded systems that use x86/x64 or ARM Cortex-A chips will most likely have 512 MB up to 8 GB of RAM. Low-power embedded systems running Cortex-M or RV32IAM chips will have 32 KB to 256 KB RAM.

Input/Output Devices

Input/output (I/O) devices are components that interact with the actual hardware. The AGC described previously had an I/O device for

- The display and keyboard interface DSKY

- The hand controller for the manual control of the spacecraft

- The rendezvous radar

- The landing radar for the lunar module landing

- The telemetry receiver for communication with the ground control

- The engine command for controlling the engines

- The reaction control system for maneuvering the spacecraft

Nowadays, systems have I/O devices for controlling actuators and reading data from sensors. As embedded systems are used in conjunction with various peripherals, from simple ones such as thermistors or photoresistors to more complex ones, such as gyroscopes and LCDs, several standards have been designed for talking to devices. UART (serial), SPI, I²C, Ethernet, and USB are the most commonly used ones. Depending on its capabilities, each device implements a subset of the existing standards.

The Storage Space

Usually, embedded systems have some way of permanently storing software that has to be run. This comes as an Electrically Erasable Programmable Read-Only Memory (EEPROM). Even though it is not an actual read-only memory, reading from it is easy while writing requires special software controls and sometimes special hardware. In common words, this is called the flash of the system, the term emerging from the flash memory technology that is the basis for the EEPROM manufacturing.

There is a little bit more to discuss when it comes to storage space. General-purpose CPUs, like x86/x64 and Cortex-A, do not have any embedded store space. As these CPUs are meant to be used in powerful computers, it is assumed that some storage space will be provided by some external device. This can be either a hard drive, an SSD, network storage, or something similar. Running software on these chips requires a full-fledged operating system that has, among others, the task of loading programs from a storage space into RAM and executing them. The CPUs only work directly with the RAM. Anything else requires drivers and additional hardware.

AVR, PIC, and Cortex-M/Cortex-R MCUs are designed for lower-end embedded systems and have integrated some internal storage. These processors were designed to run simple software, sometimes without any operating system, so usually loading programs from external storage is not feasible. This is why these devices have a small integrated storage space. Sizes vary from a few tens of KB to a few MB. This storage space is mandatory and will be present in all Cortex-M/R MCUs, and it is designed to store the applications that have to be run.

Note   There are some MCU's, like the RP2040 used by the Raspberry Pi Pico, that do not have any internal storage space. In this case, it is up to the device manufacturer to integrate a permanent storage along the MCU. For instance, the Arduino Nano RP2040 Connect integrates a 16 MB storage along the RP2040 MCU, while the Raspberry Pi Pico integrates only 2 MB of storage.

The Interrupt Controller

Even though it is an actual I/O component, the Interrupt Controller stands out of the crowd. Its primary purpose is to signal the CPU that some I/O device or peripheral needs some attention. Figure 1-4 shows the interaction between the CPU and the Interrupt Controller.

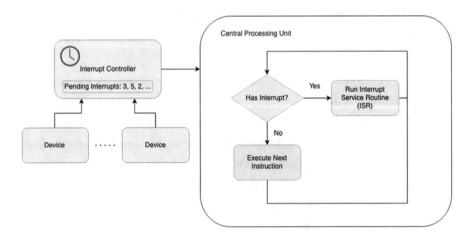

Figure 1-4. *CPU and Interrupt Controller (IC) interaction*

To better understand this, we need to dig a little bit into how the CPU works. Under standard operation, the CPU reads software commands, called instructions, one after the other, and executes them. Now let's imagine a soda dispenser in a fast-food restaurant. In its idle state, when no one wants any soda, it just displays some advertising on the screen. In other words, it takes instructions from the software and generates some images that customers see. What happens when a glass is placed underneath? The advertising stops, and the customer is asked to select the desired drink. The soda dispenser's CPU was interrupted from the normal execution and started executing the software part that asks customers about their drink choice.

In technical terms, the soda dispenser had a sensor connected to an I/O device. The I/O device is connected to the Interrupt Controller and has a unique interrupt number assigned.[6] When the customer placed the glass underneath the sensor, the sensor informed the Interrupt Controller that it requires attention, as it needs to send some information to the CPU. The Interrupt Controller stores the sensor's interrupt number in a list of pending interrupts and signals the CPU.

In simplified terms, the CPU runs a continuous loop through three significant steps:

1. Check if the Interrupt Controller has signaled that it has pending interrupts and, if required, execute an Interrupt Service Routine (ISR).

2. Execute the next instruction.

3. Rewind the loop.

Of course, this is a simplified way of looking at things. First, the CPU checks if the Interrupt Controller has any pending interrupts. If it does, it asks the Interrupt Controller to send the number of the following pending interrupt via the bus. The CPU holds a table, called Interrupt Vector, with a function pointer for every interrupt number. Upon receiving the interrupt number from the Interrupt Controller, the

---

[6] These numbers are described in each system's datasheet.

CPU executes the interrupt-associated function, called Interrupt Service Routine (ISR). When done, the CPU starts all over again and checks if the Interrupt Controller has any more pending interrupts.

If there is no interrupt pending, the CPU reads the next software instruction and executes it.

Note   This is a simple way of describing how interrupts work. In real systems, interrupts have priorities assigned. Higher-priority interrupts can interrupt Interrupt Service Routines (ISR) of lower-priority interrupts.

The Debug Interface

Another vital component is the debug interface. This allows an external device to take complete control over the functioning of the embedded system. Software developers use this interface to connect the embedded systems to a computer, load programs and data into it, and debug the software step by step. As we can notice, the debug interface is useful during the development steps.

There are several different standard debug interfaces available, the most common being

- JTAG, named after its developer, *Joint Test Action Group*

- SWD, Single Wire Debug

As development computers usually do not have hardware devices that can interface these debug interfaces, several hardware producers offer external USB devices, called debuggers and programmers.

Some embedded systems are shipped together with onboard debuggers that can be detached (mechanically separated) when shipping the device in production. Figure 1-5 shows the STM32 Nucelo429ZI board with the onboard debugger. The right part of the platform, where the debugger is located, can be ripped off before using the platform in production, thus disabling any external debug systems.

The debug interface has to be disabled by hardware to prevent end users and unauthorized technicians from tampering and modifying devices in production environments. From the security point of view, this debug interface is a significant security risk. Disabling it in the production system has to be a top priority.

Figure 1-5. *The STM32 Nucelo429ZI platform with the detachable debugger (right) attached*

Microcontrollers, Computers, and Hybrid Systems

Today, we can more or less distinguish two types of embedded systems:

1. Based upon microcontrollers, which we will simply call microcontrollers

2. Based upon computer systems, which we will call computers

3. And recently systems that are a mix of the two, which we will call hybrids

Microcontrollers

Microcontrollers are less powerful processing units that run at speeds ranging from a few MHz to a few tens of MHz and have a limited amount of RAM and a small amount of flash memory. What they lack in processing power they make in having the ability to interface many I/O devices out of the box. They are found in systems that have the task of precisely controlling hardware. Usually, these systems are named microcontroller unit (MCU). Examples of such systems are AVR, PIC, ARM Cortex-M, ARM Cortex-R, and RV32IAM.

Usually, microcontrollers are used inside simple devices that need to fulfill one specific task (e.g., alarm system, measure humidity, etc.). Inside IoT systems, microcontrollers are mainly used at the sensing layer, inside complex sensors that gather various environment information and transmit it to the gateway via multiple protocols. The applications run are quite simple, mostly focusing on collecting and transmitting data.

Computers

On the other side of microcontrollers, we have computers. These have CPUs that are very similar and sometimes identical to standard computers. They run at high frequencies, around 1 or 2 GHz, but they lack the ability to control hardware directly. The Raspberry Pi[7] is a perfect example: it has four cores that run at 1.2 GHz and has up to 8 GB of RAM, so it can perform a lot of data processing, but it needs a lot of extra I/O device connectors to be able to interface hardware properly.

---

[7] The Raspberry Pi foundation, www.raspberrypi.org/

The main difference from standard computers is that these systems are packaged in what is called a System on a Chip (SoC). In a typical computer, a mainboard connects the CPU with the RAM and the other hardware inside. For the embedded system, vendors embed the whole mainboard, CPU, RAM, and other devices into a single chip, hence the name.

Note   There might be some confusion around the Raspberry Pi. The *original* Raspberry Pi should not be confused with the Raspberry Pi Pico. The first one is a full-fledged embedded computer using an ARM Cortex-A CPU capable of running an operating system like Linux, while the second one is a microcontroller system using an ARM Cortex-M MCU that can run an embedded operating system.

In most systems' documentation, you will find the name of the CPU or MCU and the name of the SoC. The CPU is the actual processing unit, while the SoC is the processing unit bundled into a single chip with all the peripherals. Figure 1-6 shows the SoC used for the first Raspberry Pi. The SoC's name is BCM2835; it contains an ARM 1176JZF-S CPU, a VideoCore GPU, a Samsung RAM memory, and other devices.

Examples of such systems are ARM Cortex-A and RV64IAM.

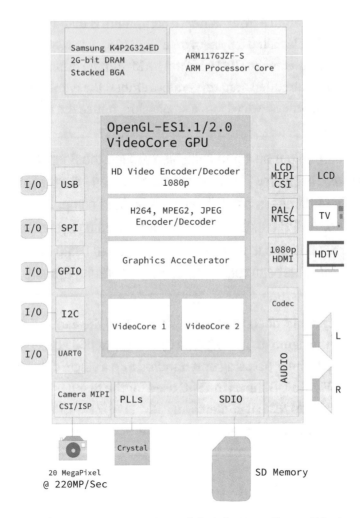

Figure 1-6. *The BCM2835 SoC used for the Raspberry Pi v1*

Inside an IoT system, the embedded computers are used at the edge or fog layer, where data coming from the peripherals based on microcontrollers is processed and some simple system logic is implemented. What is more, these devices are used to communicate with the Cloud, both for sending data and for receiving commands (e.g., turn on lights controlled from a smartphone app). Because of the advanced capabilities, these devices can implement complex protocols and security policies.

The main difference between the embedded computers and the microcontrollers is that the first are designed to run an operating system and multiple processes simultaneously, while the latter can run only one program.

Hybrids

Lately, a lot of very powerful microcontrollers have emerged. We are talking about microcontrollers that run at speeds close to 1 GHz and have a few hundred MB of RAM. The authors of this book call them hybrids: they have all the features of microcontrollers, which means they can fully control hardware but have a decent amount of processing power. Examples of such systems are the iMX-RT platform from NXP or the STM32H747XI from STMicroelectronics found in the Arduino Portenta H7 platform.

These devices have the capability to run complex programs that simulate an operating system and multiple processes being run at once.

Embedded Systems Platforms

All the major processing hardware manufacturers have a stake in the embedded systems space. The platform that does stand out is indisputably ARM (Advanced RISC Machine). They provide both microcontrollers with the Cortex-M and Cortex-R series and computer CPUs with Cortex-A series. For the time being, we strongly recommend using the ARM platform for any new embedded system design.

Classic CPU manufacturers such as Intel and AMD have a particular platform for embedded systems. These are mainly standard computer CPUs adapted for lower power consumption and with some additional I/O capabilities.

As this book is not about the industry standard, we find it mandatory to talk about the new architecture that is emerging, RISC-V. Developed at the University of California, Berkeley, and named the fifth RISC architecture, RISC-V is an open standard Instruction Set Architectures (ISA). This does not mean that RISC-V CPUs are open source, just that anyone can produce a CPU that knows how to run the RISC-V instructions without paying any license for doing that.

Several manufacturers are already providing RISC-V systems, the most notable of them being SiFive and lowRISC. We do expect to have many more providers in the future.

Summary

As this book will focus on building secure applications for embedded systems, this chapter is designed to give us an overview of the existing hardware platforms and their capabilities. Although we will focus on the software side from this point on, the first step in building an efficient and secure system is to be aware of the hardware capabilities and adapt the software accordingly.

The main characteristics of the embedded devices lie in the CPU architecture and capabilities, memory, and the supported I/O devices. Based on this, we can place any embedded device in one of the three categories: microcontroller, computer, or hybrid. While microcontrollers are simple devices, having reduced capabilities that can run only one application at once, embedded computers can run full-fledged operating systems and multiple processes. Finally, hybrid devices are microcontrollers with advanced capabilities, enabling us to build IoT systems at a reduced cost.

From the CPU point of view, we notice ARM-based devices are by far the most popular. Therefore, in the following chapters, we will use two ARM-based platforms to run the applications we develop: micro:bit v2 and Raspberry Pi Pico.

CHAPTER 2

Embedded Systems Software Development

Hardware systems are very important but pretty much useless nowadays without the proper software to make them run. Hardware is more or less like a framework that provides functions. At the same time, the software does most of the heavy lifting and actions, and with all these new programming languages available, developing applications seems to be easy. If we take a closer look, we can see that it is not. In this chapter, we will focus on presenting the characteristics of the software platforms designed for embedded systems.

What About the Software?

In any system, the central processing unit (CPU), sometimes called the microprocessor, executes the software. At a glance, the CPU can execute instructions. This means simple commands that perform mathematical operations (usually arithmetic) move data between different components (load and store) or instruct the CPU where to find the next instruction to be executed (branch). Table 2-1 describes an example of CPU instructions using a simple simulator created by Marco Schweighauser and licensed under the MIT license. The collection of instructions that a CPU can execute is called the instruction set. The virtual CPU used in the example has an elementary instruction set, having around 30 instructions.

© Alexandru Radovici and Ioana Culic 2022
A. Radovici and I. Culic, *Getting Started with Secure Embedded Systems*,
https://doi.org/10.1007/978-1-4842-7789-8_2

Table 2-1. *CPU instructions sample*

Instruction	Description	Type
add a, 120	Adds 120 to the value from ax	Arithmetic
mov a, 120	Stores (moves) the value 120 into the a register	Load and store
jmp 120	Instructs the CPU to read the next instruction starting at the address 120	Branch

The AGC (see Chapter 1) that landed a man on the moon had 11 basic instructions and 4 extended ones. In contrast, nowadays, CPUs support thousands of instructions.

Development Languages

With an increasing number of programming languages being developed, programmers nowadays can choose from a great variety based on their needs. When it comes to embedded systems, it is essential to consider that these devices are limited in resources. What is more, energy consumption is also an important factor as embedded devices are designed to be deployed and work autonomously for long periods. Further on, we will explore the development languages used for programming embedded devices.

Assembly Language

Writing software for microprocessors implies writing code using assembly language. The instruction set together with a specific set of rules forms the assembly language of a microprocessor. Each microprocessor has its own instruction set and functioning rules, so each microprocessor's assembly language is very different.

When using the assembly language, developers have complete control over the microprocessor and are able to write small, fast, and efficient programs. But as always, these advantages have a cost, and writing programs in assembly language is challenging. As the instruction set and the programming rules are limited, programs end up having millions of lines of code that are difficult to follow. Moreover, the assembly language does not have the control structures exposed by other programming languages that we are familiar with (e.g., for, while, etc.). This makes writing and even reading these programs even more difficult. To give you an idea of what writing software in assembly language means, Figure 2-1 shows Margaret Hamilton next to the listing of the AGC software that she and her team at MIT created for the Apollo missions.

Even though it controlled the spacecraft that landed on the moon, the software is not that complex compared to those written today. However, it does consist of a considerable amount of lines of code, as it was written, more or less, in assembly language – each line translated to a very simple instruction or a set of instructions for the AGC. Moreover, the software was the only thing running on the AGC, meaning that besides that actual work for the spacecraft, it had to manage all the computer's resources and make sure that each part of the software was running at the exact time it was required.

Putting into perspective, if we wrote browsers like Firefox or Edge in assembly language, we would probably need a whole room to print it out. It is funny how computers shrunk in size, and at the same time, software expanded to use more and more resources.

Figure 2-1. *Margaret Hamilton standing next to the listing of the Apollo mission software that she and her team at MIT developed*

Structured Programming

As writing software in assembly language turned out to be difficult, computer system designers came up with what we call today structured programming. Instead of writing in assembly language, that is, instructions for the CPU, programmers could write in a very restricted language format based on the English language. This language is then transformed by a program called compiler into the assembly language. Besides allowing the usage of a more familiar format, programs were shorter as these languages exposed programming structures such as conditions, loops, and functions.

There are several criteria that can categorize structured programming languages. The one that presents an interest for the embedded systems is the level of abstraction, meaning how much control a developer has over the hardware. We can identify here two categories:

1. *Low-level* or *system* **languages** – These are languages that offer some level of abstraction but still allow programmers to interact directly with the hardware instructions. The best examples are C/C++ and Pascal.

2. *Higher-level* **languages** – These languages abstract the implementation details and offer developers a rich feature set at the cost of losing some control. Most of these languages use sophisticated memory management systems that come at the expense of losing performance and increasing the software size. The most important representatives of such languages are C#, Java, Python, NodeJS, and, more recently, Go.

As embedded system software usually runs in very constrained environments (low memory, low storage space, and slow CPUs), writing software for them usually implies using a low-level language, which gets us to using C/C++.

Every year, IEEE publishes a billboard[1] of the most used programming languages. At the time of writing, the top five embedded system languages are

1. Python and its smaller lightweight siblings MicroPython and CircuitPython

2. C/C++[2]

3. Arduino[3]

4. C#

5. Rust

6. Assembly language

While the first four languages have been in last year's top five, Rust is the newcomer. Rust is growing more and more in popularity, and in the authors' opinion, it will eventually replace C/C++.

Python

Python is a high-level programming language, allowing fast development and easy debugging. While these features are great, it does introduce some overhead, resulting in higher resources usage. However, Python is the recommended language for the Raspberry Pi, an embedded computer having advanced capabilities. We strongly recommend using it for any embedded system that is powered by x86/x64 or ARM Cortex-A CPUs. Using any low-level programming language like C/C++ will increase development time and most probably introduce security issues.

---

[1] IEEE Top Programming Languages – https://spectrum.ieee.org/top-programming-languages/ (select only embedded)

[2] Even though these languages have been take into account separately by the IEEE article, we can safely state that they are more or less the same, so we decided to place them together.

[3] Arduino is just a set of libraries on top of C/C++.

When it comes to lower-end systems, like the Cortex-M MCUs, Python has two lightweight flavors called MicroPython and CircuitPython. As the latter is just a fork maintained by Adafruit, when we mention MicroPython, we will refer to both of them. MicroPython works on most systems with Cortex-M MCUs and is the language recommended for education prototyping. The overhead introduced by replacing C/C++ with MicroPython is significant.

C/C++ and Arduino

For most production systems, C/C++ is still the preferred language. This is mainly because most of the embedded operating systems and software are already written in C/C++. Also, when it comes to resource constraints, C/C++ applications can be very efficient and not waste resources. However, writing applications using C/C++ brings a high development overhead, as the time taken to write and debug the programs is significantly higher when compared to other languages such as Python. What is more, many security issues in embedded systems arise from C/C++ applications that were poorly implemented.

Arduino is a set of libraries on top of C++ that was released together with the Arduino hardware platform. The simplicity of the device and the library made the Arduino the most popular educational embedded platform. When talking about implementing simple devices, such as sensors, Arduino is one of the most used solutions.

Assembly Language

As we have already mentioned, writing applications using the assembly language enables us to use the system's resources most efficiently. However, the downside of a significant development time and the difficulty of writing and reading the assembly code make the assembly language unpopular.

C#

A high-level language, similar to Java, C# is mostly used for the development of Windows applications. Embedded computer systems, such as ATMs, that provide a user interface and run Windows are developed using C#. Microsoft provides a lightweight .NET Micro Framework which enables C# on microcontrollers. Just like Python, it provides an easy way of developing applications while introducing a considerable overhead. MCU systems designed to run C# are provided by Wilderness Labs.[4]

Rust

Rust is a very different story. While it offers most of the features of a high-level language like Python, it has no overhead and allows the same level of control as C/C++. This is why Rust is the second highest-growing language on GitHub.[5] More and more developers are now switching from C/C++ to Rust. Rust is so powerful that developers have started using it for writing whole operating systems. Tock is one of these systems.

There are a lot of other languages supported on low-end embedded systems, a few examples being

- **JerryScript** – A small and efficient JavaScript machine

- **Lua** – A scripting language used mostly in games

- **TinyGo** – A version of the Go language designed for MCUs

---

[4] www.wildernesslabs.co/

[5] The language with the highest growth is Dart, but this is due to the fact that Flutter, a cross-platform framework for mobile devices, is written using Dart.

Caution   MicroPython makes running Python on devices possible, but running the Python programs that a developer writes requires the MicroPython interpreter installed on the device. The same applies to JavaScript and the JerryScript interpreter.

Having discussed these languages, we think that Rust is one of the best languages for embedded systems. Designed with safety in mind, it offers all the advantages of a high-level language while still allowing developers full control over the hardware and software.

A Few Words About Security

This subject is extremely sensitive, especially as embedded systems are becoming a constant presence in people's lives. From systems that control our homes to health tracking devices, we are exposing ourselves to outside threats with each such device that we acquire. While this might seem scary and make us think of dropping the technology for good, this is not the solution. As the IoT market evolves, more and more emphasis is placed on security and mitigation, so using the devices carefully and updating them regularly can keep us away from many attacks.

Note   Throughout this book, we will only focus on the security issues that arise from writing code. To avoid confusion, we refer to these issues as safety issues. This is in no way the only part where security issues are found. Besides code errors, security faults are in network protocols, use handling of devices, etc.

C Programming and Safety

As most of the programs for embedded systems are written in C, it is important to analyze the impact this programming language has on the security of these platforms.

Note   The following thoughts represent the authors' vision of the subject, which might differ from other opinions.

First of all, C is an old but very powerful language. Even though it has been around since the 1970s, it has constantly been evolving, and new standards like C99, C11, and C 18 have been developed. Even more, the C++ language is adding several powerful features to it. At the time when C was developed, computers were used either by universities and research centers, like NASA, or in high-tech industrial systems like the Apollo spacecraft. As there was no public Internet and the great majority of people did now even know what a computer is, computer security was not paramount. The only way to actually *hack* a computer was to access it directly. And let's face it, for embedded systems at the time, that was almost impossible. Therefore, developers were focused on making the software work.

As computer-controlled devices became more and more mainstream, as most electronic appliances contain a computer, and with the widespread use of the Internet, nowadays, *hacking* a system does not require physical access anymore. Now security is a serious issue. The tricky part is that the operating systems running on these embedded platforms are all written in C, a language that was designed almost half a century ago. Despite the numerous programming languages available today, none of them allows the precise hardware interaction and control necessary to write an operating system. Of course, a lot has been done to improve the safety of C. Safe programming patterns have emerged, but *eventually, a developer will make a mistake* that will allow exploiting the system.

Here are a few safety issues that, from the authors' point of view, emerge due to the C programming language:

1. There is no standard memory management system. It is up to the developer to handle memory allocations as they wish. Yes, good practice patterns exist, but the compiler does not strongly enforce them.

2. Pointer arithmetics is another issue. Programmers are allowed to access memory in multiple ways, making it almost impossible for the compiler to track it and report errors.

3. Function definitions do not include any information about the relationship between the input parameters and the output values. If the source code of a function is not available to the compiler, and in most cases, it is not, it cannot make any assumptions about these relationships. Most probably, this is the single most problematic thing when programming in C and C++.

4. Backward compatibility in the Application Binary Interface (ABI) makes it difficult to patch design errors. As libraries and programs in C are designed to interact at a binary level, the whole source of the system is not available to the compiler. Not much can be changed here. A modification requires recompiling all the software.

5. A lot of source code is written using macro definitions, which in C are highly unsafe. The preprocessor simply replaces the macro definitions without enforcing the correctness of the generated code.

The list is way longer, and we could debate a lot about these safety features (or lack thereof). One thing is sure, C is fast and, so far, the only language that allows writing operating systems.

Beware of Rust

The Mozilla Foundation has always focused on providing tools for open and secure access to the Internet. While developing and improving their main product, the Firefox browser, they quickly realized that they had to write it in C/C++ due to performance issues. The downside of writing the browser engine in C/C++ is security issues. Even by following the best development patterns available, Firefox, and browsers in general, had a large amount of exploitable code.

Note   Browsers are very resource-consuming pieces of software as they are comparable in complexity to an operating system. They run web pages instead of applications, but nowadays, most *applications* are used in the browser. Your email, documents, and even games are accessed through the browser.

Around 2006, Mozilla employee Graydon Hoare started a personal project to build a new programming language called Rust with the purpose of having a language built with security from the ground up. Mozilla began sponsoring the project in 2009 and decided to use the Rust language to develop its new browser engine for Firefox called Servo. In the beginning, Rust was not significantly different from modern languages, using a runtime and a garbage collector for memory management.

In 2020, AWS, Google, Huawei, Microsoft, and Mozilla founded the Rust Foundation[6] as an independent entity to support the development of Rust. At the same time, Ferrous Systems has started working to certify a functional-safety compiler of Rust, called Ferrocene.[7]

As speed became an essential factor for Rust, the original runtime was dropped, and garbage collection was replaced by a very powerful compiler that is able to manage memory at compile time. This made Rust more or less the first language that could directly compete and replace C/C++.[8] Now we have operating systems, such as Redox and Tock, that are entirely written in Rust, without including any line of C code.

Note   Garbage collection is a technique used to automatically clean up memory that is not being used anymore. While its use significantly improves development speed and prevents memory errors, it does consume a lot of resources, making programs running slower and, sometimes, unpredictably stopping them in the middle of execution to clean up memory.

Rust is a *low-level* or *system* language that offers most of the features of a *high-level* language while maintaining a low memory footprint, full control, and fast performance. It does have a drawback, which is the steep learning curve. But then again, C/C++ is not exactly the most friendly language for beginners. To sum up, we now have a new language that can be used for writing operating systems, and this book is about Rust and its usage in embedded systems.

---

[6] The Rust Foundation, `https://foundation.rust-lang.org/`
[7] Ferrocene: Rust for critical systems, `https://ferrous-systems.com/ferrocene/`
[8] `www.drdobbs.com/jvm/the-rise-and-fall-of-languages-in-2013/240165192`

Note   Firefox Quantum was the first version to use the new browser engine.

Bare Metal Embedded

Embedded systems like the AGC used to be very specific low-power computers that would control hardware. Most of the software that ran on these computers was highly customized, knowing precisely what hardware devices it would handle. This is why these systems did not need an operating system most of the time, and some simple libraries would suffice

This way of programming a computer is called bare metal. The developer is responsible for writing all the software, setting up all the hardware, and writing all the drivers. As effective bare metal programming requires a lot of lines of code, several libraries have been developed to provide starting frameworks and useful functions to make the programmers' job easier.

The Arduino Library

The Arduino Library is probably the most used library for bare metal programming. It was designed to be used by developers that are just beginning their journey into embedded systems programming. At first, it was available only for the Arduino hardware but was adapted by several hardware manufacturers as the de facto standard for getting started.

The library is actually just a layer on top of some libraries provided by the hardware manufacturer. Think of it as more of a standard. If this is your first approach to embedded programming, you will want to try out this library.

CMSIS

The *Cortex Microcontroller Software Interface Standard* started as a standard specification for writing libraries for ARM Cortex-M devices. If you are planning to use ARM platforms, this is the library recommended by the manufacturer. Several embedded operating systems such as FreeRTOS and Mbed are based upon it.

This is a mature library and is the standard for ARM bare metal programming. The downside is that it is limited to ARM platforms.

OpenCM3

An alternative to the CMSIS is OpenCM3. This is an open source library for ARM platforms. Even though it is not production ready, it is a good starting point for understanding how bare metal programming works and how the ARM platform hardware-software interaction works. We do not recommend using it in production.

The Rust Embedded Devices Working Group

Rust is described as a system language, which means it can be used for direct hardware interaction. In other words, it can run on devices without the need for any extra software. Running a Rust program on a device is still not an easy task, and this is why the *Embedded Devices Working Group*[9] has been tasked with writing a few libraries as a starting point.

---

[9] *The Rust Embedded Book,* https://docs.rust-embedded.org/book/

This is a very good starting point for understanding how to use Rust with embedded systems. For each supported platform, there are usually three crates (libraries):

1. *platform_name*-rs – This allows access to the peripherals of a platform.

2. *platform_name*-hal – This uses the *rs* crate and exposes higher-level functions; consider it as a small driver layer.

3. *platform_name*-rt – This performs all the initializations necessary to boot up the platform.

There is a decent amount of documentation available, including three books written by the authors of the libraries. We strongly recommend anybody who wants to use Rust for embedded systems to get started with these libraries.

As Rust provides a high level of security out of the box, these libraries are worth considering for usage in production systems. Even though the libraries might not expose all the platforms' features, there is a lot of development going on to get this ecosystem of libraries to a production-ready status.

Real-Time Interrupt-Driven Concurrency

The libraries provided by the Embedded Devices Working Group allow developers to write simple programs for embedded devices. As embedded systems nowadays can have a reasonable amount of processing power, there might be a need to run several concurrent tasks in parallel. While this is rather easy when running on top of an operating system, the bare metal approach does not provide such functionality. The Real-Time Interrupt-driven Concurrency (RTIC) is a framework[10] created on top of the Rust

---

[10] *Real-Time Interrupt-driven Concurrency Book*, https://rtic.rs/0.5/book/en/

embedded libraries that allows developers to define tasks, schedule them, and exchange messages between these tasks.

Using this framework might just be enough in contrast with using an operating system. It is definitely worth trying it out.

Embedded Operating Systems and Frameworks

As embedded systems become more and more capable, developing bare metal applications has become increasingly challenging. Most of the systems that we use today need to run several tasks in parallel, much like an ordinary computer that runs several applications. As the new hardware platforms do resemble full-fledged computers, many specialized operating systems have started to emerge. In general, these are called RTOSes (real-time operating systems). The name is somehow improperly used, as not all the systems are actually real time. A better name would be embedded operating systems.

Another advantage of using an operating system is that it supports several platforms. Most of the bare metal libraries are designed for a specific platform.

Out of the hundreds of RTOSes, a few of them stand out for several reasons, and we will discuss them briefly.

FreeRTOS

This used to be the best option if you needed a production-ready RTOS. Now supervised by Amazon Web Services, FreeRTOS has been one of the first embedded operating systems. Released in 2003, this is the most mature RTOS. It lives up to its name and is a real-time operating system designed to run on time-sensitive systems. It is open source, written in C, and licensed under the MIT license terms.

As far as its architecture goes, the kernel is built together with all the applications into a single binary. Applications are more like threads than actual processes. From the security point of view, it has limited support for hardware memory protection.

As for the commercial aspect, it does have a long-term support (LTS) release cycle, meaning it is guaranteed that it will receive regular security updates. Out of the systems presented, it supports the most extensive set of hardware platforms.

The Zephyr Project

If you plan to build your new embedded system project, this is the RTOS that we would recommend you to use. Designed and developed by Intel in 2016, it is now governed by the Linux Foundation. Zephyr is informally called *Linux's little brother* as it mimics the design and architecture of the Linux operating system but is adapted to run on *small* devices.

From the technical perspective, Zephyr Project is open source, written in C, and licensed under the Apache 2.0 license terms. Like FreeRTOS, the kernel is compiled together with all the applications into a single binary. Security-wise, it makes limited use of the hardware memory protection available and does require some extra steps to enable it.

The Linux Foundations has started a certification process for a subset of Zephyr Project features, making it a perfect candidate for future embedded systems products. Zephyr Project also features an LTS release cycle, receiving regular security updates. One main difference between Zephyr Project and FreeRTOS is that the first one has been specially designed for Internet of Things applications, placing emphasis on security and updates mechanisms. In contrast, the latter has been designed for resource efficiency but in an *offline* environment.

Mbed OS

Being more a framework than an actual operating system, Mbed OS is ARM's software platform for its Cortex-M chips. Open source, written in C, and released under the Apache 2.0 license, Mbed OS works only on ARM systems.

Its architecture allows its usage either as a set of libraries for bare metal applications or as an operating system. Similar to FreeRTOS and Zephyr Project, it is compiled together with all the applications into a single binary. The main downside is that it does not support any memory hardware security mechanism.

From the business side, it is fully released under an LTS, having probably the best support among the systems described so far. If you are planning to use ARM platforms, it is definitely something worth considering.

RIOT

Even though it is far less popular than the previous systems, RIOT is one of the best academic embedded operating systems. Engineered initially as a research project between *Freie Universität Berlin*, *Institut National de Recherche en Sciences et Technologies du Numérique*, and *Fortbildungsakademie der Wirtschaft Hamburg*, it is a very good testing ground for new technologies, efficiency algorithms, and new platforms. It is one of the best-documented academic embedded systems.

From a technical standpoint, it is an open source project written in C and released under the LGPLv2 license. The kernel is compiled together with the applications into a single binary. It is one of the most space-efficient systems, running with as low as 1.5 KB of RAM and 5 KB of flash memory. Security-wise, it does make limited use of the memory hardware protection system.

Being an academic project, it does not have an official LTS release cycle, but there might be companies offering this as a third-party service. We recommend using it as a testing ground. Using it in production systems has to be carefully considered, as there is no official commercial support available.

Tock

Tock is neither the most popular nor the most efficient embedded operating system. Still, it is the only one that can be called a complete operating system, with a clear separation between the kernel and applications. It is also the only one written in a different language than C/C++. It is written in Rust. Started as a research collaboration project between the *University of Michigan*; *University of California, Berkeley*; and *Stanford University*, Tock paved the way to a new generation of embedded operating systems that are not written in C/C++ and are built to run untrusted applications. These applications are not directly shipped with the kernel and may be built by third parties.

Tock has been designed from the ground up with security in mind, and it uses all the hardware security features out of the box. The Rust programming language enforces drivers' security, while the clear separation between the kernel and applications, and memory hardware security features are enforcing application security.

Tock runs on top of ARM Cortex-M0+, M3, M4, and M7 and RISC-V IMC and IAMC architectures.

The Tock kernel is compiled as a separate binary and may be uploaded to embedded systems separately. Each application is compiled separately and talks to the kernel via a real system call interface. This allows developers to write applications in any language that is able to compile into machine language. For now, Tock officially supports C/C++ and Rust, while an SDK for the D language is underway.

Summary

In this chapter, we dealt with the software side of the embedded devices by emphasizing the security aspect. With an increasing number of embedded systems becoming part of our lives, securing these devices becomes of paramount importance. As many security threats are located at the software level, analyzing the operating systems and programming languages used for embedded devices can help us prevent a large number of attacks.

With C being a powerful language and one of the most used in the embedded world, some of its characteristics can lead to writing less secure code. As a result, a new systems programming language built with security in mind is gaining momentum. Developed initially by the Mozilla Foundation and handed over to the Rust Foundation, Rust has become the first programming language after C/C++ used to write an operating system, making it even more interesting. Among the operating systems written in Rust, Tock has gained popularity and is also used by important companies such as Google and Western Digital.

In the following chapters, we will dig into the internals of Tock and Rust programming for building secure embedded systems. We will analyze both the kernel and the application space of Tock and will build basic programs that can be easily integrated into a larger IoT infrastructure.

## CHAPTER 3

The Tock System Architecture

Tock is the first embedded operating system used in the industry written in another programming language than C/C++. This makes it particularly interesting from both the operating system's perspective and the embedded security point of view. In this chapter, we will dive into how Tock is built and the characteristics that make it an appropriate operating system for building secure embedded applications.

Why Tock?

Tock is an embedded operating system that has emerged out of an academic research project. Even though it might not be production ready (yet), it has one significant advantage: it is the first full-fledged embedded operating system written in another language but C. What is more, the industry is also interested in using it (Google for OpenSK and OpenTitan). It might not be the widely used operating system of the future. Still, certainly, it is the one that will open the way to other operating systems written in modern languages.

© Alexandru Radovici and Ioana Culic 2022
A. Radovici and I. Culic, *Getting Started with Secure Embedded Systems*,
https://doi.org/10.1007/978-1-4842-7789-8_3

The authors of this book believe in the importance of having a new and updated perspective on the embedded operating systems. All the current production OSes are based on the same principles developed 50 years ago. They are solid and robust but not adapted for the next generation of devices.

With this book, we try to offer you, our reader, a new perspective.

A Few Words About Operating Systems

Before we dive into how Tock is designed, we have to take a look at how operating systems are built. For this, the next section will focus on what the kernel, drivers, and application mean.

The Kernel

The operating system per se is called the kernel. This is a piece of software that runs along with your applications and manages all the system's hardware and software resources. The kernel is the one that decides which programs have to run, which programs have to wait, which programs are allowed to access resources like files or network connections. It is the kernel that performs most of the tasks on a system, such as reading and writing data from and to files, sending and receiving data to and from the network, reading keystrokes, etc.

From the developers' perspective, the kernel interacts with the hardware and exposes two standard interfaces, called Application Binary Interface (ABI) and Application Programming Interface (API), toward the programs that run on top of it. This makes the developer's life easy. Were it not for the kernel, a developer would have to write a lot of lines of code to be able to interact with the hardware. Each piece of hardware is different and has to be interfaced differently.

Note   The ABI represents the standard used by the process to send requests to the kernel (system calls) and to receive returned values from the kernel. On the other hand, the API represents the set of requests that a process can send to the kernel.

Just to give you an example, think about a sound card. Based on its manufacturer, each sound card exposes a different interface which means that it is controlled using different functions. When using a kernel, the kernel *knows* the type of the sound card and how to interface it or, in other words, what functions to call. It then exports the *sound API* to the developer. As long as it is a sound card, developers will use the same kernel API and don't have to worry about the actual hardware. The same program will run on any system that runs a kernel that exports the same *sound ABI*.

As long as the system works, the kernel is entirely invisible to the developer and the user. The user notices the kernel only in the case of a complete failure, such as the *Blue Screen of Death* (Windows) or *Panic* (Linux and macOS).

The Drivers

Now that we have established what the kernel does, the following question will pop up: *how does the kernel know how to interface every possible piece of hardware?* The answer is simple: *it doesn't.* The kernel has a set of standard device interfaces that it *wants* to support. Examples of such interfaces are *disk drives, sound cards, graphic cards, network, etc.* Depending on the actual kernel used, these so-called device interfaces vary a lot.

For each of these interfaces, the kernel allows developers to load *plugins,* also called *drivers.* These drivers are the ones that are capable of interfacing with the hardware and report to the kernel. As long as the kernel has a driver for a specific piece of hardware, developers and programs are able to use it. If there is no driver loaded, the kernel will not be able to interface it and export it to the developers and programs.

Think of the kernel as an extensive framework that connects drivers to programs using standard interfaces for both of them: the driver interface toward the drivers and the API toward the developers.

The Applications

The actual programs that are running on a system and interact with the user are called *applications*. They use the kernel ABI and API for interacting with the hardware and are usually portable. That means that as long as we have the same operating system (kernel), the application should run, regardless of the hardware platform.

While some applications are shipped together with the operating system (but are not an actual part of it), most applications are installed by the user.

Services

A service is a program that usually does something in the background and does not interact with the user. Examples of such programs are web servers or backup systems. These interact with several applications and provide services to them.

The Tock System Architecture

Tock is an embedded operating system (OS) that has its roots in the academic environment. It began as a research project meant to implement a new OS capable of leveraging modern microcontroller (MCU) features such as more flash and RAM or the existence of a user-mode and memory protection unit (MPU). Most existing OSes, like FreeRTOS and Zephyr, do support these new features, but developers have to do a lot of work to enable them as plugins. Tock offers all these features out of the box.

Another exciting feature that makes Tock unique is the separation between the kernel and the applications. While for standard (computer) OSes, this seems something normal – you have an OS like Windows, Linux, or macOS on top of which you run several applications that you install separately – for an embedded OS, this is not. The general idea for MCUs is that the operating system comes as a single binary that bundles all the applications and services. When building an application, you are actually building the whole operating system.

When it comes to Tock, the kernel is built separately and uploaded to the device. Afterward, each application is individually built and uploaded separately to the board. This process mimics the behavior of a regular OS and makes application and service updates more manageable.

Note   What makes Tock really stand out is that it is entirely written in Rust, without any single line of code written in C. This is a significant change as C/C++ has been, for the last 50 years, the only language that operating systems were written in. While a very powerful and stable programming language, C is old and not really adapted for modern times. Memory management is left completely at the programmers' will, making it impossible for the compiler to check programs for memory errors. Don't get us wrong, at the time when C was created, there was no other option.

Figure 3-1 shows the full Tock stack. At the bottom, in red, we have the hardware device, the MCU. It is composed out of a processing unit (CPU) and several peripherals that add functionality (random number generator, RNG; encryption, AES) and allow it to interact with other hardware (GPIO, USB, I2C, ADC, SPI, UART).

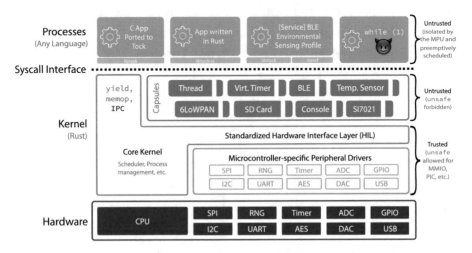

Figure 3-1. *The Tock stack (source: `https://github.com/`*
`tock/tock`)

On top of the hardware, we have, in orange, the low-level drivers that interact directly with the hardware and expose a Hardware Interface Layer (HIL) to the kernel and the capsules. The actual kernel, in teal, sits mostly between the low-level drivers and the capsules. It provides the process scheduler, inter-process communication (IPC) driver, and memory management. The upper part of the kernel, in blue, are the capsules. These are the upper-level drivers that provide services to each other via HILs and provide the API to the user space. Applications, in light green, run above the kernel. Rather than being linked into the kernel, applications use the API to request services from the kernel.

User Space

At the top of the Tock stack, we have the applications and services. These are the programs that run on top of Tock. Each of them can be written in any programming language (as long as it can be compiled for the device's MCU architecture) and is built separately, just like a typical computer application.

The applications and services are running in a restricted mode, which means that they have access only to the resources that they have been granted by the OS and cannot directly interact with the hardware. They can only use the OS system calls interface as defined by the ABI. Processes may also only access memory provided to them by the kernel and may not access memory belonging to the kernel or other applications.

As they run with some restrictions, it is said that they run in *user mode*. As such, all these applications and services are sometimes called the operating system's user space.

Note   Tock tries its best to restrict applications' access to resources. This requires some hardware support, specifically the MPU. Tock assumes that all MCUs that it is running on will have this hardware capability.

While Tock does run on some MCUs without memory protection, like some Cortex-M0 devices, it cannot restrict memory access for applications when no MPU is present.

The Tock Kernel

As we mentioned earlier, the kernel runs on top of the hardware, and it is responsible for

- **Scheduling applications and services** – It decides when each application or service is allowed to use the CPU for processing.

- **Memory management** – It allocates memory for applications and services and restricts unauthorized access to it.

- **Inter-process communication** – It sends messages between applications and services.

- **Providing an interface for hardware access** – For drivers (not applications and services) called **Hardware Interface Layer** (HIL).

- **Providing an interface for applications and services** – To access functions exposed by drivers called **system call interface** (syscall).

As it can be seen, the Tock kernel does not know how to access hardware but exposes a Hardware Interface Layer (HIL). Low-level drivers (Figure 3-1 – in orange) provide an interface to the hardware for the upper-level drivers (Figure 3-1 – in blue), called *capsules*. As we will detail later, the Tock kernel does not actually broke these services, but it only provides a common interface for the capsules and the drivers to talk to each other.

As the kernel requires complete device and memory access, its code runs without any memory or access restrictions. Technically, it could perform any action, which could be a security issue. As it is written in Rust, it must comply with Rust's compiler memory safety rules. This means that the kernel's code is being checked and validated for memory errors at compile time. This is a considerable increase in security compared to any code written in C.

There is a catch, though. Since the kernel has to perform some specific system management tasks, it needs to access memory directly from time to time. In Rust, this can be done using the *unsafe* block. Inside this block, the Rust compiler does not perform any checks. The Tock team has tried to minimize the number of *unsafe* blocs in the kernel, but they do exist, and they will not go away. It is simply not possible to perform some tasks without this feature.

Hardware Drivers

Depicted in orange in Figure 3-1, hardware drivers are small plugins that interact directly with hardware components. They implement a HIL, expose functionality to the kernel, and talk directly with the hardware interface on the other side.

As for the kernel, interfacing hardware requires specific memory access that in Rust translates to *unsafe* blocks. To minimize the number of *unsafe* blocks, the kernel exposes a register interface that drivers can use. This allows all drivers to use more or less the same method and code to access the hardware directly. From a security standpoint, while a bug in the register interface affects all drivers, the fix is also applied to all drivers at once.

Caution   Even though the Tock kernel exposes a register interface, drivers may have to implement additional functionality that requires *unsafe* blocks. This brings driver's code more or less to the level of security as C code. Still, once written, drivers seldom change, and their code is presumably tested by many developers.

Capsules

The upper-level drivers, called capsules, are responsible for offering the actual ABI toward the applications and services running in the user space. They use hardware drivers and other capsules via the HIL interface and provide system calls. To make things clearer, capsules are divided into two categories:

- **Syscall capsules** – These provide system calls to applications and services within the user space. These capsules usually provide a standard API for applications and forward requests to a service capsule that interfaces an actual device.

- **Service capsules** – They provide services to other capsules (both types of capsules, syscall, and service). These capsules usually know how to interface a specific hardware device via some standard bus (SPI, I2C, serial, etc.).

Figure 3-2 shows an example of how capsules connect. In the user space, we have an application that requires data from the motion sensors (acceleration, magnetic orientation, and gyroscope). The application makes a system call to the **NineDoF** (nine degrees of freedom) capsules. This capsule does not know what sensor the device actually has, but it is consuming a service from the **Fxos8700** capsule via the **NineDoF HIL**.

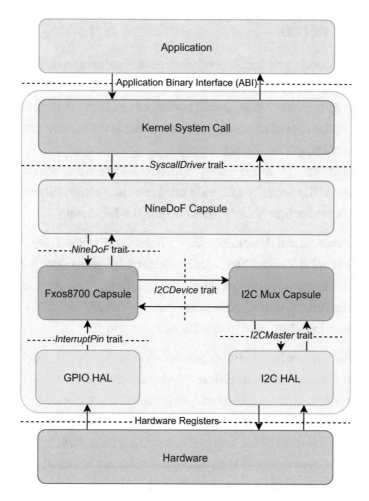

Figure 3-2. *Capsule interconnection for a motion sensor*

On the other hand, the Fxos800 capsule knows how to interface with the Fxos8700 sensor located on the board. This sensor communicates via I2C, so the Fxos8700 capsule sends and receives data to and from the sensor using the **I2C Mux** capsules via the **I2C HIL**.

Security Facts

Security is becoming an increasingly important subject as most devices today are connected to a network or the Internet. While in the early days of computing, security issues would result only in some computers not running and the loss of some documents, nowadays security can have a much greater impact on the real world.

Tock has taken a few interesting approaches when it comes to security. A quick view of the security methods used is illustrated in Table 3-1. The basic security rules that Tock is based on are the following:

- **No external dependencies** – All the code of the Tock kernel is located inside its repository. It has no external dependencies except the Rust core library. This means that all the kernel code is available to developers and vendors that want to use Tock.

- **No unsafe inside the capsules** – While the Tock kernel does need to access some memory locations directly, by using the unsafe blocks, capsules are not allowed to do that. The Rust compiler is set up to refuse the compilation of any capsule containing an unsafe block. This guarantees that capsules are memory safe and have access to hardware only via a HIL.

- **Applications and services run in user mode** – This implies that they cannot access hardware directly. They can only access their own memory and may not bring down the system. However, this requires hardware support. User space security is a much larger topic, and we will discuss this in detail further in this book.

Table 3-1. *Security facts sheet for each of Tock's components*

Component	Security mechanism	Hardware support required
User space Applications and services	Memory protection unit User mode execution	Yes
Kernel	Rust compiler (with *unsafe*) (code has to be fully trusted)	No
Hardware drivers	Rust compiler (with *unsafe*) (code has to be fully trusted)	No
Capsules	Rust compiler (will not compile if *unsafe* is used)	No

Even though the kernel uses some unsafe blocks, the amount of code within them has decreased in time, as the Tock developers have found ways to avoid some of them or optimize them. Unlike kernels written in C, the Rust compiler can guarantee memory safety and consistency for most of the source code. This is a huge advantage, and you can think of it as a computer that proofreads the kernel before it builds it.

The Tock User Space Architecture

So far, we have discussed only what happens inside the Tock kernel. While the kernel's job is to manage resources and assure application safety, most of the devices' logic is located within the applications that run on top of the kernel. As described before, applications run in a restricted environment that is well controlled by the kernel. They cannot access hardware directly and have to use the kernel API, the actual drivers, to perform several tasks.

Note   Before we dive in, we have to define the term *process*. A process is one single instance of a program that runs on Tock. This is slightly different from an *application*. An application is a generic term for something that *the device does*. It can be composed out of one or several processes that have a common goal and perform a joint action.

The Tock kernel identifies each process by an *AppId* structure. This is a unique opaque structure and should be treated as such. No assumptions should be made about it.

Process States

The kernel stores the state for each process. Table 3-2 describes all the possible process states. While there are several states available, the essential ones are *Running* and *Yielded*. These two states are the ones that are visible to application developers.

Table 3-2. *The process states*

State	Definition
Running	The process is ready to execute. This does not necessarily mean that the process is the one currently executing code on the MCU; it is just ready to run anytime
Yielded	The process is waiting for an event and is not ready to execute. This can happen in one of the two cases: 1. The process has called the *yield* system call 2. The process has finished executing and does not have to be scheduled again. In this case, the process never expects to have any callback function scheduled
StoppedRunning	The process was stopped while it was running. This means that the process will not be scheduled again until it is manually resumed. If the process needs to be scheduled again, it must be put back in the *Running* state Usually, the kernel will never stop a process. This has to be done from within a driver. The *ProcessConsole* has a function to stop processes
StoppedYielded	The process was stopped while it was yielded. This means that the process will not be scheduled again until it is manually resumed. If the process needs to be scheduled again, it must be put back in the *Yielded* state Normally the kernel will never stop a process. This has to be done from within a driver. The *ProcessConsole* has a function to stop processes

(*continued*)

Table 3-2. (*continued*)

State	Definition
Faulted	The process has generated a fault, probably a faulty memory access, and was stopped by the kernel. Based on the *FaultResponse*, the kernel might 1. Panic, print a fault message, and halt the system 2. Try to restart the process a certain number of times 3. Stop the process
Terminated	The process has executed the *exit-terminate* system call
Unstarted	The process has not yet been started

Tock processes are single threaded, which means that they can run only one code instance at a time. The process execution can be interrupted by the kernel or by interrupts, but execution continues from the same point where it was interrupted. A process can schedule functions that should be called when several events happen, but they only get called when the process asks for them.

Note   The process states in Tock are a little bit different from the classical process states. In classical OS like Linux, the *Running* state is called *Ready*, while *Yielded* is called *Waiting* or *Blocked*. There is no corresponding state for Linux's *Running* process state. This is because Tock is a single-threaded OS, and no kernel action can be executed in parallel with any process. Table 3-3 shows the correspondence.

Table 3-3. *The Tock and Linux process states correspondence*

Tock process state	Linux process state
Running	Ready and Running
Yielded	Blocked
StoppedRunning	Terminated (while it was in Running)
StoppedYielded	Terminated (while it was in Blocked)
Faulted	Terminated (faulted)
Terminated	Terminated
Unstarted	New

System Calls

A Tock process asks the kernel for services using system calls and receives back information through scheduled upcalls. The kernel provides seven system calls: *memop, readwriteallow, readonlyallow, subscribe, command, yield,* and *exit.* Table 3-4 describes each one in detail. All of these system calls are asynchronous, which means that they return a value, usually success or failure, immediately. If the kernel needs some time to process the request and cannot send back a response immediately, the process needs to subscribe and wait for an upcall from the kernel. These callbacks are scheduled and only occur after the process has called yield. In classic OS terminology, all the Tock system calls are asynchronous.

A process can only be interrupted in three specific cases:

1. The time slice has expired, meaning that the process has executed without yielding more than the kernel has it allowed to do.

2. An interrupt has arrived; the kernel will have to handle the interrupt.

3. The process faults, and the kernel puts it in the *Stopped* state.

Table 3-4. *Tock system calls*

ID	System call	Description
0	*Yield*	Puts the process in the *Yielded* state and waits for any scheduled upcall to be run. After the upcall returns, the process resumes as if it was returning from the call to *yield*
1	*Subscribe*	Allows a process to register a function that should be called when a requested action has finished This function will be run only when the process is in the *Yielded* state, meaning it has previously called the *yield* system call and is *waiting* for a scheduled upcall. Otherwise, the callback will be queued for a later yield call
2	*Command*	Requests an action from a driver. The *command* system call returns success or failure and up to three numeric values The return value usually means that the action request has been received, and the driver will try to fulfill it
3	*ReadWriteAllow*	Allows a process to share a buffer with a driver for reading and writing purposes. This is usually used for returning larger amounts of data from within a driver It is used in conjunction with *subscribe* and *command* system calls. Filling the buffer usually does not begin until a *command* is issued. The process of reading the result in the process occurs after the scheduled callback function has been called

(continued)

Table 3-4. (*continued*)

ID	System call	Description
4	*ReadOnlyAllow*	Allows a process to share a buffer with a driver for reading purposes. This is used usually for sending larger amounts of data to a driver It is used in conjunction with a *command* system call, with the driver reading the data when performing the requested action
5	*Memop*	Allows a process to request more memory from the kernel and informs the kernel about its memory layout It is used at the process' bootstrap to request heap memory from the kernel and inform the kernel about the actual stack size and data size for debugging purposes
6	*Exit*	Requests the kernel to stop the process. Depending on the system call's argument, the kernel will 0 – stop the process 1 – restart the process

Besides interrupting a process, the kernel can regain control of the MCU if the process makes a system call. This means that the process transfers control to the kernel in a voluntary way.

Note   Linux has a few hundred system calls while Tock only has seven. Linux has a different system call for every task, meaning that developers usually need to call a single system call for a task. For Tock, developers need to combine the five system calls to achieve the same result. This is very similar to CISC vs. RISC processor architectures, Tock being equivalent to a RISC.

As Tock provides only seven system calls, these have to be used together in order to achieve the same results for a standard OS. When using system calls, there are two cases: the kernel can send us back an answer immediately, also called synchronously, or it needs to initiate an action that will take some time and notify us back later. The latter one is called asynchronous.

Tip   This asynchronous system call architecture is very similar to how NodeJS works.

Synchronous System Calls

The synchronous approach is usually used to determine some system parameters that are constants. For instance, by issuing a *command* system call, a process can determine how many GPIOs or LEDs the system has connected. From the kernel's point of view, this is just a matter of returning a constant number. It does not depend on a peripheral to get a response. Whenever the kernel has to rely on some peripheral or device to transfer some data, it cannot answer immediately. An exception to this is GPIO, which can be read through a *command*.

Actions such as reading and writing to a serial port (console), a system bus like SPI, or reading sensor data (via a bus or even ADC) have to be done asynchronously. This is a lot more efficient as it allows the MCU to do some additional work until the peripheral is able to provide the requested data instead of *busy waiting* for it to finish.

Tip   This asynchronous processing pattern has been adopted by high-performance software like the NGINX web server or the NodeJS language.

To request a synchronous action from the kernel, the process has to use the *command* system call. The process will be suspended while the kernel sends the system call to the specified driver and will be resumed immediately if the time slice still allows after the driver finishes the command action. The time used by the driver to process the command request is counted toward the process' time slice.

A driver can return up to three unsigned 32-bit integer numbers or up to two unsigned 64-bit integer numbers and one unsigned 32-bit integer number via the *command* system call. Any other response that does not fit into these limits has to be reported using an *allowed* buffer. As most of the system calls that use a buffer are asynchronous, we will describe this pattern of usage in the following asynchronous system call section.

Asynchronous System Calls

The vast majority of system calls use an asynchronous pattern. In this case, the process asks something from the kernel. The kernel will acknowledge the request and notify the process via an upcall when the task has been solved. This defines a system call usage pattern, and it is an important topic. So let's get into the details of it.

First of all, let's take the example of an environment sensor. We suppose the sensor is connected via a data bus to our MCU, and it is able to read the environment temperature and humidity. We also assume that this is a new sensor, and there is no support for it in the Tock User Space Library yet. The process has to send system calls directly to the sensor.

Our intuition would suggest that the process should issue a *command* system call to the sensor driver and the driver should be able to respond with the data immediately. However, this assumption is wrong. The sensor is connected to the MCU via some data bus. Reading and writing to and from this bus take time, which the kernel and other processes can use to do other useful actions.

Instead of issuing a simple *command* system call, our process has to follow a pattern. The actual reading of data is triggered by a *command* system call, but our process needs to be prepared to get back an answer at some later point after the *command* system call has returned. For this, the first step that the process needs to take is to *subscribe for an upcall*. This implies using the *subscribe* system call that provides a pointer to a function that should be called once the data from the sensor is available. If the system call is successful, the driver knows that it has to *schedule* a call to the provided function once it has the data available.

Note   The usage of the word *schedule* is very important. A driver will never be able to actually call a function from within a process. All that the driver can do is to ask the kernel to call that function at some time. This is why the driver *schedules* a function call.

Tip   Each process has a scheduled task queue. By default, this number is limited to 10 but can be changed in the *kernel/src/process. rs* file. At the time of writing, Tock knows about two types of tasks: upcalls and IPC calls.

Once the process manages to subscribe to the sensor driver for an upcall, the next step is to send the *read command* to the driver. This is done by calling the *command* system call, and this is the actual point where the process asks the driver to perform a reading and report it back. A successful return from the *command* system call should be interpreted as *the driver acknowledging the request and performing the read action*. This does not mean that the driver will be successful or not in reading the date. The driver has only reported that it will do its best to get the requested data and that, as far as it knows at the time, there should be no error. The process can now continue doing something else, and the driver will notify it when it has the data available.

Now here comes the tricky part. The driver will do its work *in the background* while all the other processes are executing. Once it finishes reading the data, it will *schedule* an upcall to the process (considering that the process has actually subscribed to it). The process will not be notified *out of the blue*, but it has to *ask for an upcall*. We need to get into more details here. Tock upcalls are performed in a synchronous way. This means that the process will never be abruptly interrupted so that a callback function can be called. To receive an upcall, a process needs to yield. This is done by calling the *yield* system call, which will stop it and place it into the *Yielded* state. When a process is yielded, the kernel will check if it has any pending (scheduled) upcalls in its task queue. If so, the kernel will place the process into the *Running* state and call the first scheduled upcall in the queue. Then the callback function registered for the upcall returns, and the process will continue its execution as if the *yield* system call had returned. In other words, the *yield* system call returns *when a callback function returns*.

Caution   If you have some Linux background, you might think upcalls are similar to Linux signals, and callback functions are similar to signal handlers. This is not so. Linux signals are asynchronous functions that can be called at any time. The Linux kernel will stop the process at any given point and call the signal handler. The process has no idea where it was stopped, and this is why there are a limited number of actions a process can take from within a signal handler function. Tock upcalls are never called like that. They can be called only as a result of a *yield* system call. If a process never yields, it will never receive an upcall. This makes callback functions deterministic, as the process knows precisely where it has stopped to get an upcall.

If a process has several pending upcalls in its task queue, it needs to yield several times to be able to get all of them. The general rule is one yield – one received upcall. Once a callback function is called, the process is not unsubscribed. The driver will retain the pointer to the callback function until the process subscribes to a NULL pointer instead of that function. This is the action that unsubscribes a process.

A process needs to be very careful when using the yield system call. In most cases, it probably has only one possible upcall scheduled when it yields. However, there may be cases when several upcalls might be scheduled when a process yields (several drivers have some action in progress on behalf of the process). When yield returns, the process must verify that the callback function it has been waiting for was called. If not, it needs to yield again.

In other words, if a process needs to issue the same command several times, it is enough to subscribe once and issue pairs of command-yield system calls afterward. Figure 3-3 shows the system call pattern that we have discussed here.

Caution   A special note has to be given to the GPIO ports. Reading and writing the MCU's own GPIOs is really fast, and even though it could be done asynchronously, it would take more time to do that than to actually read or write them in a synchronous way. This is why accessing GPIOs and GPIO-related drivers, such as LEDs, is usually done synchronously.

On the other hand, if the GPIOs are located in an extender that is connected to the MCU via a bus, like I2C or SPI, reading and writing have to be done asynchronously as the bus data transfer takes a significant amount of time.

Shared Buffers

Looking at Figure 3-3, you might see an optional extra step in the system call pattern: the *allow* system call. Subscribed callback functions have three unsigned 32-bit (or 64, depending on the MCU word size) integers as parameters. This means that results reported using upcalls have to fit into three numbers. This is enough for our sensor, as it most probably reports two numbers but might not be enough for several other drivers, such as a network interface.

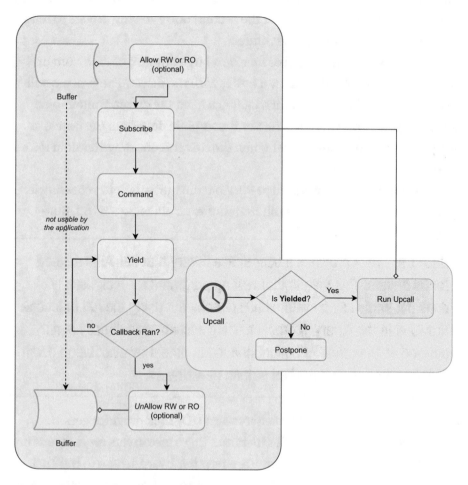

Figure 3-3. *Tock system call pattern*

To get more complex data, processes can share buffers with a driver. Unlike standard drivers in Linux or similar operating systems, Tock drivers have to obey all the Rust compiler rules while not being allowed to use the *unsafe* keyword. This means that, unlike standard drivers, Tock drivers cannot access the process' memory (even though drivers run with all memory privileges). Drivers can access the process' memory only through a kernel interface and only as long as these processes have allowed it. This is done through the *allow* system call. This system call comes in two flavors: *allow_readonly* and *allow_readwrite*, the first one allowing drivers to read data from that buffer and the second one allowing drivers to read and write data from and in that buffer.

If processes need to send or receive a large amount of data from or to the driver, they need to allow a buffer with the driver. The process still needs to subscribe and wait for a callback from the driver. Failure to do so may result in reading incorrect or incomplete data from the buffer, as the process has no control over when the driver reads or writes data into the buffer.

The application is required to *unallow* the buffer before accessing it. This means either allowing a different buffer or allowing a NULL buffer.

Caution   Tock provides a user space library that has APIs defined for its drivers. This means that writing programs for Tock usually does not imply using system calls directly but using the API functions provided in the library. Moreover, using system calls directly is not advised as the driver API might change in time. However, being aware of the pattern is useful when writing new drivers.

For several functions, like sensors and I/O, Tock provides generic drivers with a standard API. For instance, there are drivers for temperature, humidity, motion, etc. When adding a new hardware sensor to the Tock kernel, one does not need to write a new temperature driver, instead just implement the *Temperature* Hardware Interface Layer (HIL) and connect the new driver to the generic temperature driver. We will discuss this in detail further in the book.

The Process Memory

Special attention has to be paid to how memory is organized inside a Tock process. If you are coming from a Linux environment, this will be a little different. Figure 3-4 describes the memory layout for a process. As Tock is designed to run on MCUs, the process memory is split into two parts: one read only located in the MCU's flash and a read-write part located in the RAM.

The actual executable code, also known as the *text* section in Linux, is located in the flash and is read only (this means truly read only, not just marked like that). This is because the flash cannot be directly written. The flash also hosts the *rodata* section, containing constants.

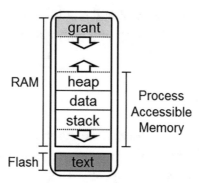

Figure 3-4. *The Tock process memory layout (source:* https:// github.com/tock/tock)

The RAM component of the process memory hosts the *data*, *stack*, and *heap* sections. Additionally, it has an extra area, *grant*, that is not accessible to the process. The first thing that can be seen is the placement of the *stack*. Instead of being placed at the top of the memory, it is placed at the bottom. This design decision has been made to enable the detection of stack overflows. The process is faulted if it tries to write outside its memory region. As the stack is at the bottom, an overflow results in a write outside the process' memory, triggering a fault. The downside of this approach is that all processes have to specify the maximum stack size they use at compile time, and they have to stick to it. Moreover, the stack memory cannot be shared with other sections.

Above the stack, we find the *data* section. This is where all the global variables are kept. The process itself manually initializes this section before the *main* function is called. The data section size is computed automatically at compile time by the compiler.

On top of the *data* section, there is the *heap*. This is where all the dynamically allocated variables are kept (*malloc*). When starting a process, Tock needs to know how much memory it needs to allocate for it.

Note   The *stack* is usually placed at the end of the process memory and grows downward. It is designed like this to allow the stack to grow as much as needed in systems with virtual memory, like Linux.

The Grant Region

A brand new approach in the Tock kernel implementation is the *grant* region. This is stored at the top of the process' memory and is not accessible to the process. Tock's kernel uses this region to store the Process Control Block (PCB) and to allocate space for drivers to store process-specific data. To understand why this region is very important, we need to dive into how the Tock kernel works.

For reliability reasons, the Tock kernel is not allowed to allocate memory dynamically. This means that all the memory used by the kernel needs to be more or less known at compile time. We are using the *more or less* term here, as the drivers do have a way to allocate some dynamic memory, but not as straightforward as using a Rust language feature.

Caution   Dynamic memory allocation can be dangerous. Imagine a driver that allocates memory each time an application requests something from it. If the driver, due to some error, does not deallocate that memory, the kernel memory will overflow eventually and cause undefined behavior. As MCU's memory is minimal, it is very easy to reach the memory limit.

Not being able to dynamically allocate memory might be a problem for some drivers. Several drivers need to store information for each process, like counters or shared buffers. Depending on the driver, the size of this stored information may vary and is not predictable by the kernel. In standard operating systems like Linux, drivers are allowed to dynamically allocate memory, precisely for these reasons.

Tock takes a different approach. Each driver has to define a Rust structure containing the data it wants to store for each process. This is called a *grant*. As there is no dynamic driver loading, the kernel knows exactly how many drivers require grants and how large each grant is at compile time. When a process starts, the kernel allocates the PCB and a pointer for each driver's grant in the *grant* region of the new process.

The first time a driver tries to access its grant for a process, the kernel will try to allocate memory space in the *grant* region for that driver's grant. If it succeeds, meaning the process is valid and enough unused memory is available in the *grant* region, the driver can store data. If the allocation fails, the driver cannot access the grant and will probably report an error to the process.

This approach ensures that a driver has either all the necessary grant memory available or has no grant available for a process. Figure 3-5 shows the *grant* region in detail. Another great advantage of using the *grant* region is that when a process is stopped, its memory is cleared by the kernel. As all the memory allocated by drivers for this process is in this process' *grant* region, there is no danger of leaking driver allocated memory. In other words, drivers can only allocate memory inside a *process' grant region*, a region that gets cleaned up when a process is stopped.

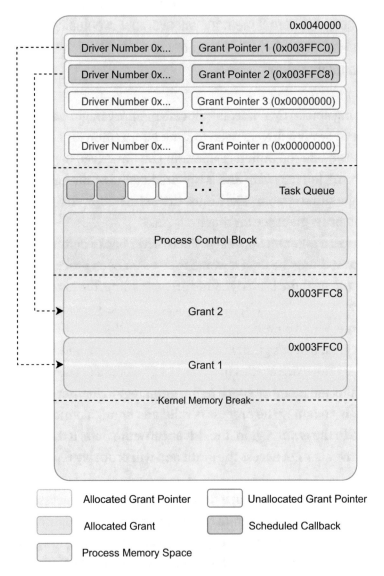

Figure 3-5. *The Grant Memory Space that stores the list of pointers toward driver grants, the task queue, and the Process Control Block*

Dynamic Grants

We stated before that drivers are not able to allocate memory dynamically. This is only partially true. Some drivers do need to allocate some extra memory that cannot be predicted at compile time. Tock offers a *DynamicGrant* structure for that. This works the same way as regular *grants* but allows drivers to ask for some extra space in the process' *grant region*.

Note   At the time of writing, none of the capsules in Tock actually use the *DynamicGrant.*

Whenever a driver needs some extra memory, it first has to enter its *grant*. Once its grant is allocated and available, the process can ask the kernel for some extra space. The kernel will try to allocate this extra space inside the *grant region* of the process. If it succeeds, it returns a *DynamicGrant* to the driver. The driver is responsible for storing it somewhere.

The *DynamicGrant* can be accessed in the same way normal *grants* are used. The kernel will ensure that the driver cannot access a *DynamicGrant* allocated in a no longer valid process. We will discuss the details of this in this book.

Note   Usually *DynamicGrants* are stored inside the normal *grant*, as it is strongly tied to a process.

Tock Application Package

One key differentiator of the Tock operating system is the ability to build and deploy applications separately from the kernel. This is very similar to how Linux and other operating systems ship applications. Before we dive in, we have to define two terms: the application *executable* and the application *package*. The first one defines a file that usually contains the binary executable code together with some initial data, while the latter contains the executable together with other files necessary to run the application. This includes data files like images, videos, sounds, and others.

While for most operating systems, the executable file is pretty standard, like PE for Windows, ELF for Linux, and MachO for macOS, the package file varies greatly. Windows uses mostly *MSI* packages; Linux, depending on the distribution, uses *DEB*, *RPM*, *snap*, and many others; macOS uses *DMG* or *PKG* packages. Mobile systems like iOS use *IPA* packages, and Android uses *APK* packages.

Most of the embedded operating systems provide a single binary file, stored in the *Intel HEX* or *UF2* file, that contains the kernel and all the apps, tightly linked together. Tock takes a different approach, providing a binary file for the kernel and separate particular files for the applications.

Tock Binary Format

While the Tock kernel is a regular binary, applications are very different. Tock defines an executable file format, named *Tock Binary Format*, used for storing an application. This file contains the executable code, initial data, and several headers describing how the applications should be loaded. Figure 3-6 (a) illustrates this format. The file starts with a TBF Header, which contains information on how the application should be loaded. Following the header, we have the binary executable code. The file ends with a padding as it has to be aligned to a four-byte boundary and possible MPU restrictions.

Tip   For Cortex-M devices, the alignment has several restrictions due to the MPU region size restrictions. One of the restrictions is that an MPU region needs to have the size of a power of two.

As applications are compiled separately from the kernel, the kernel has no way of knowing how large an application is, how much memory it needs, or what name it has. This is solved by adding a few headers inside the TBF Header of the binary file. Figure 3-6 (b) illustrates the format of the TBF Header. It starts with a fixed TBF Header Base, detailed in Figure 3-6 (c), which bears header format and size information. Several *type-length-value* (TLV) elements follow the TBF Header Base. The structure of a TLV element is described in Figure 3-6 (d).

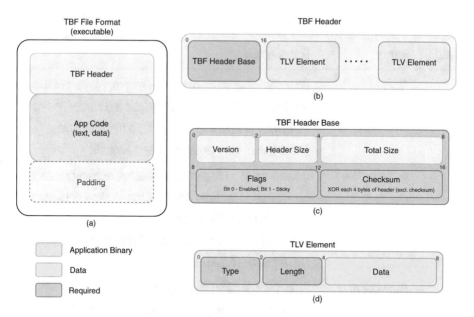

Figure 3-6.   *The Tock Binary Format and TBF Header Format*

Each one of these TLV elements has a *type*, a *length*, and a *data* payload. The type defines how the kernel should interpret the information from the data payload, and the length provides the size of the data payload. Table 3-5 describes the types that can be used.

There are two types of Tock applications: *relocatable* and *fixed address*. The first ones are the actual Tock standard applications that can be loaded into any address in memory and flash. They are built in a particular way, allowing the applications to work correctly regardless of where they are loaded. The second category is mostly a fallback. Due to some compiler issues, some applications cannot be built in this way and have to know the load memory and address at compile time. For the time being, Rust applications, due to an LLVM issue, and RISC-V, due to the compiler's lack of proper relocation, are *static address* apps.

Table 3-5. *TLV element types*

Type	Name	Description
1	*Main*	Provides information about the memory layout of the application. This TLV is required, as the kernel has no other way of knowing the required memory layout There has to be exactly one *main* element
2	*Writable flash region*	Defines an MCU flash region that the application should be allowed to write to. This is used to store persistent data between MCU reboots There may be several *writable flash region* elements, one for each requested region
3	*Package name*	Stores the application's name There has to be exactly one *package name* element

(*continued*)

Table 3-5. (*continued*)

Type	Name	Description
4	*Fixed address*	This is present only if the application is not *relocatable* and has to be loaded at a fixed memory and flash location There may be at most one *fixed address* element. Otherwise, the kernel will try to relocate the application.
5	*Permissions*	Specifies a set of capsule numbers and their command numbers that the application is allowed to call. Tock 2.0 does not yet implement these restrictions
6	*Persistent ACL*	Provides the access rules for the storage space. Tock 2.0 does not yet implement any restrictions based on the information within this header
7	*Kernel version*	Ensures that the application is compatible with the running kernel version. Tock uses an Application Binary Interface (ABI) between kernel and applications. As the kernel and the applications are compiled separately, the kernel has to make sure that the application was compiled using the same ABI; otherwise, applications might not run properly

We will discuss all these elements in detail in the chapter about application building.

Note   The types presented in Table 3-5 were valid at the time of writing. As there may be some additional types defined after the book has been written, we recommend that you look them up in the Tock official documentation.

Tock Application Bundle

As Tock runs on several different MCU architectures, the application binary code can be very different, depending on the platform. Tock allows developers to build an app bundle and distribute it for several platforms. This is done by using a file format called Tock Application Bundle (TAB).

The file format is a tar archive containing several TBF files, one for each supported platform, and a manifest describing each TBF. The TAB file is interpreted by tockloader, a command-line tool used for deploying Tock on the devices. When programming a device, tockloader will read the TAB file, select the corresponding TBF file for the platform, and upload it.

Binaries inside the TAB file have to be named using the following format: *<architecture>.<anything>.tbf*. The *anything* part from the file name may be any string value.

Flashing the System

An essential step in embedded systems development is writing the software to the device. This process is usually called *flashing* or *programming* the device. For Tock, it means loading the binary code of the kernel and the application's TBF files to the MCU's flash memory. While for most embedded systems, the two terms *flashing* and *programming* are usually interchangeable, the terminology used in Tock clearly separates them. In Tock terminology, flashing means to load code via JTAG, while programming means to load code through a serial connection to a bootloader.

For the time being, we will use the term *upload* to define the process of writing the software parts to the MCU's flash. Figure 3-7 shows the two ways in which software can be uploaded: *flashing* or *programming*.

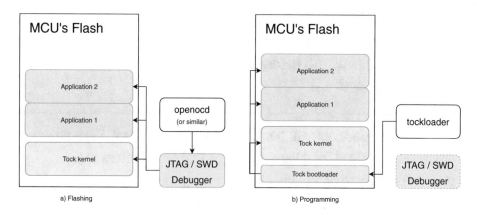

Figure 3-7. *Flashing (a) and programming (b) the Tock kernel and applications*

The Debug Chip

When writing software for computers, the operating system provides some primitives that allow a debugger software, *gdb*, for instance, to stop a program at a certain point, read its memory, display register values, etc. This is very important as finding errors in programs is not an easy task. The alternative for using a debugger software is to make a lot of prints on the screen.

When it comes to microcontrollers, debugging becomes more difficult. First of all, unlike computer software where the code runs on the same machine, microcontroller code runs on different hardware from the one you are working on. Second, microcontrollers do not usually have a *screen* where programs can print debug information. To overcome this problem, microcontrollers have a dedicated debug interface that allows an external device to stop them at a certain point, read memory, or register values. There are several standards for debugging interfaces, the most common being JTAG or SWD (ARM specific).

Even though the debug interface is present on all microcontrollers, to be used, it needs to be connected to a hardware debugger, such as SEGGER JLink or STM ST-Link. This hardware debugger is in turn connected to the computer's USB port.

Note   Some development boards, like the micro:bit v2, have an onboard embedded hardware debugger that allows them to be directly connected and debugged from a computer. Other boards, like the Raspberry Pi Pico, do not have this onboard and require external hardware before being debugged using a computer.

Flashing

When it comes to Tock, *flashing* means writing Tock software, kernel, and apps, using the hardware debug interface. This requires special software, like *OpenOCD*,[1] and special hardware, like JLink or ST-Link. This method is not specific to Tock, as any executable code can be uploaded via this method. Figure 3-7 (a) displays this method.

However, there are two advantages when flashing:

1. The microcontroller does not need any additional software running on it, and all the available flash memory can be used.

2. There is no way to lock you out, meaning that whatever goes wrong, one can always reflash the microcontroller.

---

[1] OpenOCD (Open On-Chip Debugger) is an open source on-chip debugger that links a software debugger like *gdb* to the hardware debugger on the device.

The second point is very important. Things can go wrong when writing software to the flash memory. For instance, you can have a power failure that leaves the flash only half-written. This will prevent the microcontroller from functioning properly. When using a hardware debugger, there is no problem. You can simply try again.

Programming

Programming a microcontroller means writing software onto its flash without the need for a hardware debugger. This lowers the cost of the system but does imply some restrictions. The microcontroller has to run a small piece of software called a *bootloader*. The bootloader works in the following way: when the microcontroller starts, it quickly checks if there is an update request. The way the update request is signaled differs from design to design. Some bootloaders check if a button is pressed, others check if there is data on the serial port, etc. If an update request is detected, the bootloader starts reading data from a communication port and performs several actions requested by the computer. Think of the bootloader as a small *server* receiving commands from a computer. If there is no update request, the bootloader simply runs the standard microcontroller software placed on top of the bootloader.

Tock has its own bootloader, *tock-bootloader*, together with dedicated software, *tockloader*, that perform these management tasks. *Tockloader* is able to update the Tock kernel, load, delete, update, activate and deactivate applications, and read board information.

This method of uploading software to the microcontroller is called *programming*. It does not need any special hardware, but it does need the small piece of bootloader software.

There are two drawbacks when using this method:

1.   The *tock-bootloader* takes up some space inside
     the flash.

2.   If *tock-bootloader* has an error and overwrites itself
     while writing to the flash memory, a hardware
     debugger is required to restore it.

While the bootloader might be capable of updating itself, a hardware
debugger is usually required to flash the bootloader for the first time.

The Safe Way

The safest way of developing and prototyping apps is to use both *flashing*
and *programming*. Flashing allows debugging, disaster recovery, and more
flash memory, while programming is better suited in production.

To be able to leverage the advantages of *flashing* and using the
tockloader software to load apps dynamically, *tockloader* can use the
hardware debugger to upload the kernel and applications, as if it were
programming the device via a *tock-bootloader*. Figure 3-8 describes
this method.

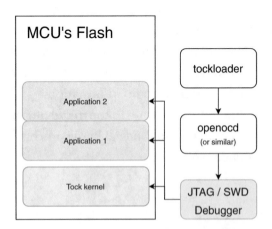

Figure 3-8. *Using tockloader with the hardware debugger*

Tockloader can issue commands to a debugger software, like *OpenOCD* or *jlink,* and can perform more or less the same tasks as a regular bootloader. The only downside is that it cannot autodetect the device; it needs to be told which debugger software to use and what board it has to deal with.

This is the method that we will be using for the *micro:bit v2* and the *Raspberry Pi Pico.* However, we need to keep in mind that for the Raspberry Pi Pico, we have to use a standard Raspberry Pi board as a programmer, as solely the Pico does not have a hardware debugger integrated.

Summary

In this chapter, we have described the general architecture of the Tock embedded operating system, pointing out several differences from classical operating systems like Linux. Throughout this book, we will discuss in detail each of the subjects presented here and provide several development examples about their usage.

We will start with setting up the development environment, uploading the Tock kernel, and uploading example apps written in C and Rust. Further on, we will discuss how to write capsules and add functionality to the Tock kernel and how to use these from the C and Rust user spaces.

Nevertheless, we will provide some guidelines on designing and implementing complex services and applications, providing examples for ARM, using micro:bit v2 and the Raspberry Pi Pico.

CHAPTER 4

Rust for Tock

We have reached the point where it's time to start writing code for the Tock kernel. As Tock is an operating system written in Rust, this will require some basic Rust programming knowledge. Therefore, this chapter focuses on some of the important aspects that the Rust programming language brings to the table. When describing Rust particularities, we assume that the reader is familiar with other compiled programming languages like C/C++ and knows how pointers and memory allocation work. Some basic knowledge about Rust's language constructs like data types, structs, enums, and traits is also required.

This chapter details only essential aspects of Rust's basic data types, structures, enums, and traits. We will focus on Rust's references and lifetimes.

Introduction to Rust

First of all, we have to get through some basic Rust notions. Please keep in mind that this is a very brief introduction. We strongly recommend you to read the introduction of *The Rust Book*.[1]

Rust is a programming language that focuses on being highly secure without compromising performance. While several programming languages like Java or Python provide a high degree of safety, it comes

---

[1] The Rust Book - `https://doc.rust-lang.org/book`

© Alexandru Radovici and Ioana Culic 2022
A. Radovici and I. Culic, *Getting Started with Secure Embedded Systems*,
https://doi.org/10.1007/978-1-4842-7789-8_4

at a cost: performance. Rust offers the same security guarantees without sacrificing performance by imposing strict programming patterns that allow the compiler to make several assumptions at compile time. In other words, it is as fast as C, as secure as Java, but more challenging to learn.

For the remainder of this chapter, we will assume the reader is familiar with basic Rust language syntax, like variable declarations, function declarations, and control flows (e.g., *if, for,* and *while).*

Further on, we will describe Rust by making analogies to C/C++ and Java.

Rust Primary Data Types

Rust provides a limited set of data types that are considered *primary*. They represent numbers and characters. Table 4-1 describes these types.

Table 4-1. *Rust primary data types and their value range*

Name	Description	Values
()	Unit	()
char	One Character in UTF-8 format (4 bytes)	UTF-8 code point
bool	Boolean value	true, false
u8	Unsigned byte integer	0 … 255
u16	Unsigned 2 bytes integer	0 … 65535
u32	Unsigned 4 bytes integer	0 … 4_294_967_295
u64	Unsigned 8 bytes integer	$0 … 2^{64}-1$
u128	Unsigned 16 bytes integer	$0 … 2^{128} - 1$
i8	Signed byte integer	-128 … 127
i16	Signed 2 bytes integer	-32768 … 32767

(continued)

Table 4-1. (*continued*)

Name	Description	Values
i32	Signed 4 bytes integer	−2_147_483_648 ... 4_294_967_295
i64	Signed 8 bytes integer	-2^{63} ... $2^{63}\text{-}1$
i128	Signed 16 bytes integer	2^{127} ... $2^{127}\text{-}1$
usize	Pointer size unsigned integer	0 ... $2^{pointer\_size}\text{-}1$
isize	Pointer size signed integer	$-2^{pointer\_size-1}$ ... $2^{pointer\_size-1}\text{-}1$
f32	Single precision (4 bytes) floating point	
f64	Double precision (8 bytes) floating point	

Note   Contrary to what C does, similar to Java, Rust makes a clear difference between the boolean and numeric types. Numeric values are not automatically transformed into booleans and vice versa. In other words, 0 is not considered to be equal to `false`.

Special attention has to be paid to the character (char) type. Rust uses UTF-8 characters, while C uses ASCII and Java uses UTF-16. While in C a character is 1 byte long and in Java 2 bytes long, a character can be up to 4 bytes long in Rust. The char data type is always 4 bytes long to be able to accommodate any Unicode character encoded using UTF-8.

Note   UTF-8 allows encoding of Unicode characters using variable length. A character may be 1 byte long (ASCII characters) up to 4 bytes long.

Mutability

Rust defines a concept that is not available in C or Java: mutability. By default, all declared variables are considered *immutable*. This means that once assigned, their value cannot be modified. Listing 4-1 outlines this concept. Variable v is immutable and cannot be reassigned. On the other hand, variable v2 is declared as mutable (using let mut) and is reassignable.

Listing 4-1. Rust mutability example

```
fn main() {
    let v = 1;
    v = v + 1; // ERROR: v is immutable
    println!("v {}", v);

    let mut v2 = 1;
    v2 = v2 + 1;
    println!("v2 {}", v2);
}
```

Rust infers the actual data type of variables v1 and v2. The Rust compiler can determine that the data type of the two variables is u32 by looking at the value assigned to them. If we want to use different data types, we have to either declare the variable's data type or add a data type to the constant. Listing 4-2 displays a rewrite of Listing 4-1, with v having a declared type and v2 having a constant with a data type.

Listing 4-2. Rust data types

```
fn main() {
    let v: u8 = 1;
    v = v + 1; // ERROR: v is immutable
    println!("v {}", v);
```

```
let mut v2 = 1u8;
v2 = v2 + 1;
println!("v2 {}", v2);
}
```

Note For integers, Rust will automatically use the u32 data type, while for floats, it will use f64.

Another interesting aspect is that reference data types (&Type and &mut Type) have mutability information. For instance, in let vr = &v, the type of vr is &u32, while in let vr2 = &mut v2, the data type of v2 is &mut u32.

Note Even though constants can be considered immutable variables, there is a difference between them. The compiler places the constants in a separate memory space, while immutable variables are standard variables, just that the compiler does not allow them to be reassigned. While constants need to have a known value at compile-time, immutable variables do not.

Who Owns A Value?

Rust introduces the concept of ownership. For every value, there can be only one owner. For instance, if we declare a variable v and assign it a value, v owns the value assigned to it. An interesting question pops up when we assign another variable to a variable. Listing 4-3 describes this problem.

Listing 4-3. The Rust ownership problem

```
fn main() {
    let v: u32 = 1; // v owns the value
    let v2 = v; // who owns the value, v2 or v?
}
```

First, the value 1 is assigned to the variable v. That means that v owns the value. In fact, it owns any value that is stored at that memory location. Now what happens when v2 is assigned the value of v? Rust applies the following rules:

1. If it can make a copy of the value, it copies it before assigning it; v2 now owns a copy of the value;

2. If it cannot make a copy of the value, it will move it. The owner of the value will be v2 instead of v. Any further use of the v variable will generate a compiler error.

The question that now follows is: *how does Rust know if it can copy or not a value?* This brings us to tackling the *traits* aspect. In simple words, traits describe a set of functions that can be applied to a data type. If you are familiar with Java, traits are similar to interfaces. A class is said to implement a particular interface if it defines all the methods described in that interface. In contrast to Java, traits can be described for any data type. We will cover Rust traits in depth later in this chapter.

When it comes to a copy or move, the Rust compiler will check if the data type implements the *Copy* trait. If it does, it will copy the value. Otherwise, it will move it. All primitive data types shown in Table 4-1 implement the *Copy* trait, and this means that the example described in Listing 4-3 will perform a copy of the value.

Listing 4-4. Copying a value in Rust

```
fn main() {
    // v owns the value
    let v: u32 = 1;
    // who owns the value, v2 or v?

    let mut v2 = v;

    v2 = v2 + 1;

    println!("v {}", v);
    println!("v2 {}", v2);
}
```

To make it clear that Rust performs a copy, Listing 4-4 goes further with the example and changes the value of v2. When printed, v will have the value 1, while v2 will have the value 2 as it was incremented.

While primitive data types implement *Copy* by default, complex types do not. Listing 4-5 shows an example where we define a complex data type, a structure containing a number. We assign a structure (the value) to the variable v, then assign variable v to v2. The Rust compiler will check whether the Number structure implements *Copy*. As it does not, it will move the value. When trying to print the number within the variable v, the compiler issues an error as the variable v does not own the value anymore and cannot be used.

Listing 4-5. Moving a value in Rust

```
struct Number {
    n: u32
}

fn main() {
    let v = Number {n:1};
    let v2 = v;
```

```
println!("v.n {}", v.n); // ERROR - v does     //not own the
                                               value, it was
                                               moved to v2

println!("v2.n {}", v2.n);
}
```

Strings

Being able to store text is a very important feature of any language. Rust provides two distinct data types to handle Strings: the String data type, and the String slice (&str). The String data type is defined in Rust's standard library (std) and uses heap allocation. On the other hand, a String slice is a reference to a memory location of an array ([u8]) that contains a text and that has a fixed length.

The Heap-Allocated String

Similar to Java, Rust provides a particular type called String that can store a series of characters. Internally, Rust stores three values: a reference to a buffer, the length of the stored String (in UTF-8 code points), and the capacity (in bytes). Listing 4-6 shows (empirically) how the String is defined. The & sign represents an array slice, and we will discuss this later. For now, just think of it as a reference towards an array of bytes (the same type as char[] in the C language).

Listing 4-6. The empirical definition of the Rust String type

```
struct String {
   buffer: &[u8],
   len: usize,
}
```

Note   The C language does not actually provide a String type, it uses the normal array of characters (char[ ]) and has a special convention to describe the end of the String. This is one of the most dangerous aspects of C and is most probably the primary vector of attacks.

Further on, let's take a closer look at the elements of the String structure. The buffer property is the actual storage space. This is somehow similar to the C Strings, as it is a simple character array that holds bytes. The useful length of the Strings is stored by len. This means how many useful characters the String has. Remember that each character is a UTF-8 code point, so a character might be 1 up to 4 bytes.

Now, what about the third value? We mentioned earlier that the String stores three values, but the structure defines only two. The third value, the *capacity* of the String, is the array size in bytes. Unlike C arrays, Rust arrays and array slices (references) are described by two values: the actual data they hold and their length. By using buffer.len(), we can retrieve the array's length.

An essential difference between Rust Strings and C or Java Strings is how individual characters are accessed. Both C and Java use array access by s[position]. This works in C as Strings are just arrays, and in Java, as Strings store Unicode characters, each of them occupying precisely 2 bytes. As Rust stores UTF-8, the character length is variable. Accessing a random element in the String's buffer might not be at a character boundary, it might be in the middle of a UTF-8 code point. This is why Rust Strings provide an iterator that is able to go through all the characters. Using standard iterator functions, we can get a specific character. Listing 4-7 illustrates such an example.

Listing 4-7. Create a new String and access a character

```
fn main() {
    let s = String::from("Hello from Rust, ☺ how are you?");

    println!("{}", s[10]);
    // ERROR - does not implement the Index trait
    println!("{}", s.chars(). nth(10).unwrap());
    // uses an iterator
    println!("{}", s);
}
```

Note   New Strings are created using the from method. Simply assigning s = "..." will not generate a new String but a String slice (&str).

An important characteristic is that String does not implement *Copy*, which means that Strings will be moved upon assignment. This decision has been made due to performance issues, as copying a String requires some processing time for copying the buffer. Listing 4-8 outlines this.

Listing 4-8. String assignment is a move

```
fn main() {
    let title = String::from("The Title");
    let the_title = title;

    // ERROR
    // title does not own the value anymore
    println!("title {}", title);
    println!("the_title {}", the_title);
}
```

There might be cases where we want to copy the String instead of moving it. For that, String implements the Clone trait, which provides the clone method that can perform a copy (Listing 4-9).

Listing 4-9. Moving a String in Rust

```
fn main() {
    let title = String::from("The Title");

    let the_title = title.clone();

    println!("title {}", title);
    println!("the_title {}", the_title);
}
```

String Slices

Slices are a special kind of reference mostly used for arrays and String variables. In the case of String, a slice is a reference towards the inner buffer of the String. Unlike a reference to a String, slices only store a length parameter. Their size cannot be changed.

The String slice has its type, &str. In most cases, this is what functions will take as parameters. Rust types constant Strings as &str. This is why we used let a = String::from ("...") instead of let a = "..." to define a String, like in Listing 4-10.

Note   Rust will automatically typecast String references (&String) to String slices (&str).

Listing 4-10. The difference between a String and a String slice (&str)

```
fn main() {
    let string = String::from("The Title");
    let string_slice = "The Title";

    // use these to display the types
    // let _: () = string;
    // let _: () = string_slice;
}
```

Tock does not use `String` as this data type is part of the standard library (`std`) which is not used. The `String` data type is not available unless the standard library is included because it uses heap allocation. This requires a heap allocator, which is available in the standard library. On the other hand, Tock does use String slices (`&str`) that are allocated in the data section (constant Strings " . . . . . ").

Note   The difference between a reference to a String (`&String`) and a String slice (`&str`) is subtle. As `&String` is a reference to a `String`, anyone borrowing the String in a mutable way may change it in any way. When using a String slice (`&str`), its length cannot be changed, even if it is mutable (`&mut str`).

Borrowing

Now that we understand value ownership, we have to discuss an important usage of values: passing them as arguments to a function. Let's take the example in Listing 4-11, which describes a function that adds two numbers. The question that pops up is what happens with the ownership of the values of a and b. The rules applied by the Rust compiler for function arguments are the same as for assignments. If the data types implement the *Copy* trait, values will be copied. Otherwise, they will be moved.

Listing 4-11. A function that computes the sum of two numbers

```
fn sum(a: u32, b: u32) -> u32 {
    a + b
}

fn main() {
    let a = 1;
    let b = 2;
    let s = sum(a, b);

    println!("sum {}", s);
    // works as the value has been copied to sum
    println!("a {}", a);
}
```

In this example, everything works fine as u32 is a primitive type and primitive types implement the *Copy* trait. Now, let's take a look at what happens when we use String instead of numbers. Remember, String does not implement the *Copy* trait. Listing 4-12 declares a function that *sums up* two String variables. When the string_sum is called, the arguments' values are moved to the function and are not available anymore. This means that the a and b variables cannot be used anymore.

Note   The format! macro works just like println!, except that it returns a newly allocated String with the text instead of printing the formatted text.

Listing 4-12. String arguments are moved to the function

```rust
fn string_sum(a: String, b: String) -> String {
    format!("{}{}",a, b)
}

fn main() {
    let a = String::from("The");
    let b = String::from(" Title");
    let s = string_sum(a, b);

    println!("sum {}", s);

    // ERROR
    // the value has been moved to string_sum
    println!("a {}", a);
}
```

The question is, how can we solve this problem? One idea would be to clone the arguments before we send them, but this is not efficient. Moreover, the function only needs the arguments temporarily while it creates a new String with the contents of the parameters. When the function has finished executing, the two variables should be usable again.

This is where the concept of *borrowing* comes into play. Rust allows us to *borrow* the values to the function while it needs them. This means that we still have ownership of the values. We just might have some restrictions on using them while they are borrowed.

Note While other languages like C or Java use the *sending a value by reference*, Rust takes this a step forward to the concept of borrowing. In other words, a borrow of a value is a reference to the value together with an annotated mutability that respects a set of rules. At any given time, there can only be one single mutable reference or as many immutable references.

Rust has two essential rules when it comes to borrowing. At a certain point, there can be:

- any number of immutable borrows;
- one single mutable borrow.

As long as we follow these rules, Rust will guarantee memory safety at compile-time, without any need for a runtime library or garbage collection.

To use borrowing, we just have to modify the function parameters so that they receive a reference towards a String. Listing 4-13 shows the modified function.

Listing 4-13. Borrowing a String

```
fn string_sum(a: &String, b: &String) -> String {
    format!("{}{}", a, b)
}
fn main() {
    let a = String::from("The");
    let b = String::from(" Title");
    // immutable borrow a and b
    let s = string_sum(&a, &b);
```

```
    println!("sum {}", s);
    // works as a still owns the value
    println!("a {}", a);
}
```

This might not seem very different from other languages, but there is more to discuss about borrowing and references and how Rust can provide security guarantees. We will discuss this in the *Lifetimes* section.

Slices

A slice is a reference towards a part of the array. Besides the actual reference, the slice stores its length. Listing 4-14 defines a function that returns the highest number in an array. If we take a better look, instead of receiving an array, it receives an array slice. From the function's point of view, this is the whole array. The slice has a fixed length, and its index starts at 0.

Listing 4-14. Passing an array slice as parameter

```
fn max_num(v: &[u32]) -> u32 {
    println!("length {}", v.len());
    let mut max = v[0];
    for n in v {
        // let _:() = n; use this to determine the type of n
        if max < *n {
            max = *n;
        }
    }
    max
}
```

```
fn main() {
    let v = [5, 4, 1, 2, 3];

    //slice from the whole array
    let m = max_num(&v);
    // slice from position 3 to 5 (exclusive)
    let m_part = max_num(&v[3..5]);

    println!("m {}", m);
    println!("m_part {}", m_part);
}
```

The example uses the function twice. First, it creates a slice from the whole array, which is defined exactly the same as a reference to the array. The second time, it creates a slice starting from the 4th element in the array (index 3) to the 5th (up to, but without, position 5).

By using slices that store the length, the Rust compiler is able to generate code that immediately panics if an access beyond the slice's length is made.

As Rust data types are inferred mainly by the compiler, it is sometimes difficult to understand which data type the compiler has inferred. To print the actual data type of a variable, we can use a trick. Declare a variable _ of type () and assign it the variable whose type we are trying to find out. As long as the variable type is not (), the compiler will print an error pointing out the actual data type. Listing 4-14 has a comment using this trick to find out the variable type of n. From the error message, we can see the data type of n is &u32. Listing 4-15 shows such an example.

Listing 4-15. Use an error to print the type of a variable

```
5 |           let _: () = n; // use this to determine the type of n
  |               --  ^ expected `()`, found `&u32`
  |               |
  |               expected due to this
```

Lifetimes

Handling references is one of the most important tools that Rust provides. This allows the compiler to offer several memory guarantees and automatic memory allocation at compile time. For this section, we assume that the reader is familiar with C language memory allocations (`malloc` and `free`). We will compare all the examples only to C examples as Java has garbage collection and automatically handles memory safety and allocation (with a heavy performance toll).

Who Is Responsible for Deallocation?

In Rust, each variable has a lifetime. The lifetime of a variable is defined as the program span from the point when a variable is created until it is dropped.

Note   Deallocating a value, or in other words, freeing it, is defined in Rust as *dropping*. Dropping is done automatically by the compiler.

We will start by presenting several examples in C while pointing out some memory allocation issues.

Function Parameters and Return Values

The first example is presented in Listing 4-16. We have (an external) function, `without_first_word,` that returns a pointer to a String (char*) representing the sentence stored in the parameter s, excluding the first word.

Listing 4-16. The problem of who has to deallocate a returned value in C

```c
#include <stdio.h>
#include <string.h>
#include <stdlib.h>

char * without_first_word (char *s);

int main ()
{
    char * s = strdup ("We love Rust");
    char *wfw = without_first_word (s);
    // free (s);    <-- before printf ?
    printf ("%s\n", wfw);
    // free (wfw); <-- after printf ?
}
```

By analyzing this example, two questions pop up. First, who has to deallocate the returned value? Second, does the function keep a reference to the supplied value s after it returns? Such an example is the strtok function.

In the case of the first question, is the returned value wfw a pointer within the allocated String s, or is it a copy of the word that the function has allocated? Listing 4-17 presents the version where the returned value is a pointer within the supplied value s. In this case, freeing the returned value will fail, as that value has never been allocated using malloc. Moreover, deallocating the initial value s before the returned value is used will result in a dangling pointer. The returned value will point towards an area of memory that has been deallocated.

Listing 4-17. Case one: the returned value is a pointer within the original value s in C

```c
char * without_first_word (char *s) {
    int pos = 0;
    for (unsigned int i=0; i < strlen (s); i++) {
        if (s[i] != ' ') pos = pos + 1;
        else break;
    }
    return &s[pos];
}
```

The second variant is presented in Listing 4-18. The returned value is a copy (newly allocated) of the original value. This means that the initial value s can be deallocated at any time after the function returns. In contrast to the previous version, in this case, the returned value wfw also has to be deallocated after it is not used anymore to avoid memory leaking.

Listing 4-18. Case two: the returned value is a pointer within the original value s in C

```c
char * without_first_word (char *s) {
    int pos = 0;
    for (unsigned int i=0; i < strlen (s); i++) {
        if (s[i] != ' ') pos = pos + 1;
        else break;
    }
    return strdup (&s[pos]);
}
```

Regarding the second question, whether the function keeps the pointer for further use after it returns, even though we cannot be sure, judging by the function's name, most probably it will not keep a pointer to the variable value s after it returns. We will have another example where this is not deductible.

Now, here comes the important part. We were able to decide how to handle the deallocation of s and wfw based on the contents of the function. If we had only the function declaration, as shown in Listing 4-18, we would not be able to decide what to do. The problem is that the C compiler has access only to this declaration, so it does not know how to handle it. This is left at the developers' decision. Moreover, as a developer usually includes a lot of libraries in the application, it is almost impossible to read all the source code of all the used functions.

Rust solves this problem by using lifetime annotations. Every reference used in Rust has to be annotated with a lifetime. This concept might be the key difference between Rust and any other compiled programming language. In a nutshell, giving each reference a lifetime allows the Rust compiler to observe and impose the connections between a function's input parameters and its output. Listing 4-19 shows the same example as Listing 4-18, but written in Rust. In this case, the compiler knows that the output is connected to the input parameter and the input parameter cannot be freed until the function's output is freed.

Listing 4-19. Rust lifetime annotations

```
fn without_first_word<'a>(s: &'a str) -> &'a str {
    // ...
}

fn main() {
    let s = String::from("We love Rust");
    let wfw = without_first_word (&s);
    // drop(s); equivalent of free (s)
    println! ("{}", wfw);
    // drop(s); equivalent of free (s)
}
```

To answer the question *who is responsible for deallocation?* Rust takes a look at the lifetime annotations. If the output (return value) of a function has the same lifetime annotation as one of the inputs, it is clear that the deallocation is necessary only for the input parameter. Moreover, the input parameter will be safely deallocated only when the output value of the function is not used anymore.

Let's take another example involving function parameters (Listing 4-20). We define a function that appends a String slice to a String and returns a slice to the String. The function uses the same lifetime annotation for all input parameters and the output. If we take a close look, this might not seem the best idea. While the function's output is indeed a slice, it is actually a reference to the first parameter s and has nothing to do with the second parameter n. Since we have defined the same lifetime for both parameters, s and n, the Rust compiler will not allow us to drop n until we drop the function's returned value. To make it clearer, from within the main function, we cannot drop s2 until we drop title, even though title is a reference to s1 and has nothing to do with s2.

Listing 4-20. Append a String slice to a String

```rust
fn append <'a>(s: &'a mut String, n: &'a str)  -> &'a str {
    s.push_str(n);
    s
}
fn main() {
    let mut s1 = String::from("ip");
    let s2 = String::from(" workshop");
    let title = append(&mut s1, &s2);
    // let t1 = s1; equivalent of free(s1)
    let t2 = s2; equivalent of free(s2)
    println!("{}", title);
}
```

To solve this problem, Listing 4-21 displays the append function with the correct lifetime annotations. The returned value and the s parameter have the same lifetime annotation as they are connected. The n parameter has a different lifetime annotation has the returned value of the function has nothing to do with it. In this way, the main function can drop s2 without having to drop title first.

Listing 4-21. The right way to append a String slice to a String

```
fn append <'a, 'b> (s: &'a mut String, n: &'b str)  ->
&'a str {
    s.push_str (n);
    s
}
```

Lifetime Elision Rules

Writing lifetime annotations can make the code less readable. Many times lifetime annotations follow a template. This is why the Rust developers have defined three lifetime elision rules. These allow us, developers, to elide the annotations of some references:

1. All the parameters of a function that do not have a specified (elided) lifetime receive a lifetime of their own.

2. If the parameters of a function have exactly one lifetime, elided or not, this lifetime is assigned to all the elided lifetimes of the return value.

3. If the parameters of a function have more than one lifetime, elided or not, and one of these parameters is &self or &mut self, the lifetime of self is assigned to all the elided lifetimes of the return value.

Listing 4-22 shows an example for each of the three rules.

Listing 4-22. Examples for lifetime elision rules

```
// Rule 1
fn ex(&p1, &p2);
fn ex<'a, 'b>(&'a p1, &'b p2);

// Rule 2
fn ex(&p) -> (&p1, &p2);
fn ex<'a>(&'a p) -> (&'a p1, &'a p2);

// Rule 3
fn ex(&self, &p1) -> (&p1, &p2);
fn ex<'a, 'b>(&'a self, &'b p1) -> (&'a p1, &'a p2);
```

Generics and Trait Objects

One of the most used programming techniques is Object Oriented Programming (OOP). This allows developers to reuse code or variants of the code that they have already written. The two main advantages of OOP are inheritance and polymorphism. While inheritance enables developers to write less code and reuse already written code, polymorphism allows developers to substitute similar structures (more precisely objects) among each other.

A Kind of Inheritance

Rust does not support inheritance. This is a deliberate design choice. Instead of inheriting a structure, Rust favors structure composition. Listing 4-23 provides an example, written in Java, where MicroBit inherits Device.

Listing 4-23. Example of Java inheritance

```java
class Device {
    String mcu;
    int pins;

    int getPinsCount () {
        return this.pins;
    }

    void setPin (int pin, int value) {
        // ...
    }
}

class MicroBit extends Device {
    int leds;
}
```

In Rust, we cannot inherit a structure, but we can compose them as shown in Listing 4-24.

Listing 4-24. Example of Rust composition

```rust
struct Device {
    mcu: String,
    pins: usize
}

impl Device {
    pub fn get_pins_count(&self) -> usize {
        self.pins
    }
```

```rust
    pub fn set_pin(&self, pin: usize, value: usize) {
        // ...
    }
}

struct MicroBit {
    device: Device,
    leds: usize
}

impl MicroBit {
    pub fn get_pins_count(&self) -> usize {
        self.device.get_pins_count ()
    }

    pub fn set_pin(&self, pin: usize, value: usize) {
        self.device.set_pin(pin, value);
    }
}
```

Similar to Python and unlike Java, Rust requires functions to define the self parameter. While in Java, the compiler automatically adds this as a reference to the current object, Rust provides three ways of defining self: self, &self, and &mut self. These three have different meanings and are used in different situations:

- self is used when the value of the variable on which a function is called has to be *consumed*. In other words, if we call value.use(...), the variable value will not be available anymore, as it was moved to the function use;

- &self is used when the value of the variable on which the function is called is borrowed in an immutable way. This means that if we call value.use(...), the function use may access the value in a read-only mode;

- &mut self is the equivalent of self in Python and this in Java. In Rust, this means that if we call value.use(...), the function use borrows the value in a read-write way.

While this might seem strange and somehow counterintuitive, Rust does nothing else than expose to the developer more or less what happens in C++ and Java. Whenever a class inherits another class, the C++ and Java compiler transforms it into a composition underneath.

Note   The C++ compiler performs an actual composition of non-virtual classes where the inheriting class contains the inherited one. For virtual classes, the C++ compiler merges the inheriting and inherited classes and generates a compatible vtable. All classes in Java are virtual and, as such, use the merge approach.

The downside of this is that, yes, we have to write some more lines of code. For the MicroBit, we have to call the functions from the device manually. This is done automatically in Java. The advantage is a little more subtle. To avoid the *Diamond Problem*, Java allows only simple inheritance. That means that a class cannot inherit more than one class (Listing 4-25). On the other hand, Rust does not allow inheritance and makes the developer explicitly include the two *inherited* structures as elements in the new structure. When calling a method that should have been inherited, the developer has to explicitly call one or the other, as shown in Listing 4-26.

Listing 4-25. The Diamond Problem

```
class Device {
    protected:
        string mcu;
        int pins;
```

```cpp
    public:
        Device (int pins) {
            this->pins = pins;
        }

        int getPinsCount () {
            return this->pins;
        }
};

class MicroBit : public Device {
   public:
        MicroBit () : Device (10) {

        }
};

class RaspberryPiPico : public Device {
   public:
        RaspberryPiPico () : Device (20) {

        }
};

// this is illegal in java, but legal in C++
class DevelopmentBoard : public MicroBit, public
RaspberryPiPico {

};

int main () {
   DevelopmentBoard board = DevelopmentBoard ();
   printf ("pins %d\n", board.getPinsCount());
   return 0;
}
```

Note   In OOP, the diamond problem is one of the significant limitations of multiple inheritance. Let's say we have the class Device and two classes, MicroBit and RaspberryPiPico, that inherit Device, and the class DevelopmentBoard that inherits both MicroBit and RaspberryPiPico (Listing 4-25). The problem is the following: after compilation, DevelopmentBoard contains both MicroBit and RaspberryPiPico. When asked about the pins count using the getPinsCount function, the class has no idea how to respond. It does not know which of the two objects it contains: MicroBit or RaspberryPiPico.

Listing 4-26. Rust's solution for the Diamond Problem. Developers have to clearly state what happens when a function exported by both inherited structures is called

```
struct DevelopmentBoard {
    microbit: MicroBit,
    raspberry_pi: RaspberryPiPico
}

impl DevelopmentBoard {
    pub fn get_pins_count() {
        self.microbit.get_pins_count() + self.raspberry_pi.get_
        pins_count()
    }
}
```

Traits

Despite the advantages, composition has a limitation. While in Java, any value of type Device can be assigned an object of type MicroBit, this is not possible in Rust. For instance, let's write a free-standing function (in Java, this will be a status method in the class Main) that sets all the pins of a device to zero. Listings 4-27 and 4-28 show the functions in Java and Rust.

Listing 4-27. Setting all the pins to zero in Java

```
public static void setPinsZero(Device device) {
 for (int i=0; i < device.getPinsCount(); i++) {
    device.setPin (i, 0);
 }
}
```

Listing 4-28. Setting all the pins to zero in Rust. We use a reference to Device as the function only borrows Device

```
fn set_pins_zero(device: &Device) {
    for pin in 0..device.get_pins_count() {
        device.set_pin(i, 0);
    }
}
```

In Java, we can call the method setPinsZero on any object that extends Device. In Rust, this is not possible. Rust uses composition, so each structure is a different data type. To solve this issue, Rust implements *traits*.

Whenever we work with a structure, we usually interact with its methods or functions, never directly with the properties. It is very seldom that we have a public property. Rust is based on this assumption.

A *trait* is similar to (but not the same as) Java interfaces. It is a definition of methods. It can be considered similar to (but in no way the same as) a C header. Whenever a structure states that it implements a trait,

it has to implement all the methods that the trait defines. Listing 4-29
illustrates an example of a Pins trait that provides pin manipulation
functions.

Listing 4-29. The Pins trait

```
trait Pins {
    fn get_pins_count(&self) -> usize;
    fn set_pin(&self, pin: usize, value: usize);
}
```

Note   The C header is only an empirical example. A trait is very
different from it. The similarity is that they both export function
definitions.

Now that we have a trait, let's implement it for our structures. Unlike
Java, where interfaces are implemented directly inside the structure, in
Rust, each trait implementation has a separate block (Listing 4-30).

Listing 4-30. The implementation of the trait Pins for Device,
MicroBit, RaspberryPiPico, and DevelopmentBoard

```
impl Pins for Device {
    fn get_pins_count(&self) -> usize {
        self.pins
    }

    fn set_pin(&self, pin: usize, value: usize) {
        // ...
    }
}
```

```
impl Pins for MicroBit {
   fn get_pins_count(&self) -> usize {
       self.device.get_pins_count ()
   }

   fn set_pin(&self, pin: usize, value: usize) {
       self.device.set_pin (pin, value);
   }
}

impl Pins for RaspberryPiPico {
  fn get_pins_count(&self) -> usize {
      self.device.get_pins_count()
  }

  fn set_pin (&self, pin: usize, value: usize) {
      self.device.set_pin (pin, value);
  }
}

impl Pins for DevelopmentBoard {
   fn get_pins_count(&self) -> usize {
       self.microbit.get_pins_count() + self.raspberry_pi.get_
       pins_count()
   }
   fn set_pin(&self, pin: usize, value: usize){
       if pin < self.microbit.get_pins_count() {
           self.microbit.set_pin(pin, value);
       }
       else
       {
```

```
        self.raspberry_pi.set_pin(
          pin -
              self.microbit.get_pins_count(),
          value
        );
      }
    }
}
```

Once we have implemented the Pins trait, all our structures have a common ground. The next step is to rewrite the set_pins_zero function. Listing 4-31 displays two examples of how any programmer would think to implement the function. However, both are not correct and cannot be compiled.

Listing 4-31. Two incorrect examples of set_pins_zero implementation

```
fn set_pins_zero(device: Pins){
    for pin in 0..device.get_pins_count() {
        device.set_pin(pin, 0);
    }
}
fn set_pins_zero(device: &Pins){
    for pin in 0..device.get_pins_count() {
        device.set_pin(pin, 0);
    }
}
```

As the trait is not an actual structure but just a definition, the code above does not work. The Rust compiler needs to know at compile-time the size of all parameters for a function. In the first example, as Pins might be replaced with any structure that implements the trait, the compiler has no way of knowing its size. In the second example, the compiler knows the exact size as &Pins is a reference (pointer to the data and pointer to vtable) and only throws a warning requiring us to use the dyn keyword. In future editions of Rust, this will be an error.

In this context, there are two ways of writing the function: one is by using generics, and the other one uses trait objects. Further on, we detail both approaches, each one with advantages and disadvantages.

Generics-Based Implementation

Listing 4-32 displays the implementation based on generics. We define a function template rather than an actual function. As the example shows, we use the data type P, where P can be any data type that implements the Pins trait. All three variants of the template function are identical. Which to choose is just a matter of preference and has no impact upon the compiled code.

Listing 4-32. Function implementation using generics

```
fn set_pins_zero<P: Pins>(device: &P) {
    for pin in 0..device.get_pins_count() {
        device.set_pin(i, 0);
    }
}

fn set_pins_zero<P>(device: &P)
    where P: Pins
{
    for pin in 0..device.get_pins_count() {
        device.set_pin(i, 0);
    }
}
```

```
fn set_pins_zero(device: &P impl Pins) {
    for pin in 0..device.get_pins_count() {
        device.set_pin(i, 0);
    }
}
```

When the template function is used, the compiler will create and compile the actual function by replacing P with the actual type that is being supplied. Listing 4-33 shows the function calls. For the first one, the compiler will generate a set_pins_zero function where the type P is replaced by MicroBit. For the second call, the compiler will generate another set_pins_zero function where the type P is replaced by RaspberryPiPico. In the compiled code, there will be two differently declared set_pins_zero functions.

Listing 4-33. Implementing generic functions

```
let microbit = MicroBit { /*...*/ }
let raspberrypi = RaspberryPiPico { /*...*/ }

set_pins_zero(&microbit);
set_pins_zero(&raspberrypi);

// The compiler defines
fn set_pins_zero__microbit(device: &MicroBit) {
    for pin in 0..device.get_pins_count() {
        device.set_pin(i, 0);
    }
}

fn set_pins_zero__raspberrypipico(
        device: &RaspberryPiPico
    ) {
```

```
for pin in 0..device.get_pins_count() {
    device.set_pin (i, 0);
}
}
```

This approach has an advantage related to speed and optimization. Since the compiler knows the exact type used when the function is called, using any function of type P results in a direct function call. The compiler knows the exact offset (place) of the function within P. Remember, we have two different functions: one that uses the type MicroBit and the other that uses the type RaspberryPiPico. These two functions will use different offsets when calling the get_pins_count and set_pin functions.

The compiler knows the exact offset of each function at compile-time, which provides it with a full view of the function calls and allows it to highly optimize the function calls.

As everything comes at a cost, this approach has some disadvantages. First, the source code looks cluttered and might become difficult to understand. This example uses a single generic, but if more were used, this would become increasingly difficult to read and follow. The second drawback is that the compiled code consists of distinct functions for every type used when calling them. This might take up some additional space in the compiled code. On the other hand, the optimizations that the compiler can perform usually outweigh the extra space.

While using the generics approach seems a better solution most of the time, using a trait approach has its advantages too. For instance, when using many different types for the generic parameter, the resulting code can be massive, as Rust implements a different structure with different functions for each type. In this case, using a trait object approach can reduce code size significantly.

Implementation Using Trait Objects

Listing 4-34 illustrates the implementation using trait objects. This is more or less what a developer should be used to if programming in Java. Using the dyn keyword, we instruct the Rust compiler to accept any type that implements Pins. This keyword can be used only when borrowing items, it can never be used stand-alone. While this sounds very similar to the previous example, which uses generics, it has a slight difference. The compiler will generate only one function but expect to receive any (reference) data type that implements Pins. As it does not know the size of the data type and the offsets of the functions that are called upon at compile-time, it will add a function index table to the data type. This table is known as *vtable*.

Listing 4-34. Function implementation using trait objects

```
fn set_pins_zero(device: &dyn Pins) {
    for pin in 0..device.get_pins_count() {
        device.set_pin(i, 0);
    }
}
```

While this approach can make the code more readable and generate one single function, it does add some space overhead due to the *vtable*. Before calling any of the two functions, get_pins_count and set_pin, the compiled code has to search the *vtable* for the actual function offset and then call it. This results in a small overhead in execution time.

Tip   Unless the speed and other resource constraints of the device are critical, we recommend using the object-based trait approach, at least while getting started, as it makes code more readable.

While on a desktop or server computer, the two approaches are similar, and disadvantages are negligible, when running on microcontrollers, the impact is measurable.

Caution   If a data type that implements a trait or the trait itself uses Self in one of its function's signatures (parameters or within the return type), using it as a trait object is not possible.

Rust Standard Traits

Unlike C++, Rust only allows a constrained subset of operator overloading by using standard traits to implement operators.

An important trait that we need to focus on is Debug. Rust has a very powerful formatter system that allows developers to print a value to streams like the console or files. As Listing 4-35 shows, one important usage is println!. In this example, we have a structure that implements a complex number by storing its real and imaginary parts as f32.

When we want to print the number, we will use the println! macro (notice the ! at the end, that means a macro, something that will be replaced at compile time). Similar to printf in C, this takes as its first argument a constant String format (slice) and a list of other parameters that will orderly replace the {...} items in the format.

Listing 4-35. Print data using the Rust formatting engine

```rust
struct Complex {
    re: f32,
    im: f32
}

fn main() {
    let number = Complex {re: 1.0, im: 2.0};
```

```
    // manually print them
    println!("re: {}, im: {}", number.re, number.im);

    // print display
    println!("number: {}", number); // ERROR:
    //Complex does not implement Display

    // print debug
    println!("number: {:?}", number); // ERROR:
    //Complex does not implement Debug
}
```

Note   The main difference between `println!` and `printf` is that the Rust compiler replaces `println!` at compile-time and verifies that the format is a constant String (no variable allowed) and that the number of following parameters is correct.

While there are several format specifiers in Rust, two of them are of great interest: {} - the standard format and {:?} - the debug formatter. To be able to format a data type using the standard formatter ({}), the type needs to implement the Display trait, while to be able to format it using the debug formatter ({:?}), it needs to implement Debug.

Note   The Display trait is somehow similar to the `toString` function used in Java to transform objects into a String representation. It does work differently under the hood.

While Display has to be manually implemented by the developers, as they are the only ones with the idea of how they want to format the data type, Debug may be automatically implemented by the compiler using the *derive* mechanism. The implementation will simply print all the fields of a data type and their values. Listing 4-36 shows a modified version of Listing 4-35 where Complex is derived using Debug, and Display is implemented.

Note   Deriving may be used only by the Eq, PartialEq, Ord, PartialOrd, Copy, Clone, Hash, Debug, and Default traits and only if all the elements of the data type are themselves derivable with the same trait or implement the trait.

Listing 4-36. Implementing Display and deriving Debug

```rust
use std::fmt::{self, Display};

#[derive(Debug)]
struct Complex {
    re: f32,
    im: f32,
}

impl Display for Complex {
    fn fmt(&self, f: &mut fmt::Formatter<'_>) ->
                                    fmt::Result {
        if self.re == 0.0 {
            write!(f, "{}i", self.im)
        } else if self.im > 0.0 {
            write!(f, "{}+{}i", self.re, self.im)
        } else if self.im == 0.0 {
            write!(f, "{}", self.re)
        } else {
            write!(f, "{}{}i", self.re, self.im)
        }
    }
}
```

```
fn main() {
    let number = Complex { re: 1.0, im: 2.0 };

    // manually print them
    println!("re: {}, im: {}", number.re, number.im);

    // print display
    println!("number: {}", number); // number: 1+2i

    // print debug
    println!("number: {:?}", number);
    // number: Complex { re: 1.0, im: 2.0 }
}
```

Note   Primary data types implement both Debug and Display by default.

Generic Structures

Just like functions, type definitions (structures and enums) can contain generic types. Listing 4-37 illustrates an example implementation for MicroBit. As there are several types of *micro:bit* boards having different MCUs, we define a property named mcu. As MCUs can be very different, we only need a data type that implements the Mcu trait. Listing 4-37 provides an example of this approach using generics. The drawback of this is that the code becomes more difficult to read, as each impl block has to declare the generics.

Listing 4-37. Structure definition using generics

```
trait Mcu {
    // ...
}

struct MicroBit<M:Mcu> {
    mcu: M
    // ...
}

impl<M:Mcu> MicroBit<M> {
    // ...
}
```

On the other hand, we can use trait objects at the cost of the *vtable* and indirect function calls (Listing 4-38). This makes the code more readable. As trait objects have to be borrowed, we have to define a lifetime parameter for the structure.

Listing 4-38. Structure definition using trait objects

```
struct MicroBit<'a> {
    mcu: &'a dyn Mcu
}

impl<'a> MicroBit<'a> {
    //
}
```

Caution   This approach is possible only if the data type that implements the Mcu trait has no function that contains Self in its signature.

Another use of generics is const genetics. In Rust, data types can be parametrized using constants. Let's take the example of micro:bit. For now, there are two versions of micro:bit, v1, and v2, but in the future, there might be other versions added. To avoid creating a new structure every time a micro:bit is released, we can parametrize it using constants. As Listing 4-39 shows, we define two constant generic parameters: the version and the number of pins.

One of the MicroBit structure's fields is an array of pins with different lengths depending on the number of pins available for each MicroBit. This is now defined using the constant generic parameter PINS.

Listing 4-39. The usage of constant generics

```
struct MicroBit<const VERSION: usize, const PINS: usize>{
    pins: [Pin; PINS],
    // ...
}

impl MicroBit {
    pub const fn version() -> usize {
        VERSION
    }
    // ...
}

fn main () {
    let microbit: MicroBit<2, 20> = MicroBit{}
}
```

Associated Types

Another kind of generic type is the *Associated Type*. Let us take the example of the MicroBit structure. Instead of using generics for the MCU, we can define the MCU as an associated type, as shown in Listing 4-40. Using associated types restricts the implementations of a structure to one. If we use generic types, we can define multiple implementations for a data type based on the trait bounds that we set. For instance, if we define the MicroBit structure in Listing 4-37, we can write two implementations: impl<M: Nrf> MicroBit<M> {/* ... */} and impl<MCU: Stm> MicroBit<M> {/* ... */}. This means that the compiler will use different functions depending on which trait bound the actual data type M will implement. In the case of associated types, we cannot have several implementations depending on the actual M data type.

Another small advantage of using the approach is the improved code readability. The associated type does not have to be declared as a structure parameter or its default and trait implementations.

Listing 4-40. Associated type example

```
struct MicroBit {
    type M: Mcu;
    mcu: Self::M
    // ...
}

impl MicroBit {
    // ...
}

fn main() {
    let microbit: MicroBit<M=Nrf52833> =
                                    MicroBit{}
}
```

We have to declare the actual type in a similar way as a generic when we create a new structure. In most cases, that type might also be inferred by the compiler.

Note   Using associated types is only valid for structures and traits.

Null Values and Error Reporting

Rust does not have a concept similar to the C and Java NULL values. If a variable is a reference to a value, that reference has to be valid. The NULL reference is not a valid value and will throw an error when dereferenced. In C, dereferencing a NULL reference will most likely result in a *segmentation fault* while Java throws a *NullPointerException*.

To represent a non-existing value, Rust uses the templated Option enum shown in Listing 4-41. The actual value that Rust stores is one of the two options of the enum: Some(T), which is a value that wraps a valid value, or None, which represents NULL.

Listing 4-41. The Option enum used to represent NULL references

```
enum Option<T> {
    Some(T)
    None
}
```

To use the value, developers have to wrap it using an if let or a match statement, as illustrated in Listing 4-42.

Listing 4-42. Value unwrap examples

```
//unwrap the value using if let
if let Some(inner_value) = value {
    // use inner value
}
else
{
    // the value is NULL
}
// unwrap the value using match
match value {
    Some(inner_value) => {
        // use inner value
    },
    None => {
        // the value is NULL
    }
}
```

The Option enum has the following convenience functions associated: is_some, is_none, map, map_or, and map_or_else. The first two functions are more or less self-explanatory, is_some returns true if the value stored is Some(T), and is_none returns true if the value stored is None.

The map functions are a little more complicated. These are not specific to the Option trait but are used for most of the types that wrap a value. We will discuss them in detail in the *Rust concepts used in Tock* section.

Another set of functions tied to Option are unwrap and expect. These are two convenience functions that directly unwrap the inner value or panic in case the value is None. While unwrap panics with a default message, expect prints a message sent as an argument. Listing 4-43 shows an example of their usage.

Listing 4-43. Example of usage for the unwrap and expect functions

```
let inner_value value.unwrap();
let inner_value value.unwrap_or(default_value);

let inner_value value.expect("Value is None");
```

Note   While using unwrap and expect seems pretty strightforward, we strongly recommend using other ways of retrieving the inner value, methods that do not panic.

Another important feature of Rust is the way error reporting works. When it comes to C, error reporting has no standard. It is up to the developers to document what functions return and which values represent errors. For instance, the C standard library and POSIX library state that functions usually return a negative number in case of an error and 0 or some useful positive value otherwise.

The way C reports errors has been the source of several security issues. An improvement to this mechanism is represented by the C++ and Java exceptions. This states that functions should always return valid results and, if this is not possible, throw exceptions. In other words, this means that functions have two ways of returning data: the simple return statement or throwing exceptions. While this may seem a good idea, it makes the compiler's job difficult and makes it hard to interact with other languages. Moreover, it generates significant overhead.

In contrast, Rust takes a different approach by making use of an enum. Listing 4-44 displays the Result type that is used for errors. It takes two generics: S and E, and all functions that might encounter errors should return this type.

Listing 4-44. The Result enum used for error reporting in Rust

```rust
enum Result<S, E> {
    Ok(S),
    Err(E)
}
```

An example of a function that might return an error is presented in Listing 4-45. The function `division` tries to divide the two numbers, a and b. If b is not 0, the function succeeds, otherwise it fails. In C, there is no way to report the error, and in Java, this function should throw an exception. In Rust, instead of returning an `i32` number, the function returns `Result<i32, &s>`. If the division is not possible, the function returns `Err(&str)`, wrapping the error message. If the division is possible, it returns `Ok(i32)` containing the actual number.

Listing 4-45. Using Result to return errors in Rust

```rust
fn division(a: i32, b:i32) ->
        Result<i32, &'static str> {
    if b == 0 {
        Err("Division by zero")
    }
    else
    {
        Ok(a / b)
    }
}
```

Unwrapping the actual value is very similar to `Option`. The first way is by using the `match` statement as presented in Listing 4-46. The second way of verifying whether there was an error or not is by using the `is_ok` and `is_err` functions. These functions return `true` depending on the Result variant that is being used. The third way of unwrapping values is by using the unwrap and unwrap_or functions. These work the same way as for Option, meaning they panic if the value stored is Err(E).

Listing 4-46. Using a match statement to unwrap a function Result

```
match value {
    Ok(innver_value) => {
        // use inner value
    }
    Err(error) => {
        // use error
    }
}
```

As Result is a type that wraps values, the map, map_or, and map_or_else functions are also available. These functions will be discussed in detail in the *Rust concepts used in Tock* section.

Using Option and Result usually tends to complicate code a lot due to the if let and match statements used to check for errors (Listing 4-47). To streamline code writing and make code more readable, Rust introduced the ? operator. In most cases, if a function call returns an error, the function where the call happens should also return the same error. This is more or less how exceptions work in Java. If a called function throws an exception, the caller function either catches it or throws it further down the stack.

Listing 4-47. Examples of value unwrapping

```
// use match to unwrap the value
fn mathematics(numbers: &[i32]) ->
                Result<i32, &'static str> {
    let mut s = 1;
```

```
    for n in numbers {
        match division (s, *n) {
            Ok (nr) => s = s + nr,
            Err (error) => return Err (error)
        }
    }
    Ok(s)
}

// use expect to unwrap the value
fn mathematics(numbers: &[i32]) ->
            Result<i32, &'static str> {
    let mut s = 1;
    for n in numbers {
        s = s + division(s, *n).expect(
                "Division by zero"
        )
    }
    Ok(s)
}
// use ? to return errors
fn mathematics (numbers: &[i32]) ->
            Result<i32, &'static str> {
    let mut s = 1;
    for n in numbers {
        s = s + division(s, *n)?;
    }
    Ok(s)
}
```

The example in Listing 4-47 illustrates the usage of the ? operator. The mathematics function receives a slice of numbers and uses the division function to perform some computation. On the other hand, the division function might return an error if the supplied argument is 0. Alternatives to using the ? operator are also shown. The first example uses match statements, but the code gets a little longer and harder to read. The other version uses the expect function. The code is shorter and easier to read, but it panics if the division cannot be made. This means that the program is stopped. From the user experience point of view, this is not recommended.

Rust Concepts Used in Tock

The goal of this chapter is to give readers an idea about the most relevant Rust features. Instead of a conclusion, we will present some of the features that are heavily used within Tock. The understanding of these features and their usage is essential for developing drivers and applications.

Interior Mutability

This is a heavily used feature of Rust within Tock. Tock has defined all the HILs using functions that receive an immutable, &self, reference to the structure they are implemented for. This means that drivers that implement these traits are not able to modify any value inside their structure. Listing 4-48 displays an example for the ft6x06 touch panel driver.

Listing 4-48. An example of a driver trying to modify a value using an immutable reference to it. This will not compile as Rust requires a mutable reference

```
pub struct Ft6x06<'a> {
    // ...
    num_touches: usize,
    // ...
}
```

```
impl<'a> i2c::I2CClient for Ft6x06<'a> {
    fn command_complete(
        &self,
        buffer: &'static mut [u8],
        _status: Result<(), i2c::Error>
    ) {
        self.num_touches = buffer[1] & 0x0F) as usize;
        // ...
    }
}
```

Simple Values

The driver's structure defines a variable num_touches that memorizes
the number of touchpoints that the panel can handle. This information
depends from panel to panel, so the driver has to ask the hardware for
it. This is done using an I2C command. The I2CClient trait that is used
to receive the I2C response defines the command_complete function with
the first parameter as an immutable reference &self. This prevents the
driver from modifying the num_touches value. To be able to modify it, the
function should have been defined with a mutable reference &mut self.

The question that pops up is *why the HILs have been designed like this?*
The answer is simple: due to the asynchronous design of Tock. Several
entities need to hold references to the same driver that implements a HIL.

To solve these kinds of problems, Rust uses the concept of interior
mutability. As Listing 4-49 displays, instead of defining a variable of a
type T, we use generics and define a variable of type Cell<T>. When using
an immutable reference &self, the variable num_touches is immutable,
but it provides two functions get and set. These two functions allow
developers to modify the value that is stored inside the Cell type. The
value Cell<T> is immutable from the outside, but inside, the T type is
mutable through the set function.

Note   Most useful methods of Cell require the T type to implement
the Copy trait.

Listing 4-49. An example of a driver using interior mutability to
modify a variable

```
pub struct Ft6x06<'a> {
    // ...
    num_touches: Cell<usize>,
    // ...
}

impl<'a> i2c::I2CClient for Ft6x06<'a> {
    fn command_complete(
        &self,
        buffer: &'static mut [u8],
        _status: Result<(), i2c::Error>
    ) {
        self.num_touches.set((buffer[1] & 0x0F) as usize);
        // ...
    }
}
```

Tip   One may say that using the get and set functions generate
overhead. However, this is, on most occasions, optimized by the
compiler.

Optional Values

Sometimes drivers need to store values that might or not have an actual value. Listing 4-50 shows an example using the same touch panel driver. The driver receives touch events and forwards them to its client. The client is a data structure that gets the processed touch information from the driver. From the driver's point of view, this client may or may not be set. Based on the previous example, the straightforward way is to use a `Cell<Option<T>>`. The `Cell` wrapping offers interior mutability, while the `Option` provides the possibility of not having an actual value.

Listing 4-50. An example of using an optional mutable value

```
pub struct Ft6x06<'a> {
   // ...
   touch_client: Cell<
     Option<&'a dyn touch::TouchClient>
   >,
   num_touches: Cell<usize>,
   // ...
}
```

Tock defines its shorthand version of this called `OptionalCell` (Listing 4-51). This is what most of the drivers use. Accessing data within an `OptionalCell` is done using the `map` functions that we will discuss later.

Listing 4-51. An example of using the OptionalCell data type

```
pub struct Ft6x06<'a> {
   // ...
   touch_client: OptionalCell<
     &'a dyn touch::TouchClient
   >,
   num_touches: Cell<usize>,
```

```
  // ...
}

impl<'a> i2c::I2CClient for Ft6x06<'a> {
    fn command_complete(
      &self,
      buffer: &'static mut [u8],
      _status: Result<(), i2c::Error>
    ) {
        self.num_touches.set((buffer[1] & 0x0F) as usize);
        self.touch_client.map(|client| {
          // ...
        });
        // ...
    }
}
```

Buffers

Another important discussion focuses on buffers. In most cases, drivers receive buffers at initialization and pass them up or down to several other components. For instance, we take the example presented in Listing 4-52, which is part of the serial port driver. At initialization, inside the new function, the driver does not receive a buffer. Whenever someone wants to write a buffer to the serial port, it calls the transmit_buffer function. This is the function that receives a buffer that the driver stores.

Listing 4-52. An example of buffer handling taken from the UART driver

```
pub struct UartDevice<'a> {
    tx_buffer: TakeCell<'static, [u8]>,
    // ...
}
```

```
impl<'a> UartDevice<'a> {
    pub const fn new(
        mux: &'a MuxUart<'a>,
        receiver: bool
    ) -> UartDevice<'a> {
        UartDevice {
            tx_buffer: TakeCell::empty(),
            // ...
        }
    }

    // ...
}

impl<'a> uart::Transmit<'a> for UartDevice<'a> {
    /// Transmit data.
    fn transmit_buffer(
        &self,
        tx_data: &'static mut [u8],
        tx_len: usize,
    ) -> Result<(), (ErrorCode, &'static mut [u8])> {
        self.tx_buffer.replace(tx_data);
        // ...
        Ok(())
    }
}
```

As the example shows, the driver does not use the Cell or
OptionalCell for storing the buffer. From Rust's point of view, it could
easily do that. There is a problem though, types using these two wrappers
need to implement the Copy trait. This means that each time data is taken
out or put in, the actual data is copied. When using buffers, this approach

has two problems: copying buffers is not ideal as it takes time, and most importantly, we do not want to have several copies of a buffer as they occupy a lot of memory.

To overcome these, Tock introduced two special wrappers: TakeCell and MapCell. They have the same semantics as Cell and OptionalCell but do not require the inner value to implement the Copy trait. The internal value can be accessed either by taking it out by using the take function or by using it in the map function's closure. Listing 4-53 shows an example using the same touch panel driver.

Listing 4-53. An example of using TakeCell for a buffer

```
pub struct Ft6x06<'a> {
    // ...
    buffer: TakeCell<'static, [u8]>,
    // ...
}

impl<'a> gpio::Client for Ft6x06<'a> {
    fn fired(&self) {
        self.buffer.take().map(|buffer| {
            // ...
            match self.i2c.write_read(buffer, 1, 15) {
                // ...
            }
        });
    }
}
```

```
impl<'a> i2c::I2CClient for Ft6x06<'a> {
    fn command_complete(
        &self,
        buffer: &'static mut [u8],
        _status: Result<(), i2c::Error>)
    {
        // ...
        self.buffer.replace(buffer);
        // ...
    }
}
```

Another difference between the standard Cell and TakeCell or
MapCell is the definition. As these were designed for holding buffer
references, they assume that they will store a reference, so the generic
parameters are a lifetime and a type to which a mutable reference will be
stored. The example also uses a function called take. The two wrappers
for buffers own the reference. Whenever the map function is used, the
reference is borrowed to the closure and is taken back when the closure
finishes execution. Sometimes, drivers need to pass a buffer to another
driver. This means that the driver first has to take ownership of the buffer,
which is what the take function does. When called, the function replaces
the inner value with None and returns the reference *with ownership*.
Whoever stores the return value of take will now own the buffer.

Note   The take function returns an Option<&'a mut T> as
TakeCell or MapCell might not have an actual reference.

This is precisely what the example in Listing 4-53 does. It calls take,
which returns an Option, and then calls map on the Option to use the inner
value. Within the map closure, it now passes the buffer to the I2C driver.

This driver will now own the buffer. When the I2C driver completes the request, it returns the buffer through the command_complete function. The touch panel driver uses the data returned and then puts back the buffer into the original TakeCell using the replace function.

All Tock drivers and the kernel rely on this pattern of using buffers.

Global Variables

Tock does not allow the usage of dynamically allocated data. This means that all the references, including drivers, have to be statically allocated. This is in contrast with Rust's philosophy that does not encourage the use of mutable global variables. In Rust, these global variables are called static variables. Safe Rust code is allowed to use only immutable static variables. Any use of a mutable static variable is considered to be unsafe.

Note   Mutable static variables are unsafe as the compiler cannot guarantee that the access to them is thread-safe and that there will be only one mutable reference to it at any given time.

Just like other Rust Embedded projects, Tock provides a macro called *static_init*. This allows the definition and initialization of global variables and returns a '*static* mutable reference to them. The usage is shown in Listing 4-54 that presents an example for the definition and initialization of the Tock kernel.

Listing 4-54. Definition and initialization of the Tock kernel

```
let board_kernel = static_init!(kernel::Kernel, kernel::Kernel:
:new(&PROCESSES));
```

The first argument of the macro is the data type, while the second argument is the initialization value. In Rust, macros have their own context. This means that each time a macro is called, the Rust compiler will build a new namespace. The macro defines a new variable having the provided type with this new context and assigns the provided value to it.

There is a caveat when using this method. The actual initialization value is first allocated on the current function' stack and then moved to the macro. Actually, this pattern is present in most of Rust's libraries. Developers rely on the fact that the Rust compiler will optimize this and place the initialization value directly in its destination place.

Note   The micro:bit will not work if Rust does not perform this kind of optimization as the kernel stack will overflow. To make sure that this optimization is done, Tock provides some specific arguments to the compiler. These can be found in the **Cargo.toml** file placed in the Tock's folder.

Using this macro, developers can create static variables from anywhere in the code. One of the most common mistakes is to consider these values local. In Listing 4-55, the board_kernel variable is local, but it is a reference to a global value.

Buffer Lifetimes

The most important difference between Tock and other embedded operating systems is that the kernel does not use any heap. All the used memory has to be statically allocated. From the programming language's point of view, this means that all the used buffers must have a 'static lifetime. Whenever the kernel or a capsule requires a buffer, its lifetime has to be 'static.

Note   The grant system presented in the previous chapter deviates a little bit from the static reference rule by allowing capsules to allocate new grants within a process's memory. The statement that the Tock kernel does not use any heap still stands, as the allocated memory belongs to the process and not to the kernel itself.

Most of the buffers supplied to drivers are defined as static mutable variables and are created within macros similar to static_init. This is why most of the drivers provide a helper macro to initialize them. Listing 4-55 shows the initialization of the buffers used by the ft6x06 touch panel driver.

Listing 4-55. An example of buffer initialization for the touch panel driver

```
// Setup static space for the objects.
#[macro_export]
macro_rules! ft6x06_i2c_component_helper {
    ($i2c_mux:expr $(,)?) => {{
        use capsules::ft6x06::Ft6x06;
        use capsules::ft6x06::NO_TOUCH;
        use capsules::virtual_i2c::I2CDevice;
        use core::mem::MaybeUninit;
        use kernel::hil::touch::TouchEvent;
        // Buffer to use for I2C messages
        pub static mut BUFFER: [u8; 17] = [0; 17];
        pub static mut EVENTS_BUFFER: [TouchEvent; 2] =
        [NO_TOUCH, NO_TOUCH];
        let i2c =
            components::i2c::I2CComponent::new(
                $i2c_mux,
```

```
            0x38
        ).finalize(
            components::i2c_component_helper!()
        );
    static mut ft6x06: MaybeUninit<
        Ft6x06<'static>
    > = MaybeUninit::uninit();
    (
        &i2c, &mut ft6x06,
        &mut BUFFER, &mut EVENTS_BUFFER
    )
   };};
}
```

Unwrapping Values

So far, we have discussed several ways to wrap mutable values
inside immutable containers. All these wrapping types, like Cell,
OptionalCell, MapCell, and TakeCell, have a set of common functions
that are heavily used throughout the kernel. We are talking here about the
map functions family, map, map_or, and map_or_else. Listing 4-56, 4-57,
and 4-58 show an example for each of these.

Listing 4-56. The simple map function

```
pub fn map<U, F>(self, f: F) -> Option<U> where
    F: FnOnce(T) -> U;

value.map(|inner_value| {
    // use inner value
});
```

The simplest of all is map. This function tries to unwrap the inner value and call the provided closure with the inner value as the argument. Listing 4-56 displays the definition of the function. The first parameter is the actual wrapper (self). This means that the map function consumes the wrapper. In other words, it will not be available anymore after the map function call. Of course, if the wrapper is still needed, the map's closure can return the value.

The function returns Option for a reason. Wrapper types might contain or not an actual value. If there is no value within the wrapper, the map function returns None.

Listing 4-57. The definition of the map_or function

```
pub fn map_or<U, F>(self, default: U, f: F) -> U where
    F: FnOnce(T) -> U;

let new_value = value.map_or(
    default_value,
    |inner_value| {
        // use inner value
        // return a value of the same type as
        // default_value
    }
);
```

One drawback of the map function is that it always returns None if there is no value wrapped. There might be situations where we would like to return a default value instead of None. This is what the map_or function shown in Listing 4-57 does. It adds an extra parameter of type U, the same type as the return type of the closure. Instead of returning None, the function returns the default parameter if there is no inner value.

Listing 4-58. The definition of the map_or_else function

```
pub fn map_or_else<U, D, F>(self, default: D, f: F) -> U where
    F: FnOnce(T) -> U,
    D: FnOnce() -> U;

let new_value = value.map_or_else(
    || {
        // return default_value
    },
    |inner_value| {
        // use inner value
        // return a value of the same type as
        // default_value
    }
);
```

The third format of the map function is map_or_else. Similar to map_or, this function is able to return a default value in case there is no inner value within the wrapper type. The difference is that instead of receiving a default value argument, it takes a closure. This function executes one of the two closures: either the one provided as the first argument if there is no value to unwrap, or the one provided as the second argument otherwise.

The first closure used for the default value does not take any arguments. The second one is called with the unwrapped value as an argument. Both closures have to return the same type.

Note   The map functions family defined for TakeCell and MapCell take as the first argument a reference to self (&self). This means that the functions do not *consume* the wrapper, it can be used after the closure returns. The closure only borrows the wrapper for its execution.

Transforming Values

One of the important features of Rust is typecasting. Rust does not perform any typecasts automatically. Developers have to specify the typecast manually. For instance, adding a u32 value to an i32 value will generate an error unless one of them is typecasted manually. While the compiler can cast number types between each other, complex types require additional code that the developers have to write.

Rust provides an interesting trait pair: From and Into. The implementation of From and TryFrom for usize and ErrorCode is illustrated in Listing 4-60. These traits provide a standard way to convert between data types. Using these traits, developers can simply write value.into() whenever a conversion is needed. In most cases, Rust will be able to infer the data type that is required and call the appropriate into function.

An interesting fact is that only the From trait must be implemented. Rust offers a blanket implementation for the Into trait for all types. As long as From is implemented, Rust is able to use the inverse.

The example in Listing 4-59 implements the From trait for generating a usize from an ErrorCode. Since the ErrorCode enum is represented as a usize, this conversion does never fail. On the other hand, converting a Result<(), ErrorCode> to ErrorCode might fail as ErrorCode can only represent errors. If the Result type returns Ok(()), there is no way to represent this as an ErrorCode. In this case, the trait used is TryFrom. This trait tries to convert the values and returns a Result. If the conversion can be done, it returns the value within an Ok, otherwise, it returns an error type.

Note   The actual error type is an associated type of the TryFrom trait.

Listing 4-59. Transforming ErrorCode using the From and TryFrom traits

```
impl From<ErrorCode> for usize {
    fn from(err: ErrorCode) -> usize {
        err as usize
    }
}

impl TryFrom<Result<(), ErrorCode>> for ErrorCode {
    type Error = ();

    fn try_from(rc: Result<(), ErrorCode>) -> Result<Self,
    Self::Error> {
        match rc {
            Ok(()) => Err(()),
            Err(ErrorCode::FAIL) => Ok(ErrorCode::FAIL),
            Err(ErrorCode::BUSY) => Ok(ErrorCode::BUSY),
            Err(ErrorCode::ALREADY) => Ok(ErrorCode::ALREADY),
            Err(ErrorCode::OFF) => Ok(ErrorCode::OFF),
            Err(ErrorCode::RESERVE) => Ok(ErrorCode::RESERVE),
            Err(ErrorCode::INVAL) => Ok(ErrorCode::INVAL),
            Err(ErrorCode::SIZE) => Ok(ErrorCode::SIZE),
            Err(ErrorCode::CANCEL) => Ok(ErrorCode::CANCEL),
            Err(ErrorCode::NOMEM) => Ok(ErrorCode::NOMEM),
            Err(ErrorCode::NOSUPPORT) => Ok(ErrorCode::NOSUPPORT),
            Err(ErrorCode::NODEVICE) => Ok(ErrorCode::NODEVICE),
            Err(ErrorCode::UNINSTALLED) =>
            Ok(ErrorCode::UNINSTALLED),
            Err(ErrorCode::NOACK) => Ok(ErrorCode::NOACK),
        }
    }
}
```

```
impl From<ErrorCode> for Result<(), ErrorCode> {
    fn from(ec: ErrorCode) -> Self {
        match ec {
            ErrorCode::FAIL => Err(ErrorCode::FAIL),
            ErrorCode::BUSY => Err(ErrorCode::BUSY),
            ErrorCode::ALREADY => Err(ErrorCode::ALREADY),
            ErrorCode::OFF => Err(ErrorCode::OFF),
            ErrorCode::RESERVE => Err(ErrorCode::RESERVE),
            ErrorCode::INVAL => Err(ErrorCode::INVAL),
            ErrorCode::SIZE => Err(ErrorCode::SIZE),
            ErrorCode::CANCEL => Err(ErrorCode::CANCEL),
            ErrorCode::NOMEM => Err(ErrorCode::NOMEM),
            ErrorCode::NOSUPPORT => Err(ErrorCode::NOSUPPORT),
            ErrorCode::NODEVICE => Err(ErrorCode::NODEVICE),
            ErrorCode::UNINSTALLED => Err(ErrorCode::UNINSTALLED),
            ErrorCode::NOACK => Err(ErrorCode::NOACK),
        }
    }
}
```

Tock uses the From trait a lot, primarily for converting error types. A very good example is the I2C driver. This driver can return several custom errors that are specific to the I2C bus. However, these errors have to be converted to ErrorCode if they have to be sent upwards the driver stack. Listing 4-60 displays this implementation.

Listing 4-60. Using the Into trait to transform an i2c::Error to ErrorCode

```
pub enum Error {
    /// The slave did not acknowledge the chip
    /// address. Most likely the address
    /// is incorrect or the slave is not properly
```

```
    /// connected.
    AddressNak,

    /// The data was not acknowledged by the
    /// slave.
    DataNak,

    /// Arbitration lost, meaning the state of
    /// the data line does not correspond
    /// to the data driven onto it. This can
    /// happen, for example, when a
    /// higher-priority transmission is in
    /// progress by a different master.
    ArbitrationLost,

    /// A start condition was received before
    /// received data has been read
    /// from the receive register.
    Overrun,

    /// The requested operation wasn't supported.
    NotSupported,

    /// The underlaying device has another
    /// request in progress
    Busy,
}

impl Into<ErrorCode> for Error {
    fn into(self) -> ErrorCode {
        match self {
            Self::AddressNak | Self::DataNak => ErrorCode::NOACK,
            Self::ArbitrationLost => ErrorCode::RESERVE,
            Self::Overrun => ErrorCode::SIZE,
```

```
            Self::NotSupported => ErrorCode::NOSUPPORT,
            Self::Busy => ErrorCode::BUSY,
        }
    }
}
```

Summary

This chapter has briefly presented some of the most useful features of Rust that Tock is using. The features presented here are the ones we encountered during our work with Tock and believe are most relevant. At first, some of them might seem difficult to understand and use, but the more readers use them, the better they understand them. This chapter's purpose is to present the minimal Rust requirements to understand how Tock works.

We strongly recommend our users to read additional Rust documentation, such as *The Rust Programming Language*[2] and *The Little Book for Macros*[3]. Our own experience is that writing simple Tock drivers is a great way of getting started with Rust and most of the features presented here.

---

[2] https://doc.rust-lang.org/book/
[3] https://danielkeep.github.io/tlborm/book/index.html

CHAPTER 5

Getting Started with Tock

This chapter will get you started with running the Tock operating system and a simple application on our devices. We will focus on running the classical "hello world" app on the micro:bit and the Raspberry Pi Pico. This will give us a head start to building more complex secure applications and modules in the following chapters of this book.

Hardware Requirements

To implement the project in this chapter, you need the following hardware components, based on the device you use:

- **Micro:bit**
    - 1 x micro:bit v2 board
- **Raspberry Pi Pico**
    - 1 x Raspberry Pi Pico board;
    - 1 x Raspberry Pi board.

© Alexandru Radovici and Ioana Culic 2022
A. Radovici and I. Culic, *Getting Started with Secure Embedded Systems*,
https://doi.org/10.1007/978-1-4842-7789-8_5

About the Tock Repository

Tock is an open source operating system with an active community of people who constantly contribute to the official repository. Therefore, when starting with using and developing applications on top of Tock, the starting point is the Github repository, where we can find the Tock source code and other additional libraries and frameworks.

By accessing the following link, we can find all the repositories published by the Tock development group: `https://github.com/tock`. Out of all the existing repositories, three are of main interest for us:

- tock - the repository containing the source code for the Tock operating system;

- libtock-c - the repository containing the libraries necessary for running C applications on top of Tock and some application examples;

- libtock-rs - the repository containing the libraries necessary for running Rust applications on top of Tock and some application examples.

As Tock and all the additional modules are still under development, it is important to keep in mind the versions used when developing the applications and pay attention to new releases and updates.

At the time of writing, the Tock operating system release is at version 2.0. However, each week new capsules are being developed and new devices being integrated, so if at a certain point you need a module that is not implemented, we suggest you pay attention to the commits and the pull requests as they might be under development and on the verge of being released.

Info   The Tock release used in this book is 2.0[1].

Similarly, suppose you aim to contribute to the tock repository. In that case, the development team encourages all contributors to share their progress so they can give timely feedback and avoid having different people working on the same feature.

The Tock Project Structure

The Tock Operating System project folder contains the source code for the Tock kernel, which is organized under the following directories:

- **arch** - It contains structures and functions that are specific to the various architectures supported by Tock. This mainly focuses on the particular registers, memory locations, permissions, system calls interface, etc. The code here addresses the minimum standard of a certain architecture. This means that any SoC will have these characteristics. Unless you aim to add support for a new MCU architecture, you shouldn't have to work in this folder.

- **boards** - This folder contains code specific to all the devices integrated into Tock. This is built on top of the **arch** and **chips** folders. The structures and functions here address the hardware components specific to each board: LEDs, pins, flashing capabilities, etc. If you aim to add support for a new device compatible with the existing architectures and SoCs, here is where you have to add the code.

---

[1] Tock 2.0 Release, https://github.com/tock/tock/releases/tag/release-2.0

- **capsules** - The capsules in the Tock kernel are similar to the drivers in other kernels. By inspecting the name of the files inside this folder, we notice that for each peripheral or communication channel that can be controlled in Tock, there is a capsule developed (e.g., button, LCD, i2c, etc.). The capsules need to use the HILs to communicate with the hardware. If you aim to add support for a new peripheral, you need to ensure there is a HIL that allows the capsule to communicate with the peripheral and create a new capsule. If no HIL addresses your need, you need to create that too.

- **chips** - The code here addresses the characteristics of each specific MCU implementation supported by Tock. This folder complements the arch folder and contains the functions specific for each SoC. As each microcontroller built on top of a generic architecture (implemented in the arch folder) has particular characteristics (e.g., pins, registers, support for various protocols such as I2C, SPI, etc.), this folder addresses these specifications.

- **doc** - It contains detailed documentation on how to use Tock and how it is built so you can contribute to it.

- **kernel** - Here we can find the implementation of the Tock kernel. The implementation for system calls, IPC, memory management, and scheduler resides here. The HILs definition files are also in this folder.

- **libraries** - These are the libraries used by all the source code in this repository.

- **tools** - These are scripts used for generating builds, testing, and other similar tools.

Figure 5-1 displays the correspondence between the main source code folders.

```
+-- tock            # kernel
|   +-- arch        # code specific to MCUs (ARM, RISC-V)
|   +-- boards      # code specific to boards (Micro:bit v2)
|   +-- capsules    # drivers
|   +-- chips       # code specific to MCUs (STM32F412G, E310, )
|   +-- doc         # documentation
|   +-- kernel      # actual kernel (scheduler, ipc, memory)
|   +-- libraries   # libraries used by all the source code
|   +-- tools       # scripts for testing on other tools
|   +-- vagrant     # VM setup (different from ours)
```

Figure 5-1. *The main Tock source code folders*

If we follow the Tock stack presented in chapter 3 (Figure 3-1) and assign each folder with one of the layers, we would have the correspondence described in Table 5-1. Based on this correspondence and the security rules, each file allows or not for **unsafe** code to be written.

Table 5-1. *The correspondence between the Tock stack and the folder structure*

Tock project folder	Tock stack layer color	Implementation rules
Arch	orange	Unsafe code is allowed but as limited as possible
boards	orange	Unsafe code is allowed but as limited as possible
capsules	blue	Unsafe code is not allowed
chips	orange	Unsafe code is allowed but as limited as possible
kernel	teal	Unsafe code is allowed but as limited as possible

In some future chapters of this book, we will work in our own capsules folder, as we will go through the steps necessary to add support for a new peripheral in the Tock kernel. What is more, we will generate a simpler project structure to work with.

The libtock-c and libtock-rs Repositories

The libtock-c and libtock-rs repositories contain the libraries that enable us to write C or Rust userspace applications on top of the Tock kernel.

Note   In this book, we will build only C applications, as the Rust library for Tock version 2.0 is still undergoing substantial changes.

Here we can find the libraries that enable the control of peripherals such as GPIO, buttons, LED, etc. What is more, both repositories contain plenty of application examples. The **README** file is also very useful in understanding how to build and deploy the applications on the devices.

Further on, we will get through the steps necessary for downloading the source code for the Tock kernel and the supporting libraries and frameworks.

Environment Setup

To get started with compiling and running the Tock kernel on our devices, we first need to install all necessary tools and libraries. This process varies based on the system that you are working on. While the setup is straightforward for Linux and macOS systems, things get a bit complicated for Windows machines. This is why we will go through two possible approaches:

1.   Make the environment setup manually;

2. Download a virtual machine that the writers of this book have prepared so you can get started with building the applications without any hustle.

Note   In this chapter, we will focus on installing the necessary tools for building and deploying the Tock kernel and applications in development mode. This means that we rely on more complex tools to control and monitor the applications we are running, in contrast with the tools necessary to deploy production applications.

In a nutshell, we need the following projects and applications on our development system, and we will detail them further in this chapter, as we get to use them:

- tock- the Tock kernel source code Github repository;

- libtock-c - the C application library repository;

- rustup - an installer for the Rust programming language;

- Rust - the compiler and tools for Rust applications;

- OpenOCD - the software that allows us to program and, most importantly, debug the devices;

- Tockloader - the tool that will enable us to manage the installation of the Tock kernel and Tock applications on the devices;

- Gcc for Arm - the C/C++ compiler for ARM, as both the micro:bit and the Raspberry Pi Pico are built with ARM processors.

The tools mentioned above are compatible with Linux or macOS systems. This means that you can install them directly on your machine and start working without any overhead. In case you are working with a Windows system, you have two possible approaches:

1. Use the Windows Subsystem for Linux (WSL);

2. Use a Linux virtual machine.

Tip   You can use the virtual machine for Linux and macOS systems if you prefer not to install the necessary tools on the physical machine. However, this might bring an overhead to the setup and device flashing processes.

The installation process is also dependent on the device you plan to use. As this book focuses on both the micro:bit and the Raspberry Pi Pico devices, we will go through all the necessary steps to build a working development setup for each of these two platforms.

Environment Setup for Programming the micro:bit Device

The micro:bit v2 is designed as an educational device that is easy to program by connecting it to the computer via USB. The device has a hardware debugger integrated, making it easy to use without any additional hardware. In our case, we can deploy the Tock kernel and applications on the device via the USB connection using the USB port on the host computer. This means that we need to install all necessary software to build the binaries on the computer.

The process is more or less the same for Linux and macOS systems, while for Windows computers, we will use a different approach.

Setup for Linux and macOS Systems

To get started on any machine running Linux or macOS, we simply need to open a terminal and run a couple of commands to install the necessary tools for debugging and programming the board.

Caution   To install tockloader, you need to have Python installed on your computer. Before running all the commands described below, please ensure that you have Python3 and pip3 installed.

Linux Systems

To install the tools for Linux, open a terminal and type the commands in Listing 5-1.

Tip   For Ubuntu 14.04 and 16.04 or distributions other than Debian, gdb-multiarch is replaced with gdb-arm-none-eabi.

Listing 5-1.   Install the necessary tools on a Linux machine

```
$ curl https://sh.rustup.rs -sSf | sh
$ sudo apt install gcc-arm-none-eabi
$ sudo apt install gdb-multiarch
$ pip3 install tockloader==1.8.0 --user
$ grep -q dialout <(groups $(whoami)) || sudo usermod -a -G
dialout $(whoami) # Note, will need to reboot if prompted for
password
$ sudo apt-get install openocd
```

Note   If you encounter an error when running the tockloader command, you might need to add it to the PATH. For this, run the following command: export PATH=$HOME/.local/bin:$PATH.

Another important configuration in Linux involves allowing OpenOCD to interact with the USB connection of the micro:bit. For this, we need to create a new file in the **/etc/udev/rules.d** directory. We call the file **tock. rules** and add the lines in Listing 5-2.

Listing 5-2. The tock.rules file

```
ACTION!="add|change", GOTO="openocd_rules_end"
SUBSYSTEM!="usb|tty|hidraw", GOTO="openocd_rules_end"

# Please keep this list sorted by VID:PID

# CMSIS-DAP compatible adapters
ATTRS{product}=="*CMSIS-DAP*", MODE="664", GROUP="plugdev"

LABEL="openocd_rules_end"
```

To load the new configuration, we need to restart the udev system running the following command: sudo udevadm control --reload-rules.

MacOS Systems

To install the tools for macOS, open a terminal and type the commands in Listing 5-3.

Listing 5-3. Install the necessary tools on a macOS machine

```
$ curl https://sh.rustup.rs -sSf | sh
$ brew tap armmbed/homebrew-formulae && brew update && brew
install arm-none-eabi-gcc
$ pip3 install tockloader==1.8.0 --user
$ brew install open-ocd
```

Note   If you encounter an error when running the tockloader command, you might need to add it to the PATH. For this, run the following command: `export PATH=$HOME/Library/Python/3.`**x**`/bin/:$PATH`, replacing **x** with the version of Python that you have installed.

Windows Systems

The tools necessary to run Tock on a device are not available for Windows systems.

However, there are a couple of ways of running a Linux machine inside the Windows environment.

Linux Virtual Machine

The easiest way to run a Linux environment on top of a Windows system is to use a virtual machine and run a Linux distribution. If you are familiar with this process and have already used Linux virtual machines, you can use one of your existing setups or create a new setup, then follow the instructions in the Linux setup section.

If you prefer to get started with a new machine, you can use an already prepared working environment that the writers of this book have prepared to make the process easier. You can download an existing virtual machine file containing all the necessary source code and libraries for both the Tock kernel and the applications. The machine runs a Linux distribution and has all the files and tools needed for running applications on top of Tock 2.0 already cloned and installed.

To download the virtual machine image, we need to access the following link: `https://tock-book.s3.us-west-1.amazonaws.com/VM/TockDev.ova`. A **.ova** file will be downloaded. Further on, we need to download the tools necessary to run the virtual machine. In our case, this would be the VirtualBox application. In addition, we have to install the VirtualBox Extension Pack that brings extra functionalities. This is necessary to enable the USB connection between the virtual machine and the device.

Note   If you are familiar with a different virtual machine application, such as VMware, you can use it. Be aware that you will need the VMware Workstation. The instructions in this book are limited to using VirtualBox and the Extension Pack as they are free.

To install the VirtualBox application, we need to access the download page[2] and select the platform package according to our host operating system. This will launch the download of the executable, which will then guide us through the installation process.

Once the installation is complete, we proceed to install the Extension Pack. This is available for download on the same page and is a generic link for all operating systems. By hitting the *All supported platforms* button, we launch the download of the *vbox-extpack* file (Figure 5-2).

---

[2]`https://www.virtualbox.org/wiki/Downloads`

Download VirtualBox

Here you will find links to VirtualBox binaries and its source code.

VirtualBox binaries

By downloading, you agree to the terms and conditions of the respective license.

If you're looking for the latest VirtualBox 6.0 packages, see VirtualBox 6.0 builds. Please also use version 6.0 if you need to run VMs with software virtualization, as this has been discontinued in 6.1. Version 6.0 will remain supported until July 2020.

If you're looking for the latest VirtualBox 5.2 packages, see VirtualBox 5.2 builds. Please also use version 5.2 if you still need support for 32-bit hosts, as this has been discontinued in 6.0. Version 5.2 will remain supported until July 2020.

VirtualBox 6.1.22 platform packages

- ⇨Windows hosts
- ⇨OS X hosts
- Linux distributions
- ⇨Solaris hosts
- ⇨Solaris 11 IPS hosts

The binaries are released under the terms of the GPL version 2.

See the changelog for what has changed.

You might want to compare the checksums to verify the integrity of downloaded packages. *The SHA256 checksums should be favored as the MD5 algorithm must be treated as insecure!*

- SHA256 checksums, MD5 checksums

Note: After upgrading VirtualBox it is recommended to upgrade the guest additions as well.

VirtualBox 6.1.22 Oracle VM VirtualBox Extension Pack

- ⇨All supported platforms

Support for USB 2.0 and USB 3.0 devices, VirtualBox RDP, disk encryption, NVMe and PXE boot for Intel cards. See this chapter from the User Manual for an introduction to this Extension Pack. The Extension Pack binaries are released under the VirtualBox Personal Use and Evaluation License (PUEL). *Please install the same version extension pack as your installed version of VirtualBox.*

Figure 5-2. *VirtualBox download page*

Once downloaded, open the file using the VirtualBox application, and you will be prompted for permission to install all the necessary tools. The final step is to hit the install button (Figure 5-3).

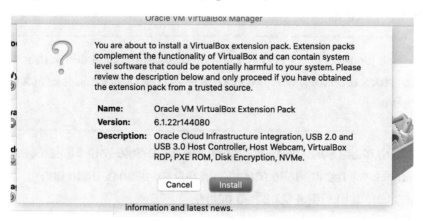

Figure 5-3. *Install the VirtualBox extension pack*

Now that we have the setup in place, we can start a generic Linux machine or the machine prepared for this book.

If you decide to use a generic Linux machine, you need to follow the instructions in the **Linux Systems** section.

To launch the prepared virtual machine, we just need to download the **.ova** file and import it by selecting the *File* ➤ *Import Appliance* options in the VirtualBox menu.

Tip   The virtual machine settings enable you to connect to it via ssh using port 2000. For this, we recommend using a remote connections application such as PuTTY[3] and connect to localhost or the IP address 127.0.0.1 and the port 2000.

Once the Linux machine is imported, we can launch it and get started with developing Tock applications as all the necessary tools are already installed.

Note   The login credentials for the virtual machine are username: tock, password: tock.

When it comes to the source code files, these are available in the **/home/tock** directory, where we can find the necessary folders: **tock** and **libtock-c**.

Tip   To make sure the repositories are up to date with the latest changes, we recommend running git pull for each of them and switching to the **tags** specified below.

---

[3]https://www.putty.org/

Install the Necessary Tools for the Raspberry Pi Pico

The Raspberry Pi Pico is the first board built with the RP2040 chip developed by the Raspberry Pi Foundation. As a recently released device, the Tock support is still undergoing changes and new implementations.

Currently, the Pico can only be programmed in development mode, which implies flashing the device using a hardware debugger. However, the board does not include one. This is why the approach we take, which is also supported by the Pico official documentation, is to connect the board to a regular Raspberry Pi device and use that as an external hardware debugger.

Programming and controlling the Raspberry Pi Pico requires a regular Raspberry Pi running a supported Linux distribution, such as Raspberry Pi OS. This implies that all the development is done on the Raspberry Pi, and the resulting binaries are flashed on the Pico board as the Pico is directly connected to the regular Raspberry Pi.

Note   Make sure that you have a Raspberry Pi running a Linux distribution and that you expanded the filesystem. You can follow the Raspberry Pi's tutorial[4] for expanding the filesystem.

If you are used to controlling your Raspberry Pi remotely, probably via SSH, we recommend you take another approach. The solution we recommend is to work on your local computer and use the Raspberry Pi only as a gateway to the Pico device. This changes a little the necessary configurations. Therefore we will present both approaches below so you can choose the one that suits you best.

---

[4] Expanding the Raspberry Pi's file system, `https://elinux.org/RPi_Resize_Flash_Partitions`

A common characteristic of both approaches is that we will use a serial connection between the Raspberry Pi and the Pico so we can view the terminal information coming from the Pico. To achieve this, the two devices will be connected via the UART pins. What is more, we need to configure the Raspberry Pi to support the UART communication. For this, we need to open a terminal on the Raspberry Pi device and run the `raspi-config` command. This will open a menu where we choose *Interface Options* ➤ *Serial Port* and select *No* when asked *Would you like a login shell to be accessible over serial?* and *Yes,* when asked *Would you like the serial port hardware to be enabled?*. The result is depicted in Figure 5-4.

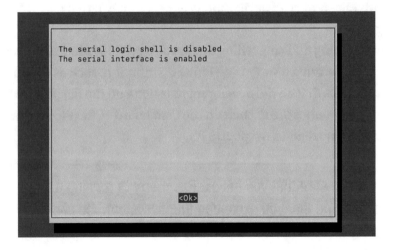

Figure 5-4. *Enable UART communication on the Raspberry Pi*

To save the configuration, select *Ok* and choose to reboot the Pi.

While this might seem enough for the UART communication to take place, for Raspberry Pi 3 and 4, the communication is not stable if the BLE is also enabled. Therefore, we also need to disable the BLE connection by inserting the lines in Listing 5-4 in the **/boot/config.txt** file.

Listing 5-4. Disable the BLE connection

```
dtoverlay=disable-bt
enable_uart=1
```

After another reboot of the device, the UART connection is configured to be stable.

Further on, we will handle the rest of the installation process differently for each approach. We either use the Raspberry Pi directly to compile and deploy the kernel to the Pico or choose to compile the kernel on the computer and deploy it to the Pico using the Raspberry Pi.

Use the Raspberry Pi Directly to Compile and Deploy to the Pico

For the case in which we use the Raspberry Pi to compile and deploy to the Pico, we need to install all the necessary tools directly on the Pi. For this, we first need to open a terminal on the Raspberry Pi, then type the commands in Listing 5-5. These will install the essential tools that we mentioned at the beginning of the chapter and some additional support tools.

Caution   You need a Raspberry Pi with more than 1 GB of RAM to install the Rust toolchain. If your device does not have this capability, we recommend following the instructions in the next section, where Rust is installed on the computer.

While most of the installed applications are from the main Raspbian (Debian) repositories, OpenOCD needs to be installed from the source code as we need the version adapted for the Raspberry Pi.

Caution   To install tockloader, you need to have Python installed on the Raspberry Pi. Before running all the commands described below, please ensure that you have Python3 and pip3 installed.

Listing 5-5. The commands that install the necessary tools on the Raspberry Pi

```
$ sudo apt update
$ sudo apt install automake autoconf
build-essential texinfo libtool libftdi-dev
libusb-1.0-0-dev git
$ git clone https://github.com/raspberrypi/openocd.git
--recursive --branch rp2040 --depth=1
$ cd openocd
$ ./bootstrap
$ ./configure --enable-ftdi --enable-sysfsgpio --enable-
bcm2835gpio
$ make -j4
$ sudo make install
$ cd ~
$ curl https://sh.rustup.rs -sSf | sh
# Proceed with installation (default)
# logout and login again after install
$ sudo apt install gcc-arm-none-eabi
$ sudo apt install gdb-multiarch
$ pip3 install --upgrade tockloader --user
$ grep -q dialout <(groups $(whoami)) || sudo usermod -a -G
dialout $(whoami)
# Note, will need to reboot if prompted for #password
$ sudo apt install minicom
```

Note Installing all these tools can take a lot of time, do not worry if the terminal seems to be stuck at a certain time.

Once the installation is done, we can get to downloading the Tock kernel and application libraries. These steps are described in the below sections called *Clone the Tock Kernel Source Code* and *Clone the Tock Additional Libraries*.

Tip Using Visual Studio Code[5] together with the Remote SSH extension is a powerful solution when developing and deploying from a Raspberry Pi that has no display.

Use The Raspberry Pi As a Gateway for the Pico

The other approach to program the Raspberry Pi Pico is to use a regular Raspberry Pi running Raspbian Linux only as a gateway between the computer and the Pico. To be more specific, we do all the development, including compiling the Tock kernel and applications, on the computer and use the Pi only to deploy the binaries on the Pico. The main advantage of this approach is that we do not need to use the Raspberry Pi as a computer (connect it to a screen, keyboard, and mouse), and we can install a Raspberry Pi OS Lite Linux distribution on it that has no UI support. This approach is recommended if you are not used to writing programs on the Raspberry Pi, as you can continue to use your favorite development setup.

---

[5] Visual Studio Code, https://code.visualstudio.com/

Note   This approach is recommended only if you have a Linux or macOS computer. For Windows systems, the setup might not work, and we recommend you do the development directly on the Raspberry Pi board.

Considering that the development and compilation are done on the computer, and the deployment is done using the Raspberry Pi, we need to install tools on both machines. On the computer, we need to clone the Tock source code and libraries and install all the tools that enable the compilation and debugging.

On the other hand, the Raspberry Pi will run the application that enables the data transfer (binaries and debugging commands and information) between the computer and the Pico board.

The Setup for Linux and macOS Systems

The process of installing the tools described at the beginning of this chapter on Linux and macOS systems is similar, the only difference being the package manager.

Linux Systems

For Linux systems, the commands that install the necessary tools are described in Listing 5-6.

Tip   For Ubuntu 14.04 and 16.04 or distributions other than Debian, `gdb-multiarch` is replaced with `gdb-arm-none-eabi`.

Listing 5-6. The commands that install the necessary tools on Linux computers

```
$ sudo apt-get update
$ sudo apt install automake autoconf
build-essential texinfo libtool libftdi-dev libusb-1.0-0-dev
$ curl https://sh.rustup.rs -sSf | sh
#Note, will need to restart terminal after installation
$ sudo apt install gcc-arm-none-eabi
$ sudo apt install gdb-multiarch
```

MacOS Systems

For macOS systems, we need to open a new terminal window and type the commands in Listing 5-7.

Listing 5-7. The commands that install the necessary tools on macOS computers

```
$ curl https://sh.rustup.rs -sSf | sh
$ brew tap ARMmbed/homebrew-formulae && brew update && brew
install arm-none-eabi-gcc
$ sudo apt install minicom
```

The Setup for the Raspberry Pi

The next step is to install OpenOCD on the Raspberry Pi. This needs to be installed by cloning the source code and compiling it, as we need to use the custom OpenOCD version, which is adapted to communicate with the Raspberry Pi Pico device. Listing 5-8 displays the commands that need to be run on the Raspberry Pi.

Note   Before running the commands in Listing 5-8 you need to connect to the Raspberry Pi via SSH

Listing 5-8. The commands that install OpenOCD on the Raspberry Pi

```
$ sudo apt-get update
$ sudo apt install automake autoconf
build-essential texinfo libtool libftdi-dev libusb-1.0-0-dev
$ git clone https://github.com/raspberrypi/openocd.git
--recursive --branch rp2040 --depth=1
$ cd openocd
$ ./bootstrap
$ ./configure --enable-ftdi --enable-sysfsgpio --enable-
bcm2835gpio
$ make -j4
$ sudo make install
$ cd ~
```

Tip   We recommend you create a new folder where you clone the two repositories: tock and libtock-c.

Clone the Tock Kernel Source Code

As new features are being pushed to the tock repository, today's version can be different from the two days ago one, and some of the changes might not be completely stable. In this context, the Tock development team issues periodic releases for the kernel. These releases consist of stable, tested features that do not change anymore. Once a release is made public, no other changes are made. Therefore, to make sure you run your applications on top of a stable system, we recommend that you use one of the releases of the Tock kernel. While this implies that all the new features will not be integrated into your system, the advantage is that you can rely on a stable version of Tock. Of course, once a new version is released, we recommend that you switch to it.

To check the current release, we select the *Releases* option on the Tock Github page[6], redirecting us to a page where each release, together with its details, is listed (Figure 5-5). Another important aspect is the name of the release, which is required to clone the appropriate source code. At the time of this writing, the release is tagged as release-2.0.

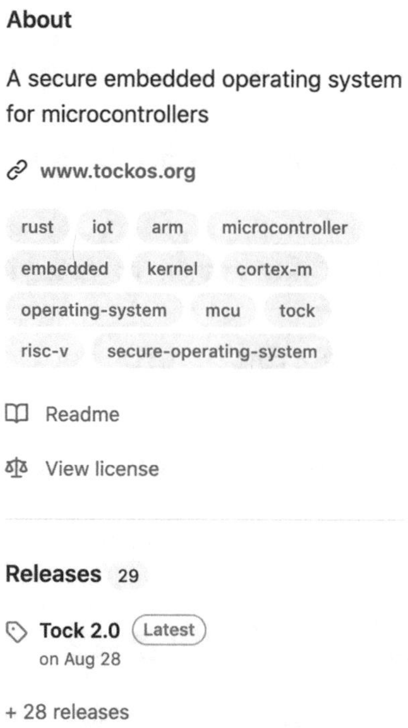

About

A secure embedded operating system for microcontrollers

🔗 www.tockos.org

rust   iot   arm   microcontroller

embedded   kernel   cortex-m

operating-system   mcu   tock

risc-v   secure-operating-system

📖 Readme

⚖️ View license

Releases 29

🏷 **Tock 2.0** (Latest)
     on Aug 28

+ 28 releases

Figure 5-5. *The release information for the Tock source code*

---

[6] Tock, `https://github.com/tock/tock`

In order to download one of the released versions of the Tock source code, we first need to clone or download the source from Github and then bring the local repository to the desired version. Listing 5-9 shows the terminal commands we need to run to use release version 2.0.

Listing 5-9. Clone Tock version 2.0

```
$ git clone https://github.com/tock/tock.git
$ cd tock
$ git checkout tags/release-2.0
Note: checking out 'release-2.0'.

You are in 'detached HEAD' state. You can look around, make
experimental
changes and commit them, and you can discard any commits you
make in this
state without impacting any branches by performing another
checkout.

If you want to create a new branch to retain commits you
create, you may
do so (now or later) by using -b with the checkout command
again. Example:

  git checkout -b <new-branch-name>

HEAD is now at 6ade39d27... Merge #2799
```

Clone Tock Additional Libraries

So far, we have downloaded the Tock kernel source code, but running the operating system alone is of little use. Therefore, the next step is to make the setup necessary for running applications. In implementing our applications, we need to use several libraries that make it possible to interface with the kernel and access the peripherals. Libtock-c and libtock-rs are the two repositories that contain the userland libraries for that, and they enable us to build c and rust applications for Tock.

Note   Since the libtock-rs library is still under development and is not stable with Tock v2.0, we will focus on building C applications using libtock-c.

Listing 5-10 shows the commands necessary to clone libtock-c for Tock v 2.0.

Listing 5-10. Clone libtock-c for Tock version 2.0

```
$ git clone https://github.com/tock/libtock-c.git
$ cd libtock-c
$ git checkout tags/release-2.0
Note: checking out 'release-2.0'.
```

We can now explore the main directories that libtock-c consists of:

- examples - it contains various C applications that can be built and uploaded on the devices; these are good starting points for building more complex apps, and we will use one of these applications in our first example;

- libc++ - this is the library for C++ applications;

- libtock - it comprises the libraries that enable the interaction with the kernel and controlling and reading data from the peripherals (e.g., gpio, i2c, led, button, etc.);

- lua53 - you can use it to write Lua applications;

- lvgl - it is built on top of Light and Versatile Embedded Graphics Library[7], a graphics library, and it enables you to write Tock applications that include visual elements;

- newlib - it is the C standard library.

Compile and Deploy the Tock Kernel and Applications

Deploying the Tock kernel on a device is similar to any other process where we have to upload a new firmware on some hardware. We basically need to compile the source code into a binary file that gets flashed on the board.

In our case, depending on the purpose we aim to achieve, we can choose between flashing using a .bin or an .elf file. While the bin file gets directly executed, the elf file is helpful for debugging as it is loaded via gdb. The file contains additional information for debugging and inspecting the program. Due to this information, gdb is able to load the binary code to the board.

When it comes to the options of flashing the device, these can be divided into two main categories: using a bootloader or without a bootloader. The bootloader is a small piece of software that runs on the device and whose primary purpose is to flash applications. Its main advantage is that applications can easily be deployed onto the hardware without the need for any external components. Without the bootloader, we need an external component called a hardware debugger that is capable of transferring our application to the device.

Based on whether we use or not the bootloader, we can define the process of transferring the executable on the device the following:

---

[7]LVGL, https://lvgl.io/

1. Flashing - This is done when there is no bootloader on the device. The kernel and applications are flashed using the hardware debug interface, which requires special hardware and software. The advantage of this approach is that there is no flash memory occupied by a bootloader software and that we can also interact with the device via the debug interface. The hardware debugger takes full control over the chip and can read and write any memory and flash locations. As its name suggests, this approach is recommended in a testing environment where we need to debug our applications.

2. Programming - The kernel and applications are deployed using a special bootloader software that needs to be previously flashed on the devices. However, if something goes wrong, we default to the first approach as by programming, we have no control over the device. This is the approach in a production environment, where the hardware debugger should not be used.

Note   When building the application for a device that will be programmed using a bootloader, we also need to consider that the bootloader takes up flash space.

In this book, we will focus on prototyping applications, so we will only flash the devices using a hardware debugger, not program them.

Flashing the devices requires special software capable of transferring the program on the chip on top of a hardware debugger. In our case, OpenOCD is the application capable of achieving that. Based on how you decide to use OpenOCD and the end goal, there are two main approaches to deploying the Tock kernel and applications on the micro:bit and the Raspberry Pi Pico devices. Each approach has its advantages and disadvantages and is suitable for a different set of tasks:

- Use gdb on top of OpenOCD – This is the option recommended when you aim to contribute to the Tock kernel as it gives you complete control over the device while the kernel is running (e.g., use breakpoints in the kernel). Its main disadvantage is that the deployment process is more complex and deploying applications on top of it can be difficult;

- Use OpenOCD directly – This option will deploy the kernel and give you no control over the device afterward. It is recommended for cases when you aim to develop applications on top of the Tock kernel without altering the kernel. Its main advantage is that it is very straightforward.

Based on each device's characteristics, the flashing process can be easier or more complicated. This is mainly because some devices have the hardware debugger integrated while others require an external device. Further on, we will go through the various possibilities of deploying Tock on the micro:bit and Raspberry Pi Pico devices in a development environment.

What is more, as running the operating system without any applications is of little use, we will also build a simple Hello World application and deploy it on both devices.

Deploy the Tock Kernel on the micro:bit

One of the main characteristics of the micro:bit v2 is that it has a hardware debugger integrated. This means that we can easily program the device without acquiring an external debugger such as Segger J-Link or Keil

Ulinkpro. We just need to use the OpenOCD application, which makes use of the board's hardware debugger to flash the device.

Next, we need to take into account that there are two main options of deploying the kernel on the micro:bit device, which we mentioned above: use OpenOCD directly, or use gdb on top of OpenOCD.

To get started, no matter the approach, we first need to connect the device to the computer via USB.

Note   To connect the device to the virtual machine, start the machine, connect the device using USB, then hit the USB icon and select the micro:bit from the dropdown list (Figure 5-6).

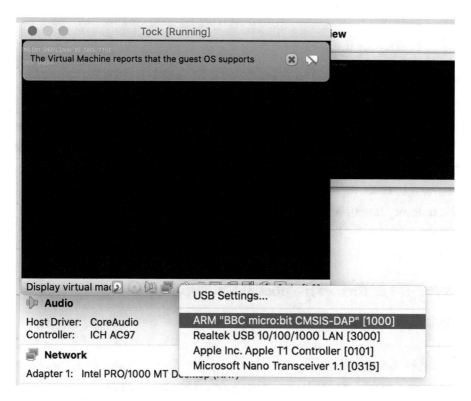

Figure 5-6. *Connect the micro:bit to the virtual machine*

189

Once the device is connected, we can move forward to compiling and deploying the kernel. Next, we will go through both approaches as some of the chapters in this book will focus on contributing to the kernel, while others will center around building applications for tock.

Use Gdb to Deploy Tock

For this case, we will take the following steps:

1. Build the kernel source code;

2. Open a connection to the device via the debugging interface;

3. Open a gdb session on the device via the debugging interface;

4. Deploy the binary via gdb;

5. Run the kernel in gdb.

To build the source code, we first need to navigate to the **boards/microbit_v2** folder in the **tock** repository. Here, we open the **layout.ld** file. This is the file that describes the memory and flash layout for the micro:bit board. The initial layout assumes that tock's bootloader is already flashed on the micro:bit. As in this approach, we will not use the tock-bootloader, the memory layout needs to be changed. To do this, we need to comment out the initial ROM layout and uncomment the specified one as shown in Listing 5-11.

Listing 5-11. Change the micro:bit memory layout

```
MEMORY
{
  # with bootloader
  # rom (rx)  : ORIGIN = 0x00010000, LENGTH = 192K
  # without bootloader
```

```
rom (rx)  : ORIGIN = 0x00000000, LENGTH = 256K
prog (rx) : ORIGIN = 0x00040000, LENGTH = 256K
ram (rwx) : ORIGIN = 0x20000000, LENGTH = 128K
}
```

Now we can build the kernel by running the make command in the same folder. As Listing 5-12 shows, a **microbit_v2.bin** file is generated. This is the kernel binary that needs to be flashed on the device. However, if we check the **release** folder where the file was generated, we notice that a **microbit_v2.elf** file is also there. The ELF file has the same binary code as the BIN file but has some additional information that can be interpreted by gdb. This is the one we will use further on.

Listing 5-12. Tock kernel compilation

```
$ cd tock/boards/microbit_v2
$ make
info: downloading component 'rust-std' for 'thumbv7em-none-eabi'
info: installing component 'rust-std' for 'thumbv7em-none-eabi'
info: using up to 500.0 MiB of RAM to unpack components
   Compiling tock-tbf v0.1.0 (/Users/tock/tock/libraries/tock-tbf)
   Compiling tock-registers v0.6.0 (/Users/tock/tock/libraries/
   tock-register-interface)
......
Compiling nrf52_components v0.1.0 (/Users/tock/tock/boards/nordic/
nrf52_components)
    Finished release [optimized + debuginfo] target(s) in 21.93s
   text      data       bss       dec       hex    filename
 106497         0     16384    122881     1e001    /Users/
tock/tock/target/thumbv7em-none-eabi/release/microbit_v2
4121b1f7ba7cb43321dd977d393923bdbbad8100e9e9febe2bdb84169476a7ab
/Users/tock/tock/target/thumbv7em-none-eabi/release/microbit_v2.bin
```

The next step is to open a new terminal window, go to the **boards/microbit_v2** folder and type the command in Listing 5-13. This will use OpenOCD to open a connection to the micro:bit. If similar messages as those in Listing 5-13 appear, the connection has been successfully established. We leave this terminal open and switch to the first one.

Listing 5-13. Use OpenOCD to connect to the micro:bit

```
$openocd
Open On-Chip Debugger 0.10.0
Licensed under GNU GPL v2
For bug reports, read
    http://openocd.org/doc/doxygen/bugs.html
Info : auto-selecting first available session transport "swd".
To override use 'transport select <transport>'.
cortex_m reset_config sysresetreq
adapter speed: 1000 kHz
Info : CMSIS-DAP: SWD  Supported
Info : CMSIS-DAP: Interface Initialised (SWD)
Info : CMSIS-DAP: FW Version = 0255
Info : SWCLK/TCK = 1 SWDIO/TMS = 1 TDI = 0 TDO = 0 nTRST = 0
       nRESET = 1
Info : CMSIS-DAP: Interface ready
Info : clock speed 1000 kHz
Info : SWD DPIDR 0x2ba01477
Info : nrf51.cpu: hardware has 6 breakpoints, 4 watchpoints
```

In the first terminal, we run the commands in Listings 5-12 to start a gdb session to the device. This session will use the OpenOCD connection to transfer the information to and from the device. We first run gdb with the **microbit_v2.elf** file as a parameter, then initiate a remote connection to localhost port 3333. This is the port where OpenOCD listens for connections.

Listing 5-14. Run Tock using gdb

```
$ arm-none-eabi-gdb ../../target/thumbv7em-none-eabi/release/
microbit_v2.elf
GNU gdb (GNU Tools for Arm Embedded Processors 9-2019-q4-major)
8.3.0.20190709-git
Copyright (C) 2019 Free Software Foundation, Inc.
. . .
Reading symbols from ../../target/thumbv7em-none-eabi/release/
microbit_v2.elf...
(gdb) target remote localhost:3333
Remote debugging using localhost:3333
<microbit_v2::io::Writer as kernel::debug::IoWrite>::write (
    self=<optimized out>, buf=...) at boards/microbit_v2/src/
    io.rs:58
58      boards/microbit_v2/src/io.rs: No such file or directory.
(gdb) load
Loading section .text, size 0x19994 lma 0x0
Loading section .ARM.exidx, size 0x10 lma 0x19994
Loading section .storage, size 0x65c lma 0x199a4
Loading section .apps, size 0x4 lma 0x40000
Start address 0x0, load size 106500
Transfer rate: 4 KB/sec, 10650 bytes/write.
(gdb) continue
Continuing.
```

Caution   The command above is run on a macOS computer.
For Linux systems, replace arm-none-eabi-gdb with gdb-
multiarch.

Once the connection is established, OpenOCD will show the message in Listing 5-15. Finally, we run *load* and *continue*, which will run the kernel on the device.

Listing 5-15. Connection established message

```
Info : accepting 'gdb' connection on tcp/3333
Warn : Unknown device (HWID 0x00000197)
```

Note   If at any time OpenOCD or gdb raise errors in connection, we recommend you reset the micro:bit and try again.

With this, we deployed the Tock kernel to the micro:bit.

Tip   To obtain additional debugging information, you can build the Tock kernel using make debug. However, this requires more stack space, so you need to open the **microbit_v2/src/main.rs** file and uncomment line 76 (or close to it), as shown in Listing 5-16.

Listing 5-16. Increase the stack size for running Tock in debug mode

```
// pub static mut STACK_MEMORY: [u8; 0x1000] = //[0; 0x1000];
// debug mode requires more stack space
pub static mut STACK_MEMORY: [u8; 0x2000] = [0; 0x2000];
```

Use OpenOCD to Deploy Tock

While the first approach also uses OpenOCD, this one does not involve additional tools to deploy the Tock kernel. The main advantage of this approach is that it is much simpler, with the downside that we cannot use any breakpoints in Tock while it is running. However, we can always use tockloader to print debug messages that we place in the code. So if you are used to debugging your applications by printing messages, this might be a fit for you.

Similar to the first approach, this one does not use a bootloader, so we will use the same flash layout as in the previous example. If you skipped it, you should take a look at Listing 5-11 to change the memory layout file.

Note   A future chapter will deal with the process of programming the devices for a production environment where the bootloader is required.

To flash the kernel, we open a terminal window and navigate to the **tock/boards/microbit_v2** file. Then, we run the make flash command as shown in Listing 5-17, and with these simple steps, we have the kernel running on the device.

Listing 5-17. Flashing the Tock kernel on the micro:bit v2

```
$ cd tock/boards/microbit_v2
$ make flash
info: syncing channel updates for 'nightly-2020-10-25-x86_64-
apple-darwin'
info: latest update on 2020-10-25, rust version 1.49.0-nightly
(ffa2e7ae8 2020-10-24)
info: downloading component 'cargo'
info: downloading component 'clippy'
info: downloading component 'rust-docs'

. . .
** Programming Finished **
verified 95181 bytes in 1.123071s (82.764 KiB/s)
shutdown command invoked
```

To verify that the flashing was completed, we can use again the *tockloader* tool to read data from the serial line. Although there is no application running yet, when resetting the device, a simple *Initialization complete.* message is emitted. Therefore, when running the tockloader listen command in the terminal, the output in Listing 5-18 will appear.

Listing 5-18. Use tockloader to check the successful flashing

```
$ tockloader listen
No device name specified. Using default "tock"
No serial port with device name "tock" found
Found 5 serial port(s).

[0]    /dev/cu.MALS - n/a
[1]    /dev/cu.SOC - n/a
[2]    /dev/cu.XXXX - n/a
[3]    /dev/cu.YYYY - n/a
[4]    /dev/cu.usbmodem145102 - "BBC micro:bit CMSIS-DAP" -
       mbed Serial Port

Which option? [0] 4

Listening for serial output.
Initialization complete. Entering main loop.
```

Note   If no message appears after you select the correct device number, reset the micro:bit by pressing the button on the back.

Hello World from micro:bit!

The next step in building a secure system is to deploy the applications on top of the Tock kernel. For this, we will use the *libtock-c* repository, where we can choose from a large set of application examples. In this chapter, we will build and deploy a simple application that prints the *Hello World!* message in the console.

Caution   To deploy the application, the Tock kernel should already be flashed on the device, as shown in the section above.

First of all, we open a new terminal and navigate to the **libtock-c/examples/c_hello** folder. Here we can find the **main.c** file containing the source code and a **makefile** for compiling it. Listing 5-19 displays the result after running the make command.

Listing 5-19. Compile the c_hello example

```
$ cd libtock-c/examples/c_hello
$ make
. . .
  DIR        build/cortex-m0
   CC        main.c
   LD        build/cortex-m0/cortex-m0.elf
  DIR        build/cortex-m3
   CC        main.c
   LD        build/cortex-m3/cortex-m3.elf
  DIR        build/cortex-m4
   CC        main.c
   LD        build/cortex-m4/cortex-m4.elf
  DIR        build/cortex-m7
   CC        main.c
   LD        build/cortex-m7/cortex-m7.elf
Application size report for target cortex-m0:
   text    data     bss     dec     hex filename
    844     208    2396    3448     d78 build/cortex-m0/
                                        cortex-m0.elf
```

```
Application size report for target cortex-m3:
   text    data     bss     dec     hex filename
    840     208    2396    3444     d74 build/cortex-m3/
                                        cortex-m3.elf
Application size report for target cortex-m4:
   text    data     bss     dec     hex filename
    840     208    2396    3444     d74 build/cortex-m4/
                                        cortex-m4.elf
Application size report for target cortex-m7:
   text    data     bss     dec     hex filename
    840     208    2396    3444     d74 build/cortex-m7/
                                        cortex-m7.elf
```

By examining the result, we notice that several elf files have been generated in the build folder. If we inspect this folder, we also see that a c_hello.tab file has been generated. This Tock Application Bundle, or TAB, is nothing more than a tar archive containing a manifest and the same TBF (Tock Binary Format) file compiled for several architectures (Cortex-M0, M3, M4, M7). This is also the file that tockloader uses to deploy the application on a device.

Therefore, the only remaining step is to run tockloader to install the application, as shown in Listing 5-20.

Listing 5-20. Use tockloader to deploy the c_hello application

```
$ tockloader install microbit_v2 --bundle-apps  build/c_hello.tab
[INFO   ] Using settings from KNOWN_BOARDS["microbit_v2"]
[STATUS ] Installing app on the board...
[INFO   ] Installing app bundle. Size: 2048 bytes.
[INFO   ] Finished in 3.825 seconds
```

After the application is flashed, we use tockloader again to listen for messages printed by the device (Listing 5-21).

Note   Tockloader also uses OpenOCD to deploy the binary.
The --bundle-apps argument is necessary due to some issue that
tockloader and OpenOCD have with the device's flash. The downside
of this is that all applications will be read from the device and
reflashed each time.

To actually see the message, we have to reset the device by pressing the
button on the back of the board after running tockloader listen.

Listing 5-21. Listen for messages from the device using tockloader

```
$ tockloader listen
[INFO  ] No device name specified. Using default name "tock".
[INFO  ] No serial port with device name "tock" found.
[INFO  ] Found 5 serial ports.
Multiple serial port options found. Which would you
like to use?
[0]     /dev/cu.SOC - n/a
[1]     /dev/cu.MALS - n/a
[2]     /dev/cu.XXXX - n/a
[3]     /dev/cu.YYYY - n/a
[4]     /dev/cu.usbmodem144102 - "BBC micro:bit CMSIS-DAP" -
        mbed Serial Port

Which option? [0] 4
[INFO  ] Using "/dev/cu.usbmodem144102 - "BBC micro:bit CMSIS-
DAP" - mbed Serial Port".
[INFO  ] Listening for serial output.
Initialization complete. Entering main loop.
Hello World!
```

Deploy the Tock Kernel on the Raspberry Pi Pico

The Raspberry Pi Pico is a device designed to be debugged via a regular Raspberry Pi device. When installing the necessary tools to deploy Tock on the Pico, we took into account the two possible approaches:

- Make the development on a regular Raspberry Pi device and deploy the resulted binary on the Pico;

- Make the development on the computer and use the Raspberry Pi only as the hardware debugging interface.

For both approaches, we first need to connect the Pico to the Raspberry Pi board. For this, we need to use the Serial Wire Debug (SWD) pins, which is the interface through which the Pico can be debugged. The SWD is standard for all Cortex-M microcontrollers, which is also the case for the RP2040.

The SWD pins on the Pico are exposed separately from the GPIO pins, while on the Raspberry Pi, the SWD is simulated by bit-banging GPIO pins 24 and 25.

In addition, we will also connect the two devices via UART, so information coming from the Pico will be displayed in a Raspberry Pi terminal.

Figure 5-7 displays how to connect the pins for both SWD and UART communication.

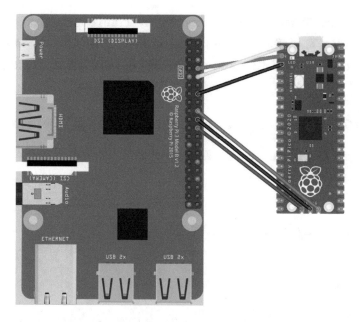

Figure 5-7. *Connect the Raspberry Pi Pico to Raspberry Pi 3 Model B via SWD and UART*

Once we power on both devices, we can get started with building and deploying the Tock kernel.

Compile and Deploy the Tock Kernel Using the Raspberry Pi

The first approach we take is to use the Raspberry Pi as the development environment, which implies that we have all the necessary tools installed on the device, together with the tock and libtock-c repository we cloned.

For this approach, we can choose among the two options we described at the beginning of the chapter. Both use OpenOCD as the main software necessary to deploy the binary on the Pico. The difference consists in the other tools used as we can use OpenOCD on its own or together with gdb, which gives us more control over the device while running the Tock kernel and applications.

In both cases, we will use the serial connection to print data coming from the Pico. Therefore, no matter the approach, the first step is to open a new terminal and run the command in Listing 5-22. This will listen for data coming from the Pico using the UART communication.

Listing 5-22. Open serial connection between the Pi and the Pico

```
$ minicom -b 115200 -o -D  /dev/serial0
Welcome to minicom 2.7.1

OPTIONS: I18n
Compiled on Aug 13 2017, 15:25:34.
Port /dev/serial0

Press CTRL-A Z for help on special keys
```

This shell instance will be used only for printing data coming on the serial line.

Use Only OpenOCD to Deploy Tock

We start with this approach as it is the more straightforward one. For this case, we compile the Tock kernel on the Raspberry Pi and deploy the resulting binary over OpenOCD. In addition, we can use the serial connection to print information messages. However, this approach does not give us any control over the device.

We recommend this approach if you are used to debugging your applications by printing messages and if you focus mainly on application development, not contributing to the kernel.

To deploy Tock in this manner, we first need to open a terminal and navigate to the **tock/boards/raspberry_pi_pico** directory, where we run the make flash command (Listing 5-23). This will compile and deploy the Tock kernel on the Raspberry Pi Pico. Once the operation is complete, the *Initialization complete. Entering main loop* Message will be displayed in the first terminal we have opened and is running minicom. This means that Tock is running on the Pico board.

Listing 5-23. Flash Tock on the Raspberry Pi Pico

```
$ cd tock/boards/raspberry_pi_pico/
$ make flash
Finished release [optimized + debuginfo] target(s) in 0.64s
   text      data      bss       dec       hex     filename
  77828        0       8192     86020     15004    /home/pi/
tock/target/thumbv6m-none-eabi/release/raspberry_pi_pico
openocd -f openocd.cfg -c "program /home/pi/tock/target/
thumbv6m-none-eabi/release/raspberry_pi_pico.elf; verify_image
/home/pi/tock/target/thumbv6m-none-eabi/release/raspberry_pi_
pico.elf; reset; shutdown;"
Open On-Chip Debugger 0.10.0+dev-gf8e14ec97-dirty
(2021-06-09-13:10)
Licensed under GNU GPL v2
For bug reports, read
        http://openocd.org/doc/doxygen/bugs.html
Info : Hardware thread awareness created
```

Use Gdb to Deploy Tock

This approach uses OpenOCD and gdb-multiarch, giving us control over the device as the kernel is run. We can use all the features of gdb (e.g., breakpoints, memory inspection) to debug the Tock kernel. While more complex, using gdb on top of OpenOCD is recommended when we aim to modify and debug the Tock kernel.

To get started, we first open a new terminal window on the Raspberry Pi and navigate to **tock/boards/raspberry_pi_pico.** In this folder, we run make. As Listing 5-24 shows, a **raspberry_pi_pico.bin** file is generated. This is the kernel binary that needs to be flashed on the device. However, if we check the **release** folder where the file was generated, we can notice that a **raspberry_pi_pico.elf** file is also there. This has the same binary code but includes additional information that can be interpreted by gdb, and this is the one we will use further on.

Listing 5-24. Compile the Tock kernel

```
$ cd tock/boards/raspberry_pi_pico
$ make
make
info: downloading component 'llvm-tools-preview'
. . .
 Finished release [optimized + debuginfo] target(s) in 5m 04s
    text        data         bss         dec         hex     filename
   57345           0        8192       65537       10001     /home/
pi/tock/target/thumbv6m-none-eabi/release/raspberry_pi_pico
6a3c56d4f78a98bcdf0f75e16d6571b3656c385a4b433675237410e6fbf11f16
/home/pi/tock/target/thumbv6m-none-eabi/release/raspberry_pi_
pico.bin
```

The next step is to open a new terminal window and type the command in Listing 5-25. This will use OpenOCD to open a connection to the Raspberry Pi Pico. If no error messages appear, the connection has been successfully established. Next, we leave this terminal open and switch to the previous one.

Listing 5-25. Start OpenOCD

```
$ openocd -f interface/raspberrypi-swd.cfg -f target/rp2040.cfg
Open On-Chip Debugger 0.10.0+dev-gf8e14ec-dirty (2021-04-18-14:57)
Licensed under GNU GPL v2
For bug reports, read
    http://openocd.org/doc/doxygen/bugs.html
adapter speed: 1000 kHz
```

```
Info : Hardware thread awareness created
Info : Hardware thread awareness created
Info : RP2040 Flash Bank Command
Info : Listening on port 6666 for tcl connections
Info : Listening on port 4444 for telnet connections
```

In the same terminal where we have built the kernel, we run the commands in Listing 5-26. By using gdb-multiarch, we can use the OpenOCD connection to transfer information to and from the device. We first run gdb with the elf file as a parameter, then initiate a remote connection to localhost port 3333. This is the port where OpenOCD listens for connections. Finally, we run load and continue, which will run the kernel on the device.

Listing 5-26. Deploy Tock using gdb-multiarch

```
$ gdb-multiarch ~/tock/target/thumbv6m-none-eabi/release/
raspberry_pi_pico.elf
GNU gdb (Raspbian 8.2.1-2) 8.2.1
. . .
Reading symbols from target/thumbv6m-none-eabi/release/
raspberry_pi_pico.elf...done.
(gdb) target remote localhost:3333
Remote debugging using :3333
0x10006ae4 in cortexm::support::atomic (f=...)
    at arch/cortex-m/src/support.rs:30
30          asm!("cpsie i", options(nomem, nostack));
(gdb) load
Loading section .apps, size 0x1 lma 0x20020000
Loading section .text, size 0x100 lma 0x10000000
Loading section .text, size 0xd024 lma 0x10000100
Loading section .ARM.exidx, size 0x10 lma 0x1000d124
Loading section .storage, size 0xecc lma 0x1000d134
```

```
Start address 0x100050f4, load size 57345
Transfer rate: 50 KB/sec, 7168 bytes/write.
(gdb) continue
Continuing.
```

As the kernel is run, the first terminal, where the serial connection was established using minicom, will show the message *Initialization complete. Entering main loop.* This means that the kernel is running on the Raspberry Pi Pico device.

Compile and Deploy the Tock Kernel from the Computer

If you work on a Linux or macOS system, you can take advantage of the support for the development tools necessary and build the Tock kernel directly on the computer. This is particularly useful if the Raspberry Pi you use does not have a user interface and the peripherals necessary to control it directly. In this case, we will use SSH to connect to the Raspberry Pi and deploy the binary on the Pico.

In this case, flashing can only be done using gdb on top of OpenOCD. Direct OpenOCD flashing is not possible in this setup.

To get started, we first open a new terminal on the computer and connect to the Raspberry Pi via SSH. What is more, we need to forward port 3333, which OpenOCD uses. Once the connection is established, we run OpenOCD, which will start a connection between the Raspberry Pi and the Pico device. On the other side, OpenOCD listens for connections on port 3333, and gdb uses this connection to send commands to the Raspberry Pi Pico. This is why we ensured that this port is forwarded to localhost, which is our machine (Listing 5-27).

Listing 5-27. Run OpenOCD on the Raspberry Pi

```
$ssh pi@<pi_IP> -L 3333:localhost:3333
$openocd -f interface/raspberrypi-swd.cfg -f target/rp2040.cfg
Open On-Chip Debugger 0.10.0+dev-gf8e14ec-dirty
(2021-04-18-14:57)
. . . . . . . . . . .
Info : Listening on port 3333 for gdb connections
```

In another terminal, we navigate to the Tock source code in the **tock/
boards/raspberry_pi_pico** folder. We build the kernel using the make
command, which will generate a binary file, as shown in Listing 5-28.

Listing 5-28. Build the Tock source code

```
$ cd tock/boards/raspberry_pi_pico
$ make
make
info: downloading component 'llvm-tools-preview'
. . .
 Finished release [optimized + debuginfo] target(s) in 5m 04s
   text    data     bss      dec     hex   filename
  57345       0    8192    65537   10001   /home/
pi/tock/target/thumbv6m-none-eabi/release/raspberry_pi_pico
6a3c56d4f78a98bcdf0f75e16d6571b3656c385a4b433675237410e6fbf
11f16   /home/pi/tock/target/thumbv6m-none-eabi/release/
raspberry_pi_pico.bin
```

If we check the **release** folder where the file was generated, we can
notice that a **raspberry_pi_pico.elf** file is also there. This has the same
binary code, but includes additional information that can be interpreted
by gdb and this is the one we will use further on.

Next, we use gdb that connects to the OpenOCD server on the Raspberry Pi to transfer the information to and from the device. We first run gdb with the elf file as a parameter, then initiate a remote connection to the Raspberry Pi on port 3333. Since port 3333 on the Raspberry Pi is forwarded to port 3333 on localhost, we will connect to localhost:3333, and all the messages will reach the Raspberry Pi. Once the connection is established, OpenOCD will show a message. Finally, we run load and continue, which will run the kernel on the device.

Caution   If you are on a Linux machine, you will use the gdb-multiarch command, while on macOS, the same is done using arm-none-eabi-gdb. Listing 5-29 shows the commands necessary for macOS. For Linux machines, replace arm-none-eabi-gdb with gdb-multiarch.

Listing 5-29. Deploy Tock on the Raspberry Pi Pico from the computer

```
$arm-none-eabi-gdb tock/target/thumbv6m-none-eabi/release/
raspberry_pi_pico.elf
GNU gdb (GNU Tools for Arm Embedded Processors 9-2019-q4-major)
8.3.0.20190709-git
. . .
Reading symbols from target/thumbv6m-none-eabi/release/
raspberry_pi_pico.elf...
(gdb)target remote localhost:3333
target remote localhost:3333
Remote debugging using localhost:3333
(gdb) load
Loading section .apps, size 0x1 lma 0x20040000
```

```
Loading section .text, size 0x100 lma 0x10000000
Loading section .text, size 0x48d8 lma 0x10000100
Loading section .ARM.exidx, size 0x10 lma 0x100049d8
Loading section .storage, size 0x618 lma 0x100049e8
Start address 0x10002640, load size 20481
Transfer rate: 20 KB/sec, 3413 bytes/write.
(gdb) continue
Continuing.
```

As the binary is flashed and Tock is run on the device, we can notice the message *Initialization complete. Entering main loop* in the terminal where minicom is running. This signals that Tock is running on the Raspberry Pi Pico.

Hello World from Raspberry Pi Pico!

Now that we managed to run Tock on the Raspberry Pi Pico, it's time to take another step and build applications on top of it. Running an operating system solely is of little use, so let's see how to deploy a simple C application that prints *Hello World* in the console.

Similar to the kernel deployment process, we will present how to deploy the application either from the Raspberry Pi or from the computer.

Deploy the Application from the Raspberry Pi

As any application deployment requires, first of all, we need to compile the source code. For this, we open a new terminal on the Raspberry Pi and navigate to **libtock-c/examples/c_hello**. This is a sample application that prints the *Hello World* message. To build the source code, we run the make command as shown in Listing 5-30.

Listing 5-30. Build the application on the Raspberry Pi

```
$ cd libtock-c/examples/c_hello/
$ make

. . .

Application size report for target cortex-m0:
   text    data    bss     dec     hex   filename
    844     208    2396    3448    d78   build/cortex-m0/
                                        cortex-m0.elf
Application size report for target cortex-m3:
   text    data    bss     dec     hex   filename
    840     208    2396    3444    d74   build/cortex-m3/
                                        cortex-m3.elf
Application size report for target cortex-m4:
   text    data    bss     dec     hex   filename
    840     208    2396    3444    d74   build/cortex-m4/
                                        cortex-m4.elf
Application size report for target cortex-m7:
   text    data    bss     dec     hex   filename
    840     208    2396    3444    d74   build/cortex-m7/
                                        cortex-m7.elf
```

The make command generates an elf file for each of the supported architectures. What the output of the make command does not show is that a TBF (Tock Binary Format) file for each of the architectures has also been generated. This is the file that we need to use. In our case, we will use the **build/cortex-m0/cortex-m0.tbf** file.

To flash the application on the device, we navigate to **tock/boards/ raspberry_pi_pico** and run the command in Listing 5-31. This will bundle the TBF file with the Tock kernel and deploy the resulted binary on the device.

Listing 5-31. Flash the Tock kernel and the application on the Raspberry Pi Pico

```
$APP=../../../libtock-c/examples/c_hello/build/cortex-m0/
cortex-m0.tbf make program
```

Once the command finishes its execution, the *Hello World!* message is printed in the terminal where minicom is running.

Caution   When flashing the device using make program, ensure that OpenOCD is not running on the Raspberry Pi. Otherwise, the flashing process will fail.

If we wish to debug the kernel and application bundle using gdb, we can take the approach described above which enabled us to deploy the Tock kernel using gdb-multiarch. The same process can be used to deploy the kernel and application bundle so you can use all gdb features to have complete control over the device.

For this, we first need to run the openocd command again: openocd -f interface/raspberrypi-swd.cfg -f target/rp2040.cfg.

In another terminal, we run gdb-multiarch but with a different elf file as a parameter. When running make program, a **raspberry_pi_pico-app. elf** file is created. Therefore, we will use the commands in Listing 5-32 to deploy the kernel and application bundle.

Listing 5-32. Deploy the kernel and application bundle using gdb-multiarch

```
$ gdb-multiarch ~/tock//target/thumbv6m-none-eabi/debug/
raspberry_pi_pico-app.elf
GNU gdb (Raspbian 8.2.1-2) 8.2.1
Copyright (C) 2018 Free Software Foundation, Inc.
(gdb)target remote localhost:3333
```

. . .

(gdb) load

```
Loading section .text, size 0x100 lma 0x10000000
```

. . .

(gdb) continue

```
Continuing.
```

The result is similar, in the third terminal where minicom runs, the *Hello World!* message is displayed.

Tip   The Pico does not have a reset button. A simple way to reset it is to run the `monitor reset init` command followed by the `continue` command in gdb.

Deploy the Application from Your Computer

Writing the source code on a regular computer rather than on the Raspberry Pi can be more efficient. We will get through the steps necessary to deploy Tock and the basic hello world application directly from the computer.

In this case, the process is not very different from deploying the Tock kernel. The only difference is that we first have to build the application and bundle it with the kernel. Once an elf file containing both the kernel and the application binary is generated, we use OpenOCD on the Raspberry Pi and gdb-multiarch on the computer to make the deployment.

To build the application, we open a terminal on the computer, navigate to **libtock-c/examples/c_hello** and run make. This is the same process as the one shown in Listing 5-30, in the previous section, and it will generate a binary file for the application.

Next, we navigate back to the **tock/boards/raspberry_pi** folder and run the command in Listing 5-31. The result seems to be a failed command, which is true. This is because make program also tries to flash the Raspberry Pi Pico, which is not possible directly from the computer. However, the **raspberry_pi_pico-app.elf** is created. This is the file that we need to flash on the Raspberry Pi Pico.

Further on, the process is similar to flashing the kernel. We first open a terminal on the Raspberry Pi by connecting via SSH and forwarding port 3333. Next, we run openocd -f interface/raspberrypi-swd.cfg -f target/rp2040.cfg.

In the terminal on the computer, we run gdb-multiarch ~/tock// target/thumbv6m-none-eabi/debug/raspberry_pi_pico-app.elf.

Once this command is successfully run, we can see the *Hello World!* message is displayed in the terminal where minicom is running.

Summary

Starting with this chapter, we can use the Raspberry Pi Pico and micro:bit v2 devices to deploy the Tock kernel and C applications on top of it. Based on the purpose, we can choose between several deployment approaches. The common ground for all of them is that we need a hardware and software debugger. While the hardware debugger is different for the Pico and the micro:bit, the software tool is the same for both devices, called OpenOCD. Further on, we can choose to use OpenOCD on its own, or together with gdb so we can make use of features such as breakpoints or memory inspection to debug our software.

This chapter might seem a bit complex for a getting started guide, but it deals with all the possible approaches of deploying Tock and its applications on the devices so you can choose the one that fits your requirements best.

CHAPTER 6

The Structure of a Custom Tock System

In the previous chapter, we followed the necessary steps to build and deploy the Tock kernel together with a simple single-process application based on *libtock-c*. To achieve this, we cloned the *tock* and *libtock-c* repositories, then we compiled and deployed the source code according to the device's characteristics and the specific use-case.

However, there is a major issue with this process. The Tock kernel that we compiled has a different folder for each device it supports, and many implemented capsules and HIL files. When we aim to run a simple application on a micro:bit or a Raspberry Pi Pico device, many of the existing files are unnecessary. Their complex structure can make the project structure hard to follow. What is more, tampering with the Tock kernel repository is not recommended. The repository should be used only as a foundation on top of which we build our projects.

In a nutshell, we need to think of a better way of structuring our projects, highlighting the files that we need to create and work with while the *tock* and *libtock-c* repositories are only as support files.

This chapter will focus on how we can create a new project with a straightforward structure and where the files we need to work with are easily accessible.

A. Radovici and I. Culic, *Getting Started with Secure Embedded Systems*,
https://doi.org/10.1007/978-1-4842-7789-8_6

To get started, we first create a new empty git repository called **project**. This is the folder where we will create the rest of the project structure. This structure can be divided into two main components: kernel and application.

Initialize the Kernel Component

The most important folder for the kernel component is the Tock kernel itself. This means that various files from the *tock repository* are needed for our project. The easiest way of having these files at hand is to add the *tock repository* as a submodule to our project. As a result, we can link any necessary file where it is needed.

For the kernel files that we change, we create a new folder called **kernel** in the root of our project. This is where we place the drivers that we write and other board-specific files.

Link the Tock Kernel Repository

To link the *tock repository*, we first need to initialize the project folder as a git repository. This enables us to use git features such as linking external repositories.

To include the *tock repository* in our project, we choose to add it as a submodule rather than downloading the source code by using the git clone command. The advantage of this approach is that we can easily keep the linked version up to date with all the changes made in the main repository. For now, we use the release-2.0 tag that is corresponding to Tock 2.0.

The commands necessary for linking the *tock repository* are illustrated in Listing 6-1.

Listing 6-1. Link the Tock kernel repository in the project folder

```
$ cd project
$ git init
$ git submodule add https://github.com/tock/tock.git
$ cd tock
$ git checkout tags/release-2.0
```

Add the Board-Specific Folder

In the Tock kernel repository, each supported device has a corresponding folder inside the **boards** directory. This is where board-specific files are located. These files usually handle the flashing and startup process, which is different for each board.

Most of the time, the projects we build target a specific device. Therefore, out of the array of available devices, we will need only one. In the case presented in this book, we will either work on a micro:bit or a Raspberry Pi Pico device. As such, we need one of the two available folders: **microbit_v2** or **raspberry_pi_pico**. As we will modify the board implementation to suit our needs, we must copy it from the t*ock repository* that we previously cloned to the **kernel** folder, as shown in Listing 6-2 or Listing 6-3.

Listing 6-2. Initialize the device folder for a micro:bit project

```
$ cd kernel
$ cp -r ../tock/boards/microbit_v2 microbit_v2
```

Listing 6-3. Initialize the device folder for a Raspberry Pi Pico project

```
$ cd kernel
$ cp -r ../tock/boards/raspberry_pi_pico raspberry_pi_pico
```

Caution   We made a copy of the board-specific folder into our project. This means that any changes to the mainstream kernel will not be reflected in our project. Whenever you update the kernel version, make sure that the board folder is compatible, and if not, make the required changes manually.

Besides the source code and other configuration files necessary for running the code on the device, this folder also contains the **Makefile** that automates the build and deployment of the kernel, and the **Cargo.toml** file necessary for building the source code.

Build Information

To ensure that the source code of the device package can be built, we need to adapt the **Cargo.toml** file.

Note   Cargo is the package (crate) manager for Rust, and **Cargo.toml** is the manifest file that contains information such as name, version, and dependencies, for the Rust crate where it resides.

The first lines in the file consist of general information about the crate, which we can leave unchanged. The following section, [dependencies], links the crates that need to be included in the build. However, since we copied the folder from the **tock** directory, we need to change the paths to target the appropriate crates in the kernel folder.

What is more, we added another crate called drivers. This points towards a folder that we create, where the capsules that we write will be placed (Listing 6-4). More information on this folder is presented in the following section.

Listing 6-4. The [dependencies] section in the Cargo.toml file

```
[dependencies]
cortexm4 = {path = "../../tock/arch/cortex-m4"}
capsules = { path = "../../tock/capsules" }
kernel = { path = "../../tock/kernel" }
nrf52 = { path = "../../tock/chips/nrf52" }
nrf52833 = {path = "../../tock/chips/nrf52833"}
components = { path = "../../tock/boards/components" }
nrf52_components = { path = "../../tock/boards/nordic/nrf52_
components" }
```

drivers = { path = "../drivers" }

Finally, we have to add two more target properties that specify details about the build process. This is necessary because the *tock repository* has a **Cargo.toml** file located in the root of the folder hierarchy, and the build information is placed there. Now, as the hierarchy changes, we need to copy that information in this configuration file.

The build target properties define how the build is done for a development or a release binary. Listing 6-5 illustrates the two targets' properties that need to be added to the file. They are the same no matter what device you use.

Listing 6-5. The complete Cargo.toml file for the device package

```
[profile.dev]
panic = "abort"
lto = false
opt-level = "z"
debug = true
```

```
[profile.release]
panic = "abort"
lto = true
opt-level = "z"
debug = true
codegen-units = 1
```

In addition to the **Cargo.toml** file, we also need to update the **Makefile** and the **layout.ld** files. They link other files in the **tock** folder, which are not directly available from this directory.

In the case of the **Makefile**, this uses another **Makefile** that is generic for all boards. This is located inside the **tock/boards** directory. Therefore, we need to change the path in line 7 to point to the correct **Makefile. common** (Listing 6-6).

Listing 6-6. The correct path in the device Makefile

```
include ../../tock/boards/Makefile.common
```

Secondly, we need to do a similar step in the **layout.ld** file. This includes a **kernel_layout.ld** file in the repository. Listing 6-7 illustrates how the last line in **layout.ld** needs to be changed.

Listing 6-7. The last line of layout.ld

```
INCLUDE ../../tock/boards/kernel_layout.ld
```

Create the Drivers Folder

In addition to the board folder where we have the configurations specific for the device, we need a folder for the drivers that we will write. For these, we create a folder called **drivers** where we will place these drivers' (capsules') files.

We build drivers as a standalone crate as we have to impose the rule of not using unsafe code. Since it is a different crate, it will have its **Cargo.toml** file and an **src** folder, where we place the source code. The entry point of the crate is a **lib.rs** file, placed inside **src**.

The Cargo.toml File

The drivers available in the *tock repository* can be found in the **capsules** folder. Here we can find a **Cargo.toml** file. This is the one we also use for our project. Therefore, we need to copy that file inside the **project/kernel/ drivers** folder in our project structure. Further on, we open the file and make some minor changes to it.

First of all, we change the name from *capsules* to *drivers,* so it reflects the name of the folder we have created. We can leave the version, authors, and edition unchanged.

Next, we inspect the [dependencies] section, where the three essential Tock components are linked: the kernel files, enum_primitive, and tickv. These paths need to point to the associated folders in the *tock repository* we cloned previously (Listing 6-8).

Listing 6-8. The full Cargo.toml file for the drivers package

```
[package]
name = "drivers"
version = "0.1.0"
authors = ["Tock Project Developers <tock-dev@
googlegroups.com>"]
edition = "2018"

[dependencies]
kernel = { path = "../../tock/kernel" }
enum_primitive = { path = "../../tock/libraries/enum_primitive" }
tickv = { path = "../../tock/libraries/tickv" }
```

> **Note**   enum_primitive and tickv are optional crates that should be included only if there is at least one driver using them.

Drivers Source Files

Our project's capsules will be placed in a different folder, which we named **src**. This is on the same level in the folder hierarchy as the **Cargo.toml** file. Here we can place new drivers that we develop. As mentioned above, the entry point to this crate is the **lib.rs** file that we put in the **src** folder.

One of the main constraints when building Tock drivers (or capsules) is that we cannot include *unsafe code*. To ensure this cannot happen, we include the constraint in the lib.rs file, as shown in Listing 6-9.

Listing 6-9. The lib.rs file

```
#![forbid(unsafe_code)]
#![no_std]
```

The first line in the file specifies that no unsafe code can be used. The second is used to exclude the *standard Rust library* from the crate. Usually, the *standard* library is included by default. However, the *standard* library depends on the operating system and since we are building one, using it is not possible in this context.

Initialize the Userspace Component

The next step after configuring the kernel component is to initialize the files necessary for building applications. For this, we will use the libtock-c library that we need to link in our applications. In addition, the capsules that we write in our project have a userspace component that enables them to be used in the applications.

Link the libtock-c Repository

To include the *libtock-c* repository in our project, we take the same approach as linking the Tock kernel. Therefore, we will add libtock-c as a git submodule to our main repository and use the release-2.0 tag.

We add libtock-c to the root of our folder hierarchy, directly in the project folder. Listing 6-10 illustrates the commands necessary to achieve this.

Listing 6-10. Link the libtock-c repository in the project folder

```
$ cd project
$ git submodule add https://github.com/tock/libtock-c.git
$ cd libtock-c
$ git checkout tags/release-2.0
```

Create the Applications Folder

We place all the source code related to the applications in a different folder that we create in the **project** directory. To make it suggestive, we call this folder **applications**.

Inside the applications folder, we place another two directories: **drivers** and **example_app**. The **drivers** folder is used to store the userspace component of the capsules that we write, while the other folder is an application.

Note   If we choose to build multiple applications as part of the project, we create a different folder for each of them.

The Driver Userspace Component

In the **drivers** folder inside **applications**, we add all the userspace files for all the drivers we create. For each such driver, we need a **.h** and **.c** file, which is the interface towards the driver. This helps us make the code modular and easy to follow. These files will implement the capsule APIs that will be used in the applications.

To get started, we create two files called **example_driver.c** and **example_driver.h**. In addition, we need a **Makefile** to build the two files. Listings 6-11 and 6-12 show the contents of the **c** and **h** files. We place there an empty function that we can start from.

Listing 6-11. The contents of example_driver.h

```
#pragma once
void example_driver_action(void);
```

The first line in **example_driver.h** specifies that this source file cannot be included more than once in the same application. For instance, if we create a file, **peripheral.h**, that includes **example_driver.h**, and another file that includes **peripheral.h** and **example_driver.h**, the compiler will ignore the second include of **example_driver.h**.

Listing 6-12. The contents of example_driver.c

```
#include "tock.h"
#include "example_driver.h"

void example_driver_action(void) {}
```

When generating the **Makefile**, we need to consider that all the files in **drivers** are exported as a library that we include in our applications. In addition, we need to link **libtock** when compiling the source code (Listing 6-13) to have access to the Tock API functions.

Listing 6-13. The contents of the drivers Makefile

```
# Base folder definitions
TOCK_USERLAND_BASE_DIR ?= ../../libtock-c
LIBNAME := drivers
$(LIBNAME)_DIR := $(TOCK_USERLAND_BASE_DIR) /../
applications/$(LIBNAME)

# List all C and Assembly files
$(LIBNAME)_SRCS  := $(wildcard $($(LIBNAME)_DIR)/*.c)

override CFLAGS +=
-I$(TOCK_USERLAND_BASE_DIR)/libtock

include $(TOCK_USERLAND_BASE_DIR)/TockLibrary.mk
```

The Structure of a Sample Application

Inside the **example_app** folder, we place the files necessary to build any C application: a **main.c** file and a **Makefile**.

Inside **main.c** we include the **example_driver** that we created and add the **main** function, as shown in Listing 6-14.

Listing 6-14. The main.c file

```
#include <stdio.h>
#include "example_driver.h"

int main(void) {
  printf ("Hello World!\r\n");
  example_driver_action ();
  return 0;
}
```

On the other hand, the **Makefile** takes into account all the necessary libraries we need to link to our application, such as **drivers** and **libtock-c** (Listing 6-15). We use one Makefile from the **libtock-c/examples** folder, modify its paths and add the **drivers** library.

Listing 6-15. The Makefile

```
# Makefile for user application

# Specify this directory relative to the current # application.
TOCK_USERLAND_BASE_DIR = ../../libtock-c

# External libraries used
EXTERN_LIBS += ../drivers

# Which files to compile.
C_SRCS := $(wildcard *.c)

# Include path for drivers library
override CFLAGS += -I../drivers

# Include userland master makefile. Contains #rules and flags for actually
# building the application.
include $(TOCK_USERLAND_BASE_DIR)/AppMakefile.mk

# Build the drivers
../drivers/build/cortex-m0/drivers.a:
        make -f ../drivers/Makefile

# Clean drivers folder
clean::
        rm -rf ../drivers/build
```

The Rust Toolchain

Once all the files are created, there is one more step to finalize the sample project structure. This is related to how the project is built, specifically, the required *Rust* toolchain.

Inside the *tock submodule* that we cloned, we can find a **rust-toolchain** file where the Rust version is mentioned. This is necessary when first installing the Rust compiler, so there are no inconsistencies when compiling the source code. Therefore, during the compilation, the make searches for the **rust-toolchain** file and installs the appropriate version on the system.

The file is assumed to be in the **root** of the project, so we bring it to the top of the project hierarchy by creating a *symbolic link* towards the file located inside the **tock** folder. The command that generates the link is shown in Listing 6-16.

Listing 6-16. Generate the rust-toolchain link

```
$ cd project
$ ln -s tock/rust-toolchain .
```

Build the Project

Now that we have defined the project folder structure, all that is left is to build it. The kernel and the applications are built separately.

Build the Kernel

To build the kernel, we go to the **kernel/microbit_v2** or **kernel/raspberry_pi_pico** folder and run the **make**. Next, we follow all the steps that have been described in the previous chapter.

Build an Application

We have to build each application individually. To build an application, we go to its folder, for example, **applications/example_app,** and run **make**. This will build the application together with all its dependencies.

Caution   Whenever changing the **drivers** library, we have to manually rebuild it before we build the application that uses it. The applications' **Makefiles** cannot dynamically determine whether we made a change to **drivers**. Rebuilding the **drivers** library means going to the **applications/drivers** folder, and running make.

Summary

In this chapter, we described all the steps necessary to build a new, standalone project based on the Tock kernel. To ensure that you followed all the steps correctly, Listing 6-17 displays the folder hierarchy starting from the project folder.

Note   For a project that uses the Raspberry Pi Pico device, the **microbit_v2** file in Listing 6-17 will be replaced with **raspberry_pi_pico**.

Listing 6-17. The project hierarchy for a micro:bit project template

```
$ tree project
$ .
├── applications
│   ├── drivers
│   │   ├── Makefile
│   │   ├── example_driver.c
│   │   └── example_driver.h
│   └── example_app
│       ├── Makefile
│       └── main.c
├── kernel
│   ├── drivers
│   │   ├── Cargo.toml
│   │   └── src
│   │       └── lib.rs
│   └── microbit_v2
│       ├── ...
│       ├── ...
├── libtock-c
│   ├── ...
│   ├── ...
├── rust-toolchain -> tock/rust-toolchain
└── tock
    ├── ...
    ├── ...
```

Tip   To use the project structure multiple times, you can upload it on Github[1] as a template project. You can also use the sample template project that the authors of this book have prepared by accessing the following link: `https://github.com/WyliodrinEmbeddedIoT/ tock-project`.

In the following chapters, we will make use of this project structure to build new drivers and applications on top of the Tock kernel.

---

[1] `https://github.com`

CHAPTER 7

Userspace Applications Development

For a process to interact with the Tock kernel, which includes the drivers, it needs to make a system call. The Tock architecture is built around seven such system calls: *yield, subscribe, command, read-write allow, read-only allow, memop,* and *exit*. In a nutshell, any application that we aim to run on top of the Tock kernel needs to make these calls to access the resources like peripherals, storage space, or sensors.

However, including the system calls in the application is a tedious process. This means that we have to carefully analyze each driver and the necessary calls together with their parameters to obtain the desired behavior.

As a result, each Tock driver has a C API library that we can use to make writing applications easier. The API libraries expose generic functions that enable the application developers to easily interact with the peripherals. These functions offer an abstraction layer on top of the drivers and the hardware that we use.

© Alexandru Radovici and Ioana Culic 2022
A. Radovici and I. Culic, *Getting Started with Secure Embedded Systems,*
https://doi.org/10.1007/978-1-4842-7789-8_7

Hardware Requirements

To implement the project in this chapter, you need the following hardware components, based on the device you use:

- **Micro:bit**

    - 1 x micro:bit v2 board

- **Raspberry Pi Pico**

    - 1 x Raspberry Pi Pico board;

    - 1 x Raspberry Pi board.

While most of the examples in this chapter are designed to work on the micro:bit and the Raspberry Pi Pico devices without external hardware required, some of them require the connection of some simple peripherals such as sensors or LEDs. When this is necessary, we specify explicitly to connect an external component and how.

Userspace Capsule APIs

When a new capsule is included in the Tock kernel, the good practice also involves including an API for it in the libtock-c and libtock-rs repositories. To better understand how API files work, we will inspect some of them.

Note   Throughout this book, we will focus on the libtock-c library, as libtock-rs is still undergoing significant changes for Tock 2.0 compatibility.

First of all, we take a look at the **gpio.h** and **gpio.c** files located in **libtock-c/libtock**. These files expose the constants and functions necessary to control and read values from the GPIO pins.

The exposed functions are declared in the **gpio.h** file (Listing 7-1).

Listing 7-1. The complete gpio.h file

```
#pragma once

#include "tock.h"

#ifdef __cplusplus
extern "C" {
#endif

#define GPIO_DRIVER_NUM 0x4

// GPIO pins exposed to userspace are defined in platform
// definitions. The index of each pin in the array corresponds
// to the value of GPIO_Pin_t in userspace.
// For example, on imix board, pin8's GPIO_Pin_t value is 6.
typedef uint32_t GPIO_Pin_t;

typedef enum {
  PullNone=0,
  PullUp,
  PullDown,
} GPIO_InputMode_t;

typedef enum {
  Change=0,
  RisingEdge,
  FallingEdge,
} GPIO_InterruptMode_t;

// Returns the number of GPIO pins configured on the board.
int gpio_count(int* count);
```

```
int gpio_enable_output(GPIO_Pin_t pin);
int gpio_set(GPIO_Pin_t pin);
int gpio_clear(GPIO_Pin_t pin);
int gpio_toggle(GPIO_Pin_t pin);
int gpio_enable_input(GPIO_Pin_t pin, GPIO_InputMode_t
pin_config);
int gpio_read(GPIO_Pin_t pin, int* pin_value);
int gpio_enable_interrupt(GPIO_Pin_t pin, GPIO_InterruptMode_t
irq_config);
int gpio_disable_interrupt(GPIO_Pin_t pin);
int gpio_disable(GPIO_Pin_t pin);
int gpio_interrupt_callback(subscribe_upcall callback,
void* callback_args);

#ifdef __cplusplus
}
#endif
```

After including the necessary libraries, we can find the definition of two enum types, one for the input modes and the other for the interrupt modes. Further on, we can find the functions exposed. These functions represent the generic operations that can be done with the GPIO pins.

To analyze the implementation of the function, we take a look at the **gpio.c** file (Listing 7-2).

Listing 7-2. Snippet from the gpio.c file

```
#include "gpio.h"

int gpio_count(int* count) {
 syscall_return_t rval =
     command(GPIO_DRIVER_NUM, 0, 0, 0);
```

```
return tock_command_return_u32_to_returncode
    (rval, (uint32_t*) count);
}

int gpio_enable_output(GPIO_Pin_t pin) {
syscall_return_t rval =
    command(GPIO_DRIVER_NUM, 1, pin, 0);
 return
tock_command_return_novalue_to_returncode(rval);
}
```

As we can notice, the functions call command with the necessary
parameters, according to the driver's implementation. However, this is not
visible to the developers using the *gpio* library.

Further on, we will analyze the most important libraries and build an
application example for each of them.

Note   Most of the functions return an integer value representing the
execution status.

The Timer Library

One of the first actions that we have to do in our application is to use
timing functions such as delaying certain actions or firing a function at a
specific moment.

All these actions are enabled by the timer library that exposes the following functions:

- `void timer_in(uint32_t ms, subscribe_upcall, void*, tock_timer_t* timer)` – Calls the `subscribe_upcall` function after ms milliseconds. The third parameter points to a structure that is passed to the callback as is, in case we need to pass any data to it. The last parameter is an alarm structure that needs to be created beforehand;

- `void timer_every(uint32_t ms, subscribe_upcall, void*, tock_timer_t* timer)` – Calls the `subscribe_upcall` function repeatedly every ms milliseconds. The third parameter points to a structure that is passed to the callback as is, in case we need to pass any data to it. The last parameter is an alarm structure that needs to be created beforehand;

- `void timer_cancel(tock_timer_t*)` - Cancels the alarm passed as parameter;

- `void delay_ms(uint32_t ms)` – Blocks the process for ms milliseconds;

Tip   All `yield` functions are used to make the process ask for any incoming interrupts and handle them.

- `int yield_for_with_timeout(bool* cond, uint32_t ms)` - It *yields* the process until the condition is met or until the specified timeout expires. Calling `yield` is necessary when the application needs to wait for an upcall. Otherwise, it will process other instructions, and the upcall will never be handled.

Note   When the main function ends, the process does not finish but automatically calls `yield`. This is due to the implementation of the **libtock-c** library. This means that if a callback function is registered, it will fire even after the `main` function finishes its execution. Please note that this might change in future versions.

The GPIO Library

The gpio library exposes functions that enable the developers to control and read data from the GPIO pins.

Note   The GPIO_Pin_t type for the pins is an uint32.

The functions that **gpio.h** exposes are the following:

- `int gpio_count(int* count)` – stores the number of GPIO pins on the device in the count variable;

- `int gpio_enable_output(GPIO_Pin_t pin)` – sets the pin in output mode;

- `int gpio_set(GPIO_Pin_t pin)` – sets the pin to HIGH;

- `int gpio_clear(GPIO_Pin_t pin)` – sets the pin to LOW;

- `int gpio_toggle(GPIO_Pin_t pin)` – toggles the pin; if the pin is set to HIGH, the function sets it to LOW, and if the pin is set to LOW, the function sets it to HIGH;

- `int gpio_enable_input(GPIO_Pin_t pin, GPIO_InputMode_t pin_config)` - sets the pin to input mode; based on the value of `pin_config`, the pin can be set to pull-down, pull-up or pull-none;

- `int gpio_read(GPIO_Pin_t pin, int* pin_value)` – reads the value from the pin; the value is stored in the `pin_value` variable;

- `int gpio_enable_interrupt(GPIO_Pin_t pin, GPIO_InterruptMode_t irq_config)` – enables the interrupt on the pin;

- `int gpio_disable_interrupt(GPIO_Pin_t pin)` – disables the interrupt on the pin;

- `int gpio_disable(GPIO_Pin_t pin)` – disables the GPIO pin;

- `int gpio_interrupt_callback (subscribe_upcall callback, void* callback_args)` – registers a callback function that is called whenever an interrupt occurs.

Application Example

To make a simple application such as an LED blink, we use both the timer and the GPIO libraries. In the application illustrated in Listing 7-3, we use `gpio_set` and `gpio_clear` to turn the LED on and off and the `delay_ms` function to make the process stop for 1 second so we can actually see the LED blinking.

Listing 7-3. An LED blink application example

```c
#include <gpio.h>
#include <timer.h>

int main(void){
  gpio_enable_output(25);
  while (1){
    gpio_set (25);
    delay_ms (1000);
    gpio_clear (25);
    delay_ms (1000);
  }
}
```

In the case of the Raspberry Pi Pico, the code above blinks the onboard LED as this is connected on pin 25. However, the pin is not exposed by default as it is mapped to the LED driver. Therefore, we need to expose the LED, then run the application. This is done by adding pin 25 to the gpio structure in the **kernel/raspberry_pi_pico/src/main.rs** file, around line 320. Listing 7-4 illustrates the new structure.

Listing 7-4. The new gpio structure for the Raspberry Pi

```rust
    let gpio = GpioComponent::new(
        board_kernel,
        capsules::gpio::DRIVER_NUM,
        components::gpio_component_helper!(
            RPGpioPin,
            // Used for serial communication. //Comment them in
            if you don't use serial.
2 => &peripherals.pins.get_pin(RPGpio::GPIO2),
3 => &peripherals.pins.get_pin(RPGpio::GPIO3),
. . .
```

```
24 => &peripherals.pins.get_pin(RPGpio::GPIO24),
25 => &peripherals.pins.get_pin(RPGpio::GPIO25),
```

For the micro:bit, we need to use one of the pins exposed by the device as there is no default LED that we can control via GPIO. We recommend connecting pin 0 to an LED via a micro:bit shield or crocodile clips and changing the GPIO number from 25 to 0 in the application code.

Note   The LEDs on the micro:bit are not directly connected one to one to the GPIO pins and can only be used with the LED driver.

The LED Library

Most of the devices we use have at least one onboard LED that can be controlled from the application. By using the **led** library, we have control over these LEDs with the help of the following functions:

- `int led_count(int* count)` – stores the number of LEDs on the device in the `count` variable;

- `int led_on(int led_num)` – lights up the LED passed as parameter;

- `int led_off(int led_num)` – turns off the LED passed as parameter;

- `int led_toggle(int led_num)` – toggles the LED passed as parameter; if the LED is turned on, the function turns it off, while if the LED is turned off, the function turns it on.

Application Example

As we specified in the section above, the Raspberry Pi Pico has an onboard LED that we can control and which is connected on pin 25. On the other hand, on the micro:bit, there are 25 such LEDs, numbered from 0 to 24.

Listing 7-5 displays an application that can be run on both devices to make the LED 0 blink every 1 second.

Caution   To run this application on the Raspberry Pi Pico, you first need to delete pin 25 from the `gpio` structure, if you added it in the previous section.

In contrast to Listing 7-3, this application uses the `timer_every` function that registers a callback every 1000 milliseconds. In the callback function, we change the LED status.

Note   Using `delay_ms` also works. We just show another way of doing this.

Listing 7-5. LED blink example using the LED library

```
#include <led.h>
#include <timer.h>

static void timer_cb (
  __attribute__ ((unused)) int arg0,
  __attribute__ ((unused)) int arg1,
  __attribute__ ((unused)) int arg2,
  __attribute__ ((unused)) void* userdata) {
  led_toggle(0);
}
```

```
int main(void){
  tock_timer_t timer;
  timer_every(1000, timer_cb, NULL, &timer);

  while (1){                          '
    yield ();
    // do other tasks
  }
}
```

Note   In this case, as the main function ends after the callback is registered, calling `yield` is not necessary. We chose to add it to the code to exemplify how this would work for other cases. Just to be on the safe side, we recommend adding this to the end of all applications that still have pending callbacks.

The ADC Library

The ADC library exposes two types of functions: synchronous and asynchronous. The asynchronous functions receive a callback as the parameter, and each time a reading or multiple readings are complete, that function is called. On the other hand, synchronous functions return the read value right away.

In Tock, ADC is exposed in the userspace through ADC channels. This might be different from what you might be used to, as most MCU boards expose ADC pins. In Tock, an ADC channel might be corresponding to a pin but might also be another piece of hardware, like the MCU's temperature sensor.

> **Note**   Exposed channels are configured within the board's interface, usually in **main.rs**.

What is more, each reading can be returned immediately, or stored in a buffer when faster sampling rates are needed.

> **Note**   The devices used in this book do not support buffered sampling.

Since buffered readings are not available when using the Raspberry Pi Pico and micro:bit devices, in this book, we will use only the synchronous functions that return the read value immediately:

- `bool adc_is_present(void)` – returns `true` if the ADC driver is present and `false` otherwise;

- `int adc_channel_count(int* count)` – stores the number of ADC channels available in the `count` variable;

- `int adc_sample_sync(uint8_t channel, uint16_t* sample)` – returns a single analog reading from the channel number passed as an argument in the `sample` variable.

Application Example

The best application example for the ADC library is in the **libtock-c/ examples/adc** directory. We recommend you copy the **main.c** file in the **applications/example_app** folder and compile it for the micro:bit or the Raspberry Pi Pico.

To connect some sensors on one of the ADC pins, you can use crocodile clips for the micro:bit and a breadboard with jumper wires for the Pico. We also recommend connecting the Pico to the Pico Explorer expansion if you have one.

The Sensor Libraries

Besides the primary libraries for GPIO and ADC readings, libtock-c provides an array of functions that abstract the interaction with basic sensors. Therefore, we can import header files that define functions for reading temperature or motion values.

Note   While this chapter focuses on the sensor libraries integrated with the micro:bit or the Raspberry Pi Pico devices, libtock-c also exposes functions for other sensors that are compatible with other devices supported by Tock.

Reading The Temperature

The **temperature.h** file exposes three main functions to be used for synchronous or asynchronous temperature readings. To use this library, the device needs to have a temperature sensor connected and the kernel to provide a driver for it. Both the Raspberry Pi Pico and the micro:bit have a temperature sensor and the driver for it. As such, both devices are capable of running applications that include this library.

The library exposes both synchronous and asynchronous functions:

- `int temperature_read(void)` – reads the temperature sensor asynchronously;

- `int temperature_read_sync (int* temperature)` – stores the temperature value in the `temperature` variable;

- `int temperature_set_callback (subscribe_upcall callback, void* callback_args)` – sets the `callback` function that will be called when the asynchronous reading is done; an additional parameter can be passed to the function via the `callback_args` structure, which can be used to send data to the `callback` function.

Reading The Motion

Tock provides a motion sensor library that can be used with devices like the micro:bit, which is equipped with a motion sensor. This translates to three different readings on the X, Y, and Z axes. The library that exposes the functions for this is called *ninedof*. The library's name comes from the *ninedof* (nine degrees of freedom) sensor that reads the acceleration, gyroscope, and compass for the three axes, resulting in nine different values.

Some devices might support only a part of the three values, like the micro:bit that has an LSM303AGR motion sensor with an accelerometer and a magnetometer. Therefore, we can use only part of the functions that the library exposes:

- `int ninedof_read_acceleration_sync (int* x, int* y, int* z)` – stores the acceleration on the three axes using the `x, y,` and `z` variables;

Note   Similarly to the ADC library, we use only the non-buffered readings that are implemented using synchronous functions.

- int ninedof_read_magnetometer_sync (int* x, int* y, int* z) – stores the magnetic field values read on the three axes using the x, y, and z variables;

- int ninedof_read_gyroscope_sync (int* x, int* y, int* z) – stores the rotation on the three axes using the x, y, and z variables.

Application Example

To exemplify the use of the sensors' libraries, we create an application that reads the values from all the sensors and prints them in the console using printf (Listing 7-6). We use only synchronous functions for this.

The complete application can be run on the micro:bit. For the Raspberry Pi Pico, only the temperature can be read, as the other sensors are not integrated into the device. For the other sensors, the driver_exists function will return false, and nothing will happen.

The gyroscope functions will return success for the micro:bit as the motion driver is present. As there is no gyroscope hardware, the returned values are only zeros.

Listing 7-6. Reading the sensors' values

```
#include <stdio.h>
#include <humidity.h>
#include <temperature.h>
#include <ninedof.h>

unsigned humi = 0;
int temp = 0;
int ninedof_accel_x = 0;
int ninedof_accel_y = 0;
int ninedof_accel_z = 0;
```

```
int ninedof_magneto_x = 0;
int ninedof_magneto_y = 0;
int ninedof_magneto_z = 0;
int ninedof_gyro_x = 0;
int ninedof_gyro_y = 0;
int ninedof_gyro_z = 0;

int main(void){
  if (driver_exists(DRIVER_NUM_TEMPERATURE)){
    temperature_read_sync(&temp);
    printf("Temperature: %d C\n", temp/100);
  }
  if (driver_exists(DRIVER_NUM_NINEDOF)){
    bool rc = ninedof_read_acceleration_sync(
        &ninedof_accel_x, &ninedof_accel_y,
        &ninedof_accel_z);
    if (rc == RETURNCODE_SUCCESS){
     printf("Acceleration: X: %d Y: %d Z: %d\n",
       ninedof_accel_x, ninedof_accel_y,
       ninedof_accel_z);
    }
    rc = ninedof_read_magnetometer_sync(
        &ninedof_magneto_x, &ninedof_magneto_y,
        &ninedof_magneto_z);
    if (rc == RETURNCODE_SUCCESS){
     printf("Magnetometer: X: %d Y: %d Z: %d\n",
       ninedof_magneto_x, ninedof_magneto_y,
       ninedof_magneto_z);
    }
    rc = ninedof_read_gyroscope_sync(
        &ninedof_gyro_x, &ninedof_gyro_y,
        &ninedof_gyro_z);
```

```
 if (rc == RETURNCODE_SUCCESS){
  printf("Rotation: X: %d Y: %d Z: %d\n",
    ninedof_gyro_x, ninedof_gyro_y,
    ninedof_gyro_z);
 }
}
 return 0;
}
```

For the micro:bit, both the temperature and the ninedof sensors are available. For the ninedof sensor, we store the return code and check that it equals to RETURNCODE_SUCCESS. This is to make sure that all three components of the sensor are working and return valid readings.

Human Interaction Libraries

In our applications, we also need to consider how the user interacts with the system that we build. Therefore, libraries that enable us to display information or read user input are also essential.

Further on, we detail the use of the libraries that enable us to print text or graphical information and read user gestures.

The Console Library

Besides displaying information to the user, printing data is also necessary during development. In this case, we need to print text information in the console to help us assess and debug the applications.

The easiest way of printing console information in the C applications that we build is by using the standard printf function. For this, we need to import the **stdio.h** library, just as for any other C application (Listing 7-6). However, the disadvantage of this approach is that printf implements a double buffering mechanism to display the information. This is why there are times when the data is not printed in the console as the buffer is not flushed.

Note   The printf function provided by libtock-c flushes the buffer when it displays a newline (\n). Flushing the buffer means sending the data to the kernel driver that actually displays it.

For some devices, the mechanism implemented by printf might be too costly, resource-wise. The alternative is to use the console library that libtock-c exposes.

The console library exposes functions that print and read data in a lightweight manner, making it appropriate for any device, no matter the constraints. What is more, it can work both synchronous and asynchronous. For the examples in this book, the synchronous functions are sufficient:

- int putnstr(const char* str, size_t len) – prints
  len characters from the text stored in str;

Caution   When using putnstr, make sure len is no longer than the text stored in str, as you risk printing data outside the buffer.

- int getch (void) – returns one character read.

Note   For reading data from the serial line, only the getch function can be used.

Application Example

Listing 7-7 illustrates an application example that prints data with the help of the *console* library. While the code is more complex than using printf, the execution is more efficient.

Listing 7-7. Print data using the console library

```
#include <console.h>

int main(void){
  putnstr("Hello world from Tock", 21);
  return 0;
}
```

The Text Screen Library

One of the simplest ways of displaying information to the user is via a text screen. However, as we will see in future chapters, text can also be displayed with the help of an LED matrix. The text_screen library is capable of operations such as moving the cursor, turning the display on or off, and printing characters, even if some of the actions might not be available depending on hardware.

The functions defined in this library make system calls to the *text_ screen* capsule that uses a driver which controls the hardware. Therefore, if the screen is an LED matrix, the calls to the capsule will light up LEDs, or if we use an actual LCD screen, the same functions will print characters on the LCD:

- int text_screen_init (size_t len) – initializes the text screen library with a buffer that is len bytes long; this buffer is used to send data to the driver;

- `uint8_t* text_screen_buffer (void)` – returns the buffer that stores the text to be displayed so that the application can access it;

- `int text_screen_display_on (void)` – turns on the screen;

- `int text_screen_display_off (void)` – turns off the screen;

- `int text_screen_blink_on (void)` – makes the screen blink, if the capability exists;

- `int text_screen_blink_off (void)` – stops the screen from blinking;

- `int text_screen_show_cursor (void)` – displays the cursor, if the capability exists;

- `int text_screen_hide_cursor (void)` – hides the cursor;

- `int text_screen_clear (void)` – erases all the information on the screen;

- `int text_screen_home (void)` – moves the cursor to the initial position, if the capability exists;

- `int text_screen_get_size (size_t* width, size_t* height)` – stores the screen dimensions in the `width` and `height` variables;

- `int text_screen_set_cursor (uint8_t col, uint8_t row)` – moves the cursor on the column and row specified by the `col` and `row` variables;

- `int text_screen_write (size_t len)` – print `len` characters from the buffer on the screen.

The Screen Library

In addition to the classical text screens, we can use more complex color screens to display text and images. The generic behavior is that we have a screen with a specific resolution that can light up pixels at a different brightness and do other similar operations.

The library uses a buffer where pixel information is stored, and by calling certain functions, the buffer is sent to the driver. What is more, we can define a limited portion of the screen as the display area, and the buffer will be mapped to that specific area. The operations that we can do using this library are pretty complex, and some of the most basic available functions are described below:

- `int screen_init (size_t len)` – initializes the screen library; needs to be called before all the other functions;

- `uint8_t * screen_buffer (void)` – returns the buffer where the information to be displayed is stored; this buffer is used to send data to the driver and might be smaller than the hardware buffer used by the screen;

- `int screen_get_resolution (size_t *width, size_t *height)` – stores the current screen resolution in the width and height variables

- `int screen_get_supported_resolutions (int* resolutions)` – stores the number of supported screen resolutions in the resolutions variable;

- `int screen_get_supported_resolution (size_t index, size_t *width, size_t *height)` – uses the previous function to retrieve a specific screen resolution that is stored in the `width` and `height` variables; `index` specifies which resolution to retrieve from the list obtained by calling `screen_get_supported_resolutions()`;

- `int screen_write (size_t length)` – writes the data stored in the buffer up to `length` bytes.

An application example of how to use this library can be found in the **libtock-c/examples/screen** folder.

Note   Since the micro:bit and the Raspberry Pi Pico do not have a screen integrated, you need to connect an external screen to use this library.

Application Example With the Pico Explorer Device

The Raspberry Pi Pico can be easily connected to a screen via the Pico Explorer expansion board. The expansion connects a colored screen to the device via SPI.

To use the screen on Pico Explorer, we need to use the board setup for that specific board. We switch the device folder from **raspberry_pi_pico** to **pico_explorer_base**. This device is implemented similar to the Pico and has all its characteristics, but it also supports the screen connection and the other integrated peripherals.

To use the `pico_explorer_base` device defined in tock, we need to copy that device in the **project/kernel** folder and adapt all the paths as shown in *The Structure of A Custom Tock System* chapter.

Further on, we can use the example application inside the **libtock-c/examples/screen** directory. Besides copying that example in the **applications/example_app** folder, we also need to configure the **Makefile**.

When analyzing the **Makefile** in the example, we notice that a custom heap size is specified. This is because the buffers used for displaying information on the screen are large, so we also need to enlarge the heap. We also need to add this line to our Makefile inside **applications/ example_app**: APP_HEAP_SIZE := 20000.

To run the application, the same process as for the Raspberry Pi Pico device can be applied.

Tip   If the device you are working with has support for graphical user interfaces, we recommend you include the **lvgl** library in your application. This enables you to build complex user interfaces. An example is provided in the **examples/lvgl** folder.

The Button Library

Besides displaying information to the user, reading input is also an important aspect of user interaction. The easiest way of doing this is through buttons.

In addition to the integrated LEDs, most devices also expose buttons that can be used in our applications. The button library enables us to read the buttons' states by using the following five functions:

- int button_count(int* count) - stores the number of buttons on the device in the count variable;

Note   No matter how each device identifies the onboard buttons, Tock exposes them using numbers. For instance, on the micro:bit, button A is 0 in Tock, and button B is 1. On the Pico Explorer board, button A is 0, B is 1, and so on.

- `int button_read(int button_num, int* button_value)` – stores the state of the `button_num` button in the `button_value` variable; the value depends on how the button is configured on the device (pull-up or pull-down);

- `int button_enable_interrupt(int button_num)` – enables the interrupt on the button so we can register an interrupt handle;

- `int button_disable_interrupt(int button_num)` – disables the interrupt for the specified button;

- `int button_subscribe(subscribe_upcall callback, void *ud)` – registers the `subscribe_upcall` function to be called each time a button interrupt is fired, usually when a button changes its state; ud is a pointer to a user-defined structure that is passed as is to the callback function if data needs to be passed to it.

In addition to the buttons, we can also make use of touch sensors. These sensors can be present on the device in multiple forms. We can have a simple touch that behaves identical to a button, or it can be integrated into the screen.

Note   Since neither the micro:bit nor the Raspberry Pi Pico have a touch screen, we will not describe it in this chapter.

Application Example

In Listing 7-8, we adapted the button example application in libtock-c to light on and off LED 0 when any onboard button of the device is pressed. In the case of the micro:bit, this means that any of the two buttons A and B, will trigger an interrupt when pressed and released.

To make sure the LED changes its state only when the button is pressed, we check that value equals to 1. This is necessary because an interrupt is generated both when we press and release the button.

Listing 7-8. Light up/off LED 0 when any button is pressed

```
#include <button.h>
#include <led.h>

static void button_callback(int btn_num,
              int val,
              __attribute__ ((unused)) int arg2,
              __attribute__ ((unused)) void *ud) {
    if (val == 1){
      led_toggle(0);
    }
}

int main(void) {
  int err;

  err = button_subscribe(button_callback, NULL);
  if (err < 0) return err;

  // Enable interrupts on each button.
  int count;
  err = button_count(&count);
  if (err < 0) return err;

  for (int i = 0; i < count; i++) {
    button_enable_interrupt(i);
  }

  return 0;
}
```

Persistent Data Storage Library

Some of the applications might require reading and storing data in the flash region of the device. This is especially useful to ensure the device restores its state when powered off and on. For example, a car computer will want to store the mileage using permanent storage.

The **app_state** library is designed to enable this by allowing the developers to declare a structure specific to the information being stored. Then, by calling a couple of functions exposed by the library, the data can be stored and read from the flash:

- `APP_STATE_DECLARE(_type, _identifier)` - this is a macro that declares all the necessary data structures; the first parameter, `_type` is the data type that is being stored, the second parameter is the name of the variable where the information is stored;

- `int app_state_load_sync(void)` – loads the information from flash into the declared variable;

- `int app_sate_save_sync(void)` – saves the data in the declared variable in the flash region.

An important aspect when reading the data is to consider if a value was stored previously or if it is the first time the process runs and there is nothing to read. Readings will never fail, even if we never wrote any data. In this case, we will simply read some random values that are stored in that location.

To prevent the application from using random information, we add a fixed value to the data we write. When reading, we compare the retrieved value to the one we expect to read. If they are the same, a previous writing has been made. If not, we have read a random value. In Listing 7-9, you can find this under the `magic` variable.

Note   This verification mechanism relies on the fact that chances are very low that a random value will equal the expected one.

Listing 7-9. Reading and storing data in the flash region

```
#include <app_state.h>
#include <stdio.h>

#define MAGIC 42

struct valuable_data {
  uint32_t magic;
  uint32_t my_value;
};

APP_STATE_DECLARE(struct valuable_data, my_data);

int main() {
  int ret;
  ret = app_state_load_sync();
  if (ret != 0) {
      printf("ERROR(%i): Could not read the flash
      region.\n", ret);
  }

  if (my_data.magic != MAGIC) {
      printf("Data was not stored\n");
  }
  else {
    printf ("Stored information: %d\n", my_data.my_value);
  }
```

```
my_data.magic = MAGIC;
my_data.my_value = 20;

ret = app_state_save_sync();
if (ret != 0) printf("ERROR(%i): Could not write back to
flash.\n", ret);
}
```

No valid data can be retrieved from the flash when first running the application in Listing 7-9. This is verified using magic. Upon reading from the flash, we verify if the magic value that we have just read is the same as the magic value that we expect. If so, we can assume we have read valid data, or at least data that we have previously written. If not, this is probably the first time this application has run, so no values will be printed. To read the values, we have to reset the device. The second time we run the application, the value will be printed on the screen.

Caution   Resetting the device while data is being written to the flash can corrupt the application. Ensure you do not reset the device before your application prints the messages stating that it has done writing in flash. In production devices, a capacitor might be added to the power system so that the device is able to finish flashing before the power runs out.

The app state driver is not the best solution to storing persistent data in the flash. Tock provides some other mechanisms to achieve this, but those drivers are not fully functional yet. We recommend taking a look at the *TickV* and *SDCard* libraries.

Summary

This chapter focuses on how Tock applications are built. To create complex applications that leverage the devices' peripherals, libtock-c exposes various libraries and functions from simple GPIO control to sensor-specific libraries that enable the reading of temperature or motion.

In this chapter, we made an overview of the most important libraries that can be used with the micro:bit and the Raspberry Pi Pico. Still, many others are available to be integrated into your projects. The integration of a new library is described in the following chapters.

Tip   For all the libraries described in this chapter, you can find application examples in the **libtock-c/examples** folder. While this chapter provides some examples for the most important libraries, we recommend you also inspect the **libtock-c** examples.

In the following chapters, we will focus on the way the Tock kernel works and how to build custom capsules that enable us to easily build secure applications on top of it.

CHAPTER 8

Synchronous Syscall Capsules

The purpose of this chapter is to get through the steps necessary for building a capsule. To exemplify this, we will focus on building a simple capsule to light up an LED matrix.

Hardware Requirements

To implement the project in this chapter, you need the following hardware components, based on the device you use:

- **Micro:bit**
    - 1 x micro:bit v2 board
- **Raspberry Pi Pico**
    - 1 x Raspberry Pi Pico board;
    - 1 x KWM-R30881CUAB or KWM-R30881AUAB LED matrix;
    - 14 x jumper wires;
    - 5 x 220 Ω resistors;
    - 2 x (or 1 x large) breadboards.

© Alexandru Radovici and Ioana Culic 2022
A. Radovici and I. Culic, *Getting Started with Secure Embedded Systems*,
https://doi.org/10.1007/978-1-4842-7789-8_8

Caution   While the hardware setup for the two devices differs, the code is mostly the same. The chapter will present the code that needs to be implemented for the micro:bit, while the final section details the changes necessary to run it on the Raspberry Pi Pico.

The Tock Capsule

Tock splits drivers into two categories: lower-level and upper-level. While the lower-level drivers are designed to interact directly with the hardware, the upper-level ones provide functionalities to other similar upper-level drivers or directly to the userspace.

Tock calls these upper-level drivers *capsules*. The name has not been randomly chosen and reflects that capsules are not allowed to include unsafe Rust code, which encapsulates them in a safe environment.

Note   Throughout this chapter, we will use the words *capsule* and *driver* interchangeably. From the Tock point of view, these two mean the same thing. There is a slight preference to call the lower-level ones drivers and the upper-level ones capsules.

As there are various types of capsules, based on their functionality, we enumerate all capsule types together with their security mechanisms in Table 8-1.

Regardless of their type, capsules, provide additional capability to the Tock operating system. The kernel itself is only a framework that drivers use to interact with each other and provide the functionality they are designed for.

Table 8-1. *Tock capsule (driver) types and their security mechanisms*

Driver Name	Functionality	Security Mechanism
Service Capsule	An upper-level driver that provides functionality to other capsules by implementing one or more kernel HILs.	The Rust type system makes sure at compile time that capsules access only data they are allowed to.
Syscall Capsules	The upper-level drivers that provide functionality to userspace processes by implementing the Driver trait and exposing system calls.	The Rust type system makes sure at compile time that capsules access only data they are allowed to.
Drivers	The lower-level drivers that interact directly with hardware components and expose the hardware functionality by implementing kernel HILs.	None, these drivers are part of the trusted code base as interacting with hardware requires direct (*unsafe*) memory access.

Why Write A Capsule?

Before starting to write a capsule, we have to understand why we would choose to do that. Tock provides Syscall Capsules for accessing all the basic peripherals of a device. By basic access, we refer to setting on and off an LED, reading and writing a value from or to a GPIO pin, transferring data using the system buses, etc.

More complex actions can always be written within a userspace process. This has two downsides: speed and space. First of all, these actions will be performed slower, as Tock has to switch back and forth between the process and the kernel. Secondly, if several processes need the same functionality, each has to include it into its code. This results in code duplication.

Note   While Tock does support some inter-process communication (IPC) mechanisms, these can sometimes be difficult to implement. We will discuss these in detail in chapter 11.

While there are disadvantages in writing code in userspace, there is one significant advantage. If the code in userspace faults, Tock will simply stop or restart the process, but the whole system will not stop. On the other hand, since Tock is written in Rust and capsules are only allowed to use safe Rust code, faults in the capsules are rare.

As a rule of thumb, whenever your system consists of several processes that need the same functionality, it might be a good idea to write a Syscall Capsule.

A Closer Look at The System Call Interface

Before we can start writing the Syscall capsule, we have to clear out how system calls work. As discussed in the previous chapters, Tock supports three system calls for capsules: `command`, `subscribe`, and `allow`. The `command` system call asks the capsule to perform an action, `subscribe` provides a mechanism for processes to subscribe to events emitted by the capsule, and `allow` makes it possible for a process to share buffers with the capsules.

Note   We will use only the `command` system call for the capsule that we are trying to build.

The *Command* System Call

The command system call is used to request actions from a Syscall capsule. Based on the actions requested, these can be performed in two ways. For short and straightforward tasks, like lighting up an LED or reading and writing the state of a GPIO, the capsule will perform the requested action immediately and return a CommandReturn structure. For more complex actions, that take some time to finish, the capsule will try to start the requested command and return a CommandReturn result informing the process whether it was able to start the action or not. While the process performs other tasks, the capsule will take care of the requested action and, upon its completion, will emit an *upcall* to the process. We will detail this process further in this chapter.

The command system call requires four arguments: the *capsule number*, the *command number*, and two word-sized arguments. Table 8-2 presents the details for each of these arguments.

Table 8-2. *The arguments of the command system call*

Argument	Name	Description
1	*capsule number*	Uniquely identifies the capsule (destination) that the system call targets
2	*command number*	The actual command. The capsule interprets this number, and an action is started or performed based upon it.
3	*argument 1*	A word-sized argument used to send data from the process to the capsule.
4	*argument 2*	A word-sized argument used to send data from the process to the capsule.

The *capsule number,* sometimes called the *driver number,* uniquely identifies each driver. When the kernel receives a system call, it reads the *capsule number,* asks the board implementation whether the system call should be allowed, and, if so, searches for the capsule with the corresponding number and sends the command to it. Figure 8-1 details the complete process flow.

First of all, the process generates a command system call and sends it to the kernel. The system call can be compared to a message that is sent from the process to the kernel. This *message* contains the capsule_number, the command_number, and two optional arguments.

Note   Even though the arguments are called optional, values need to be passed to the function. Usually, if the capsule does not use the arguments, they are set to 0.

When the message reaches the kernel, it asks for authorization to execute it and searches the *capsules list* for the specified capsule_number. If one is found, the capsule_number in the message is replaced by the process_id, and the message is forwarded to the capsule. The process_id uniquely identifies the process instance that has initiated the system call. If no capsule is found, the kernel generates an error response represented by the CommandReturn structure where the value CommandReturn::failure (ErrorCode::NODEVICE) is stored. This is sent back to the process. The complete list of CommandReturns can be found in **tock/kernel/src/syscall_ driver.rs**.

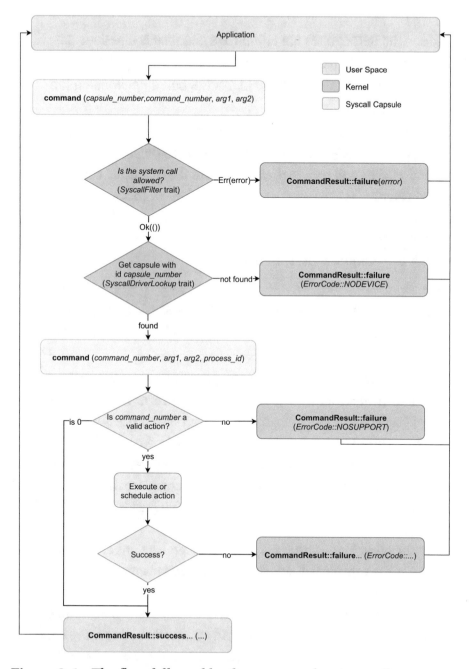

Figure 8-1. *The flow followed by the command system call*

Note   The kernel does not authorize system calls and does not keep a list of capsules. It uses the `SyscallFilter` and `SyscallDriverLookup` traits to ask the board implementation about the drivers.

Once the message reaches the destination, the capsule reads the command_number and tries to perform or start the requested command. Special attention is given to the command_number 0. Tock's convention states that all the capsules have to respond with a successful result for command_number 0. By leveraging this rule, a process can ask the kernel whether one or more capsules are present.

Note   For command_number 0, some capsules, like the GPIO or LED, return a value representing the number of available GPIO pins or LEDs.

If the capsule is not aware of the requested command_number, it will simply return an error message using `CommandReturn::failure(Error Code::NOSUPPORT)`. Most probably, in this case, the process is expecting a different capsule version from the one available in the kernel.

If the requested command_number refers to a simple, short task that can be performed synchronously, the capsule will complete the task and return the result to the process. Such actions can be GPIO reads and writes, LED control, etc.

On the other hand, if the task involves several actions and takes longer to execute, the capsule will schedule the task and respond to the process. A successful response means that the capsule has started or will start the action. The process should subscribe to an upcall event to be notified when the action has been completed. Any action that takes more time than a few tens of clock cycles is considered an action that has to be performed asynchronously.

The *CommandReturn* Structure

The command system call returns a CommandReturn structure that contains the type of the returned value (*failure* or *success*) followed by up to three arguments, each represented on 32 bits. The return type specifies whether the command was successful or not. In case of failure, the CommandReturn uses the first 32-bits argument to store an ErrorCode structure. This is mandatory and provides additional details about why the command failed.

In case of success, CommandReturn can return up to three 32-bits unsigned integer numbers. It is up to the capsule to encode the information that it wants to send back to the process in any way. It just needs to ensure that the process library corresponding to the capsule can decode the information correctly. For instance, a capsule might receive a command to return the values from an accelerometer sensor. It can decide to use each of the three arguments to return one of the values for each of the three X, Y, and Z axes.

On the other hand, the accelerometer might return the acceleration values as a group. As each of these values is encoded using 16 bits, the capsule can decide to use the first 32-bit argument to encode the acceleration for axes X and Y and the second argument to encode the acceleration for the Z axis.

Note   Whenever possible, the recommended way to return data is to use each argument for a different value.

A Capsule's Architecture

Tock capsules can be split into two categories: *syscall* and *service*. This chapter aims to write a capsule that provides a Syscall API to the userspace for displaying digits and letters using system calls.

The micro:bit v2 has a 5 x 5 LED Matrix. While not precisely a screen, this LED Matrix is good enough to display digits and letters.

On the other hand, for the Raspberry Pi Pico, we need to use an external LED matrix that we control. However, this does not bring significant changes from the micro:bit case.

Note   The last section of this chapter details how to connect the LED matrix to the Raspberry Pi Pico device.

The general architecture of the whole system is presented in Figure 8-2.

Although there are several components in the figure, we have to write only two of them:

1. The DigitLetterDisplay Syscall Capsules;

2. A test process that uses the capsule.

All the other components are already present and are part of the Tock architecture.

From a high-level point of view, the process in the userspace will send a command to the `DigitLetterDisplay` Syscall capsule asking it to display a specific digit or a letter. Upon receiving the command, the capsule will talk to the `LedMatrix` and ask it to light up the LEDs so that they generate the requested digit or letter. The Syscall capsule will use several instances of the `LedMatrixLed` service capsule (one of each LED) through the `Led` HIL, which in turn communicate with the `LedMatrix`.

The API Definition

The first step in writing the Syscall capsule is to design the system call interface, in other words, the API. As our capsule has to light up some LEDs, a task that is considered to be simple enough, we will only use the command system call. The process of defining the API involves defining the known *command numbers*, their parameters, and their functionality.

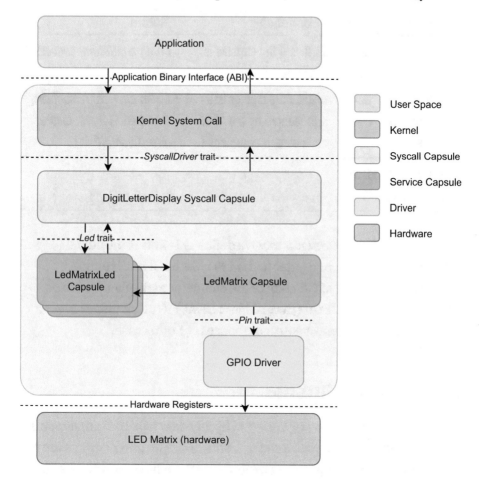

Figure 8-2. *The Architecture of the DigitLetterDisplay Capsule*

Table 8-3 shows a summary of the API. First of all, we define the *command number* 0 used to verify whether the driver exists. This command number does not receive any parameters and always returns CommandReturn::success().

Table 8-3. *The system call API for the DigitLetterDisplay capsule*

Command				
No	Arg 1	Arg 2	Description	Return
0	Not used	Not used	Verifies if the capsule is available.	*CommandReturn::success( )*
1	ASCII code for digit or letter	Not used	Display the digit or letter represented by the ASCII code sent in argument 1.	*CommandReturn::success( )* *CommandReturn:: failure (ErrorCode::INVAL)*

Subscribe (not used)

Allow (not used)

The second *command number* we define is 1. This is the actual task that writes a digit or a letter to the LED Matrix. It receives one single parameter: the ASCII code of the character to display. It returns CommandReturn::failure (ErrorCode::INVAL) if the character is not a digit or a letter and CommandReturn::success() otherwise.

Writing the Capsule

A Tock API capsule can be represented by any data type that implements the SyscallDriver trait presented in Listing 8-1. The trait provides the two functions corresponding to the possible system calls: command and allow. For our capsule, we will implement only the command function and use the default implementation for allow.

The allocate_grant function is used by the kernel when a process tries to subscribe to a driver. This function is detailed in the next chapter that presents an asynchronous capsule implementation.

> **Note**   If the process tries to use any of the two, *subscribe* and *allow*
> system calls for our capsule, the kernel for subscribe and the default
> implementation of allow will return the `ErrorCode::NOSUPPORT` error.

Listing 8-1. The SyscallDriver trait

```
pub trait SyscallDriver {
/// Request to allocate a capsule's grant for a specific process.
  fn allocate_grant(&self, appid: ProcessId) -> Result<(),
  crate::process::Error>;

/// System call for a process to perform a short
/// synchronous operation or start a long-
/// running split-phase operation
  fn command(&self, which: usize, r2: usize, r3: usize,
  caller_id: ProcessId) -> CommandReturn {
   CommandReturn::failure(ErrorCode::NOSUPPORT)
  }

/// System call for a process to pass a buffer
/// (a ReadWriteAppSlice) to the kernel, that
/// the kernel can either read or write.
  fn allow_readwrite(
      &self,
      app: ProcessId,
      which: usize,
      slice: ReadWriteAppSlice,
  ) -> Result<ReadWriteAppSlice, (ReadWriteAppSlice, ErrorCode)> {
      Err((slice, ErrorCode::NOSUPPORT))
  }
```

```
/// System call for a process to pass a read-
/// only buffer (a ReadOnlyAppSlice) to the
/// kernel, that the kernel can read.
   fn allow_readonly(
       &self,
       app: ProcessId,
       which: usize,
       slice: ReadOnlyAppSlice,
   ) -> Result<ReadOnlyAppSlice, (ReadOnlyAppSlice, ErrorCode)> {
       Err((slice, ErrorCode::NOSUPPORT))
   }
}
```

For the implementation, we use the same project folder structure presented in *Chapter 6: The Structure of A Custom Tock System*. To make a small recap, the project folder has the following structure:

- *kernel* - all the components that will be part of the operating system (kernel);

- *kernel/board* - the board implementation, the source code that initializes the device and starts the kernel;

- *kernel/drivers* - crate that contains additional drivers that are only part of this project;

- *applications* - each subfolder, except **drivers**, is a separate process;

- *application/drivers* - contains additional libraries, headers, and source files, usually for interfacing the additional drivers in kernel/drivers.

Defining the Driver

The first step in writing our Syscall capsule is to create a new file in the **kernel/drivers** project folder to store the source code. The driver is part of the Rust *drivers* crate. We name the file **digit_letter_display.rs**. Next, we need to ask the Rust compiler to parse it and include it in the *drivers* crate. This is done by adding it as a module named digit_letter_display to the main *drivers* crate file, **lib.rs**. Listing 8-2 shows the exact statement we need to use.

Listing 8-2. The declaration of the digit_letter_display module within the drivers crate

```
pub mod digit_letter_display;
```

Now that we have a file for the capsule and have declared it as a module inside the *drivers* crate, we can start writing the actual Syscall capsule.

First of all, we have to declare a data type that implements the SyscallDriver trait. We could use any data type, including an empty one, such as an empty tuple. To follow other capsules implementations and because we might need to store some additional information for the capsule later on, we choose to use a structure.

First of all, we define an empty structure called DigitLetterDisplay. Next, we implement the SyscallDriver trait for the structure. The actual functions that our driver has to implement are allocate_grant and command. The first function just returns Ok(()) as our driver does not have any grant defined.

Note   We will present grants in detail in *Chapter 9: Writing an Asynchronous Syscall Capsule.*

The command function is the heart of our driver. The initial implementation is straightforward. We perform a single match upon the command_number parameter. If it is 0, the function returns CommandReturn::success() signaling its existence to a process.

For command_number 1, the driver will have to perform the actual displaying of a digit or a letter. We choose to leave this out for now and place a TODO comment reminding us that we will have to write some code here and return CommandReturn::success() eventually.

Any other value of command_number is treated as an error, and the driver will return CommandReturn::failure (ErrorCode::NOSUPPORT), signaling the process that it has not recognized the requested action. Listing 8-3 illustrates the complete source code we have written so far.

Listing 8-3. The initial DigitLetterDisplay implementation

```
use kernel::syscall::{
    CommandReturn, SyscallDriver
};
use kernel::ErrorCode;
use kernel::process::{Error, ProcessId};

pub struct DigitLetterDisplay {
}

impl SyscallDriver for DigitLetterDisplay {
   fn allocate_grant(&self, appid: ProcessId) -> Result<(),
   Error> {
      Ok(())
   }

   fn command(
       &self,
       command_number: usize,
       r2: usize,
```

```
    r3: usize,
    process_id: ProcessId,
) -> CommandReturn {
    match command_number {
        0 => CommandReturn::success(),
        1 => {
            // TODO write the actual code to
            //display a digit or a letter
            CommandReturn::success ()
        }
        _ => CommandReturn::failure(
                ErrorCode::NOSUPPORT
            ),
    }
  }
}
```

Defining the Font

The micro:bit has a 5 x 5 LED matrix capable of displaying 25 red points. Using the LedMatrix driver, Tock exposes all the LEDs separately to the userspace. The same driver exposes a small adaptation structure called LedMatrixLed. This enables each LED to be used from within other drivers inside the Tock's kernel. As such, the kernel capsules and userspace processes can control each LED individually by setting it on or off.

In this chapter, the DigitLetterDisplay driver that we create will use the LedMatrixLed to display digits and letters. This means that we have to define a font. To be more specific, we need to define which of the 25 LEDs will be on and which will be off for each digit, from 0 to 9. Then, we need to do the same for each letter, from A to Z.

The LEDs in the matrix are numbered from 0 to 24, with LED 0 being the upper left LED and 24 being the lower right LED.

Note   The font used by the driver is inspired from `https://www.dafont.com/5x5.font`.

The easiest way to define the font is to use for each glyph (character) a u32 value. Each of the bits 0 to 24 of this value represents an LED. To make the font more readable, an inverted bits order has been used. LED 0 is represented by the most significant bit (MSB), bit 24, and LED 24 is represented by the least significant bit (LSB), bit 0. Listing 8-4 defines the arrays for each digit.

Listing 8-4. The digits font definition

```
const DIGITS: [u32; 10] = [
    // 0
    0b11111_10011_10101_11001_11111,
    // 1
    0b00100_01100_00100_00100_01110,
    // 2
    0b11110_00001_01110_10000_11111,
    // 3
    0b11110_00001_11110_00001_11110,
    // 4
    0b10000_10000_10100_11111_00100,
    // 5
    0b11111_10000_11110_00001_11110,
    // 6
    0b11111_10000_11111_10001_11111,
    // 7
    0b11111_00001_00010_00100_00100,
```

```
    // 8
    0b11111_10001_11111_10001_11111,
    // 9
    0b11111_10001_11111_00001_11111,
];
```

The same approach is taken for the letters. For simplicity, we will use only capital letters. Whenever the userspace process provides a letter, we uppercase it before displaying it.

The font defined in Listing 8-5 shows the definition for the letter *A*. We leave it as an exercise to the user to define the whole set of letters.

Listing 8-5. The font definition for the letter A

```
const LETTERS: [u32; 1] = [
    // A
    0b01110_10001_11111_10001_10001,
    // B...
];
```

Connecting the LEDs

The `DigitLetterDisplay` Syscall capsule has to control the micro:bit's 25 LEDs. This is done using the Led Hardware Interface Layer, or simply *Led* HIL. The capsule does not care how the LEDs are set up, connected, or initialized. This is a task that the board interface (the **main.rs** file in the **board** folder) has to perform. The capsule can only receive a slice containing 25 items that implement the Led trait.

Note   The capsules should interact with each other only by using HILs.

A HIL is a Rust trait defined in the `kernel::hil` crate. Using these HILs allows capsules to be loosely coupled and interchangeable. In our example, the `DigitLetterDisplay` driver will use the *Led* HIL to control each of the 25 LEDs. In a simpler use-case, each LED used by this capsule would be connected to a different GPIO pin. If this capsule were to use directly the Gpio instead of the *Led* HIL, it would not work for the micro:bit as LEDs are not directly connected to the GPIO pins. The 25 LEDs from the micro:bit are controlled by a more complex LED matrix driver. On the other hand, the matrix driver can *expose* each LED separately using the *Led* HIL.

To interact with the *Led* HIL, we have to change the definition of the capsule to something similar to what is shown in Listing 8-6. The capsule's structure receives two parameters: a lifetime for the LEDs array reference ('a) and a generic type L with the Led trait bound. L can be replaced with any concrete type that implements the Led trait.

Listing 8-6. Connecting the LEDs to the API Capsule

```
use kernel::hil::led::Led;
use kernel::syscall::{
    CommandReturn, SyscallDriver
};
use kernel::ErrorCode;
use kernel::process::{Error, ProcessId};

pub struct DigitLetterDisplay<'a, L: Led> {
   leds: &'a [&'a L; 25],
}

impl<'a, L: Led> DigitLetterDisplay<'a, L> {
   pub fn new(leds: &'a [&'a L; 25]) -> Self {
       DigitLetterDisplay { leds }
   }
}
```

Note   A more straightforward way to declare this would have been
to use trait objects and declare the structure as shown in Listing 8-7.

Listing 8-7. The definition of DigitLetterDisplay using traits

```
pub struct DigitLetterDisplay<'a> {
    leds: &'a [&'a dyn Led; 25],
}
```

While the traits-based approach in Listing 8-6 looks simpler as
there is no generic parameter, it does increase the code size and adds a
performance penalty due to the runtime calculations needed to call any
function from Led. As code size and execution speed are very important for
a small microcontroller such as the one inside the micro:bit, we prefer to
use generics despite adding more complexity to the code we write.

Inside the DigitLetterDisplay structure, we defined a field called
leds as a reference to an array of 25 references with lifetime 'a to the
data type L.

Slice vs Array Reference Usage

Instead of the array of 25 LEDs, we could have defined a slice of LEDs, as
shown in Listing 8-8. While this is perfectly valid in Rust and seems more
generic, it adds more code and a performance penalty.

Listing 8-8. The alternative that uses a slice instead of the array

```
pub struct DigitLetterDisplay<'a, L: Led> {
    leds: &'a [&'a L],
}
```

The drawback of using a slice is because the length of any slice is only known at runtime. This has two implications in our code:

1. Within the new function, we have to verify if we have 25 LEDs. If not, most probably we should panic, which is not recommended within the kernel. Using a fixed size array instead of a slice makes the compiler display an error before we even run the kernel;

2. Each time we access the slice, even if we do this within a constant bound for, the compiler inserts a bound verification and a possible panic function to be sure that we are within the slice's bounds. When using a fixed-size array, the compiler knows the size at compile time and is able to optimize the bounds check, making the code smaller and faster. The difference between using an array or a slice is outlined in Listing 8-9. The code in bold is inserted by the compiler.

Listing 8-9. The difference between using a slice and an array

```
// using a slice
for index in 0..25 {
    // the compiler does not know the length
    // of the slice at compile time and
    // inserts the if statement in bold
    if index < self.leds.len() {
        self.leds[index].off()
    } else {
        panic!("Index out of bounds");
    }
}
```

```
// using an array
for index in 0..25 {
    // the compiler knows the length of
    // the array at compile time and does
    // not need to insert as it knows that
    // index cannot exceed the length of
    // the array
    self.leds[index].off()
}
```

Controlling the LEDs

Now that we have completed the structure definition, the next step is to implement it. Inside the impl block, we define a function called new that will create a new structure of type DigitLetterDisplay. The function takes as a parameter a reference to an array of references towards L and returns a new structure instance. We use the keyword Self for the function's return type as it makes the code more readable. We could have easily written the whole data type as DigitLetterDisplay<'a, L>.

Note   While in other programming languages like C++ or Java, new is a keyword, in Rust it is just a simple function name. Rust has as a convention that functions creating data types are usually called new.

Within the new function we create a new structure instance and initializes the leds field with the received parameter. When the new function returns, we have a new driver instance connected to the 25 LEDs in the matrix.

> **Note**   If we were to use a slice instead of an array of LEDs
> references, within the new function, we would need to first check
> that the length of the supplied slice is 25, as the driver expects to
> have a 5 x 5 LED matrix (Listing 8-10). If the length is not 25, the
> driver should cause a panic, and Tock should stop and print a full
> panic debug information using the console. Even though it might be
> strange to kill the whole system due to such an error, this would have
> been fine here as the driver gets initialized only once at startup. If the
> driver cannot be initialized, the whole system does not work.

Listing 8-10. The check required inside the new function if a slice is
used instead of an array

```
pub fn new(leds: &'a [&'a L]) -> Self {
    if leds.len() != 25 {
        panic!("Expecting 25 LEDs, {}     supplied", leds.len());
    }
    DigitLetterDisplay { leds: leds }
}
```

Display Digits and Letters

Now that we have defined the capsule's data type structure and have
connected the 25 LEDs, it is time to write the actual functionality of
the driver. For this, we add three functions to the DigitLetterDisplay
implementation, which will perform the tasks. Listing 8-11 presents all the
code that we will discuss here.

Listing 8-11. Displaying digits and letters

```rust
impl<'a, L: Led> DigitLetterDisplay<'a, L> {
    pub fn new(leds: &'a [&'a L; 25]) -> Self {
        DigitLetterDisplay { leds: leds }
    }

    fn print(&self, glyph: u32) {
        for index in 0..25 {
            match (glyph >> (24 - index)) & 0x01 {
                0 => self.leds[index].off(),
                _ => self.leds[index].on(),
            }
        }
    }

    fn clear(&self) {
        for index in 0..25 {
            self.leds[index].off();
        }
    }

    fn display(&self, character: char) ->
                        Result<(), ErrorCode> {
        let displayed_character =
                character.to_ascii_uppercase();
        match displayed_character {
            '0'..='9' => {
                self.print(DIGITS[
displayed_character as usize - '0' as usize]);
                Ok(())
            }
            'A'..='Z' => {
```

```
                self.print(LETTERS[
displayed_character as usize - 'A' as usize]);
                Ok(())
            }
        _ => {
                self.clear();
                Err(ErrorCode::INVAL)
            }
        }
    }
}
```

The first function is print. Its task is to print the glyph received as a parameter to the LED matrix. The glyph is a u32 number, with its first 25 bits representing the LEDs assigned to a digit or a letter, in other words, one item from the defined font. This function always succeeds, so there is no need to return a value. Its functionality is really simple, it iterates an index from 0 to 24, verifies the value of a bit in the glyph, and sets each LED on or off accordingly. If the value is 0, the corresponding LED is turned off. Otherwise, it is turned on.

Note   While there might be some errors when setting on and off an LED, the Led HIL does not return them. From our driver's point of view, the on and off functions will always succeed.

The second function is called clear. It is very similar to the print function, except it does not receive any parameter and its behavior is to turn off all the LEDs.

The third function, display, does all the heavy lifting. It receives a character as a parameter, verifies if it is a digit or a letter, and calls the print function with the correct glyph. This function can fail if the character supplied as a parameter is not a digit or a letter. While returning a bool would have been more intuitive, this is not Rust's or Tock's way of doing things.

Functions that might return errors, or in other words fail, usually return the Result<Success, Error> type. The two generics defined here are the actual data types that should be returned in case of failure or success (this aspect is detailed in *Chapter 4: Rust for Tock*).

In our case, the function returns Result<(), ErrorCode>. If the provided character is a digit or a letter, the function succeeds and returns Ok(()), where *Success* is of type Unit. In case of failure, it returns Err(ErrorCode) containing an error code that is sent to the process.

As both uppercase and lowercase letters can be used, we first need to convert letters to uppercase. For this, we define a new variable, displayed_character, and bind it to the ASCII uppercase value of the received parameter.

Next, we perform a match on the displayed_character value. Remember, in Rust, match is an expression that returns a value. In our case, the match is the last expression of the function, so the value returned by match is the value that the function returns.

If the character is between '0' and '9', we have to display a digit. This is done by calling the print function and sending the corresponding digit from the DIGITS array. To compute the index within DIGITS, we convert the character to an unsigned integer number (which will be the ASCII code for the character as digits are all part of ASCII) and subtract the value of the ASCII code for '0'.

As the print function is always successful, we return Ok(()).

Note   Rust uses UTF-8 to represent characters. This means that a char value might be up to 4 bytes. In UTF-8, the first 127 code points are identical to the ASCII codes.

If the character is a letter between *A* and *Z*, we perform a similar task as for digits but use the LETTERS array of glyphs. As the print function is always successful, we return Ok(()).

If no match has been performed so far, that means that the provided character is neither a digit, nor a letter, so we cannot display it. First of all, we clear the display so that the user can see that the character has not been displayed. Next, we return Err(ErrorCode::INVAL), which means that the character received is invalid.

The Syscall API Implementation

Our capsule functionality is complete, it has all the LEDs connected and has all the necessary functions implemented. The next step is to expose an API for the userspace processes. This is where the SyscallDriver trait comes into play. We have already implemented the basics of the command function. All we have to do is to write the code for the match case when command_number equals 1.

Note   Parameters _r3 and _process_id are not used, thus prefixed with an underscore to prevent the Rust compiler from issuing unused code warnings.

Command number 1 is the actual display request. When the userspace process sends a command system call with value 1 to the capsule, it will use the first parameter r2 to store the character's ASCII code to be displayed. The command function converts the usize value of r2 into a char and calls the display function.

As seen in Listing 8-12, the conversion from usize to char is not straightforward. Rust cannot convert any arbitrary usize value to a UTF-8 code, as not all usize values are valid UTF-8 code points. This is why we first have to convert the usize into an u8, a byte, and then convert it back to a UTF-8 character. All u8 values are valid UTF-8 code points as they are the actual ASCII codes.

Listing 8-12. The Driver implementation for DigitLetterDisplay

```
impl<'a, L: Led> Driver for DigitLetterDisplay<'a, L> {
    fn command(
        &self,
        command_number: usize,
        r2: usize,
        _r3: usize,
        _process_id: ProcessId,
    ) -> CommandReturn {
        match command_number {
            0 => CommandReturn::success(),
            1 => match self.display(r2 as u8 as char) {
                Ok(()) =>
                    CommandReturn::success(),
                Err(err) =>
                    CommandReturn::failure(err),
            },
            _ => CommandReturn::failure(
                    ErrorCode::NOSUPPORT
                ),
        }
    }
}
```

Note   All ASCII codes are valid UTF-8 code points. When converting a usize value to u8, we might lose some information. If the number stored in the usize value is larger than 255, part of it will be lost in the conversion. In our case, this is not a problem as the userspace should send us only ASCII character codes, codes that are always represented using 8 bits. If we want to make sure that we do not lose any information due to the conversion to u8, we can add an if statement before and return an ErrorCode::INVAL if the value we received is larger than 255.

Another important aspect is how the match is used upon the self. display(...) function call. The display function returns Result<(), ErrorCode>. Within the command function, we need to decide if the function was successful and, in that case, return CommandReturn::success(). If it failed, we return the error code that was wrapped into the returned Result. This means we have to unwrap the Result value and transform it into a CommandReturn. We use a two-branches match to perform this action.

The returned value of display is either Ok(()), which leads us to CommandReturn::success(), or Err(err). In the case of an error, match assigns the ErrorCode value wrapped into the Result to the variable err and executes the code within that branch. We construct a CommandReturn::failure(err) and return it to the userspace process.

Note   As this capsule only implements command and leaves the other functions with their default implementation, the userspace processes will only be able to issue command system calls to it. Any other type of system call towards this capsule will return an error.

Registering the Capsule

Now that we have implemented that capsule, the next step is to register it with the kernel. This allows the kernel to forward command, subscribe, and allow system calls to it and send back a response to the process. The kernel does not use a list of capsules but leverages the SyscallDriverLookup trait.

Note   Each board supported in Tock has a *board implementation* that is located in ***boards/_board_name_***. In our case, *_board_ name_* is replaced with ***microbit_v2*** for the micro:bit and with ***raspberry_pi_pico*** for the Raspberry Pi.

The Board Implementation

First of all, we have to understand how Tock starts and how the kernel works. The first function called when a Tock board is powered on is main. In the **tock** repository, this function is located in **boards/_board_name_/src/main.rs**. In our project, this file is located in **kernel/_board_name_/src/main.rs**.

The main function handles all setup actions that have to be taken before the kernel starts. These actions include peripheral initialization like configuring GPIO pins, setting up the serial port at a certain speed, configuring SPI or I2C buses, starting timers and alarms, etc.

The KernelResources Trait

The Tock kernel is designed to be device-independent. This means that the same kernel has to work on all the available devices. As the kernel runs at a very low level, it has to perform some actions dependent on the platform it runs on. Actions like setting up a timer for preempting processes or managing the system's watchdog are specific to each MCU. To allow flexible downstream ports, the kernel exposes the KernelResources trait. This will enable boards to implement the following features:

- syscall drivers lookup;

- system call filter;

- process fault handler;

- the process scheduler;

- the scheduler's timer;

- the watchdog.

System Calls Filters

Whenever a process makes a system call, it is suspended, and the kernel takes back control of the execution. Depending on the actual system call made by the process, the kernel will follow one of the two paths. If the system call is yield, memop, or exit, the kernel will execute the requested action.

In case of a yield, it will suspend the process until an *upcall* is available. For a memop, the kernel will try to make the requested memory changes to the process' memory space and return the execution to the process. Finally, an exit system call will make the kernel stop or restart the process.

If the system call is command, subscribe or allow, the kernel will read the capsule_number from the system call and use the resources parameter supplied with the kernel_loop function. This provides the kernel the syscall_filter function that returns a data type that implements the SyscallFilter trait presented in Listing 8-13. This trait defines one single function called filter_sycall. The kernel calls this function and, if the function returns Ok(()), the kernel continues. Otherwise, it unwraps the returned ErrorCode and sends it back to the process. In other words, this is like a *firewall* for system calls.

Listing 8-13. The SyscallFilter trait's default implementation

```
pub trait SyscallFilter {
    fn filter_syscall(
        &self,
        _process: &dyn process::Process,
        _syscall: &syscall::Syscall,
    ) -> Result<(), errorcode::ErrorCode> {
      Ok(())
    }
}
```

Drivers Registration

If the system call is allowed, the kernel must find the driver to dispatch the system call to. This is where the SyscallDriverLookup trait presented in Listing 8-14 comes into play. The kernel asks the board implementation by calling the syscall_driver_lookup function for a reference to a data type that implements the SyscallDriverLookup trait. Now that it has a reference to a syscall driver lookup data structure, it calls the with_driver function with two arguments: the capsule_number and a function that has to be called with an Option<&dyn SyascallDriver> as an argument. The system call lookup implementation may use any means to find the requested driver and call the supplied function. This function takes an Option as an argument as the driver lookup system might not be able to find a specific capsule. If it finds the capsule, it will call the function using Some(driver). Otherwise, it will use None.

Listing 8-14. The SyscallDriverLookup trait

```
pub trait SyscallDriverLookup {
    fn with_driver<F, R>(&self, driver_num: usize, f: F) -> R
    where
    F: FnOnce(Option<&dyn SyscallDriver>) -> R;
}
```

Now, let's take the example of micro:bit. The board implementation uses the MicroBit structure shown in Listing 8-15 to store all the capsules. Each property of the structure represents one of the available capsules. In this particular example, the MicroBit has the following drivers:

- **console** - uses a serial port to simulate a screen (printf functions in the userspace);

- **gpio** - allow access to the board's pins;

- **led** - provides access to the LED Matrix;

- **button** - controls the A and B buttons;

- **ipc** - provides a mechanism for processes to send data to each other; this capsule is not related to any hardware device;

- **alarm** - provides the alarm system used to implement timing functions like the delay_ms function.

Note   The MicroBit contains several other drivers, but for the simplicity of the example, we decided to leave them out.

Listing 8-15. The definition of the MicroBit v2 structure that implements the KernelResources trait

```
pub struct MicroBit {
    console: &'static capsules::console::Console<'static>,
    gpio: &'static capsules::gpio::GPIO<
            'static,
            nrf52::gpio::GPIOPin<'static>
    >,
    led: &'static capsules::led_matrix::LedMatrixDriver<
        'static,
        nrf52::gpio::GPIOPin<'static>,
        capsules::virtual_alarm::VirtualMuxAlarm<
            'static,
            nrf52::rtc::Rtc<'static>
        >,
    >,
    button: &'static capsules::button::Button<
            'static,
            nrf52::gpio::GPIOPin<'static>
    >,
    ipc: kernel::ipc::IPC<NUM_PROCS>,
    alarm: &'static capsules::alarm::AlarmDriver<
        'static,
        capsules::virtual_alarm::VirtualMuxAlarm<
            'static,
            nrf52::rtc::Rtc<'static>
        >,
    >,
```

```
    // ...
    scheduler: &'static RoundRobinSched<'static>,
    systick: cortexm4::systick::SysTick,
    // ...
}
```

The MicroBit structure definition is particular for the micro:bit board and very different from other boards' implementations. Usually, this is the structure that implements the KernelResources trait and the SyscallDriverLookup trait.

First of all, the MicroBit structure implements the KernelResources trait. The actual implementation is presented in Listing 8-16. Each of the trait's associated types is assigned to a concrete type. Assigning Self to the SyscallDriverLookup type implies that the MicroBit structure will have to implement the SyscallDriverLookup trait. The assignment of () - Unit to SyscallFilter, ProcessFault, and WatchDog means that the default implementations of these traits will be used (as a trait cannot be implemented for a type that is not defined within the crate). In other words, all system calls will be allowed, the default process fault policy will be applied, and there is no watchdog used.

Note   Details on how fault policies work and are implemented will be discussed in chapter 12.

Next, the implementation defines the concrete types for the scheduler and the timer.

Listing 8-16. The KernelResources trait implementation for the
MicroBit v2 definition structure

```
impl KernelResources<
    nrf52833::chip::NRF52<
        'static,
        Nrf52833DefaultPeripherals<'static>
    >
  >
    for MicroBit
{
    type SyscallDriverLookup = Self;
    type SyscallFilter = ();
    type ProcessFault = ();
    type Scheduler = RoundRobinSched<'static>;
    type SchedulerTimer = cortexm4::systick::SysTick;
    type WatchDog = ();

    fn syscall_driver_lookup(&self) ->
    &Self::SyscallDriverLookup {
        &self
    }
    fn syscall_filter(&self) -> &Self::SyscallFilter {
        &()
    }
    fn process_fault(&self) -> &Self::ProcessFault {
        &()
    }
    fn scheduler(&self) -> &Self::Scheduler {
        self.scheduler
    }
```

```
    fn scheduler_timer(&self) -> &Self::SchedulerTimer {
        &self.systick
    }
    fn watchdog(&self) -> &Self::WatchDog {
        &()
    }
} }
}
```

The KernelResources trait implementation requires the `MicroBit` structure to implement the `SyscallDriverLookup` trait. The complete source is presented in Listing 8-17. By analyzing the code, we can notice that the `match` statement is used to search for a capsule. The function simply matches the provided `driver_num` argument (sometimes called `capsule_number`), representing the capsule id against all the drivers in the structure.

Listing 8-17. The SyscallDriverLookup trait implementation for the MicroBit v2 definition structure

```
impl SyscallDriverLookup for MicroBit {
    fn with_driver<F, R>(&self, driver_num: usize, f: F) -> R
    where
        F: FnOnce(Option<&dyn kernel::Driver>) -> R,
    {
        match driver_num {
            capsules::console::DRIVER_NUM => f(Some(self.console)),
            capsules::gpio::DRIVER_NUM => f(Some(self.gpio)),
            capsules::alarm::DRIVER_NUM => f(Some(self.alarm)),
            capsules::button::DRIVER_NUM => f(Some(self.button)),
            capsules::led_matrix::DRIVER_NUM => f(Some(self.led)),
            // ...
```

```
        kernel::ipc::DRIVER_NUM => f(Some(&self.ipc)),
        _ => f(None),
      }
    }
}
```

If the match in Listing 8-17 succeeds, the function calls f with
Some(driver) as an argument. In this case, the kernel will forward the
system call to the specified capsule and wait for the capsule to respond. It
is now the responsibility of the capsule to handle the system call.

If none of the drivers match, the function calls f(None). The kernel
will send an ErrorCode::NODEVICE response to the process, signaling
that there is no available driver with the requested capsule_number. The
flowchart in Figure 8-1 presents the steps we described previously.

Starting The Kernel

As the data structures required for starting the kernel are defined,
and the KernelResources trait and its associated data types are
implemented, the board implementation can initialize the drivers and
start the kernel. Listing 8-18 illustrates the initialization of the LedMatrix
capsule, the creation of the MicroBit structure, which implements the
SyscallDriverLookup trait, and the call to the kernel_loop function that
starts the kernel.

Initialization is different for each capsule. Each driver is a separate
structure with several generic parameters. What is more, their new function
takes several arguments that connect it to other drivers. Therefore, the
initialization line might be long and difficult. Tock leverages the Rust
macro system and recommends that each driver defines a set of macros
in the components crate. In the example presented in Listing 8-18,
the LedMatrix driver is initialized using the led_matrix_component_
helper macro.

Listing 8-18. LedMatrix capsule and MicroBit structure initialization

```
let led = components::led_matrix_component_helper!(
        nrf52833::gpio::GPIOPin,
        nrf52::rtc::Rtc<'static>,
        mux_alarm,
        @fps => 60,
        @cols => kernel::hil::gpio::ActivationMode::ActiveLow,
    &nrf52833_peripherals.gpio_port[LED_MATRIX_COLS[0]],
    &nrf52833_peripherals.gpio_port[LED_MATRIX_COLS[1]],
    &nrf52833_peripherals.gpio_port[LED_MATRIX_COLS[2]],
    &nrf52833_peripherals.gpio_port[LED_MATRIX_COLS[3]],
    &nrf52833_peripherals.gpio_port[LED_MATRIX_COLS[4]],
        @rows => kernel::hil::gpio::ActivationMode::ActiveHigh,
    &nrf52833_peripherals.gpio_port[LED_MATRIX_ROWS[0]],
    &nrf52833_peripherals.gpio_port[LED_MATRIX_ROWS[1]],
    &nrf52833_peripherals.gpio_port[LED_MATRIX_ROWS[2]],
    &nrf52833_peripherals.gpio_port[LED_MATRIX_ROWS[3]],
    &nrf52833_peripherals.gpio_port[LED_MATRIX_ROWS[4]]
    )
.finalize(components::led_matrix_component_buf!(
        nrf52833::gpio::GPIOPin,
        nrf52::rtc::Rtc<'static>
    ));
// ...
let microbit = MicroBit {
        console: console,
        gpio: gpio,
        button: button,
        led: led,
        alarm: alarm,
```

```
    // ...
    ipc: kernel::ipc::IPC::new(board_kernel, &memory_
    allocation_capability),
  };
// ...
board_kernel.kernel_loop(
      &microbit,
      chip,
      Some(&microbit.ipc),
      scheduler,
      &main_loop_capability,
  );
```

Note   As each capsule is different, the actual initialization code can be found in the documentation comments of the capsule's source and component. Capsules are usually found in the **capsules** folder, and components are in the **boards/components** folder.

After the initialization of all drivers, the board implementation can create the necessary structure. In our example, a new MicroBit structure is created.

The final step in starting Tock is calling the kernel_loop function. This function never returns, so invoking it has to be the last action that main takes. The function presented in Listing 8-19 launches the kernel. The function takes three arguments and the required capability.

Listing 8-19. The kernel loop function

```
pub fn kernel_loop<
      KR: KernelResources<C>,
      C: Chip,
```

```
    const NUM_PROCS: usize,
    const NUM_UPCALLS_IPC: usize,
>(
    &self,
    resources: &KR,
    chip: &C,
    ipc: Option<&ipc::IPC<
                NUM_PROCS,
                NUM_UPCALLS_IPC>
            >,
    capability:
        &dyn capabilities::MainLoopCapability,
) -> !
```

The kernel_loop's function first argument is any data type that implements the KernelResources trait as shown in Listing 8-20. The second argument is the number of processes that the kernel can load. The third argument represents the number of possible subscribe numbers that the IPC driver must be able to register. This is usually the number of processes plus one. The last argument is the MainLoopCapability required to start the kernel.

Tip   The platform-based implementation in this section is specific to the micro:bit device. If you work on a Raspberry Pi Pico, we recommend you read this to understand the concepts, then follow the last section of the chapter to adapt it for your device.

Capabilities

Suppose you are asking yourself about the meaning of the last argument of kernel_loop, the capability. In that case, this is part of a security mechanism implemented by Tock to prevent capsules from getting access to some sensible resources. From the developer's point of view, capabilities are unsafe traits. The definition of the MainLoopCapability is presented in Listing 8-20.

Listing 8-20. The definition of the MainLoopCapability capability

```
/// The `MainLoopCapability` capability allows
/// the holder to start executing as
/// well as manage the main scheduler loop in
/// Tock. This is needed in a board's
/// main.rs file to start the kernel. It also
/// allows an external implementation
/// of `Process` to update state in the kernel
/// struct used by the main loop.
pub unsafe trait MainLoopCapability {}
```

Unsafe traits can only be implemented in unsafe code. As capsules are not allowed to use unsafe code, there is no way for a capsule to implement a capability trait. Functions that perform sensitive actions, like managing processes or memory allocation, require a reference to a data structure that implements that capability. An example is the kernel_loop function in Listing 8-19. If a capsule wants to use such a function, it must provide the required reference to the capability. As the capsule is not able to create such capability, it can only call the function if it has previously received one as an argument (most probably in its new function).

From the efficiency point of view, capabilities are zero-sized structures used only by the compiler and optimized by the linker. The capability argument that a function receives is never used within the function. It only prevents the calling of the function from a context that does not have the requested capability.

You might think that this is not really helpful as:

- you can always write a capsule that receives a capability in its initialization function;

- you can inspect the source code of a capsule.

While the statements above are true, we need to look at the problem from a different angle. This approach partially solves the third-party dependency security problem. Imagine you have a system that uses a large number of third-party capsules, capsules that have not been developed by Tock's authors or by yourself. It isn't easy to go through all the capsules and audit every single line of code. As long as these third-party capsules obey the rules of not using unsafe code, there is no way that one of these capsules is able to perform a sensitive action as it does not have the required capability. The only possibility of getting a capability is to provide it to the capsule at its initialization in the board implementation (**main.rs**).

Note   Enforcing the rejection of unsafe code is easily verifiable by looking at a crate's lib.rs file and finding the #![forbid(unsafe_code)] directive.

The DigitLetterDisplay Capsule Registration

Now that we know how the driver infrastructure works, the last step we have to take regarding the kernel is to register our capsule. First of all, we have to give our capsule an *id*. Within the capsule's source file, we define a public constant called DRIVER_NUM, just like the one presented in Listing 8-21. While the actual name of the constant is not relevant, using DRIVER_NUM seems to be the standard approach in Tock.

Listing 8-21. Define a driver number for the DigitLetterDisplay

```
pub const DRIVER_NUM: usize = 0xa0001;
```

The value of the constant is relevant. Each driver in Tock has to have a unique identifier. Drivers provided by Tock have their identifiers defined in **capsules/src/driver.rs**. Third-party drivers like the one we have just created must have an identifier starting from 0xa0000. We have chosen the 0xa0001 (Listing 8-21) as this is our first (1) driver.

Tip Driver ids below 0xa0000 are reserved for the drivers that Tock provides out of the box.

The next step that we have to take is to register the driver with the MicroBit structure. We define a new field within the structure, called digit_letter_display as shown in bold in Listing 8-22. Its type is more complex. All the structure's fields are static references to the actual driver. This means that these references never go out of scope. All the drivers' references will be valid for as long as the kernel is loaded. From Rust's point of view, drivers are global variables.

Listing 8-22. The definition of the digit_letter_display field in the MicroBit structure

```
pub struct MicroBit {
 console: &'static
   capsules::console::Console<'static>,
 gpio: &'static capsules::gpio::GPIO<'static,
   nrf52::gpio::GPIOPin<'static>>,
 led: &'static
   capsules::led_matrix::LedMatrixDriver<
      'static,
      nrf52::gpio::GPIOPin<'static>,
```

```
            capsules::virtual_alarm::VirtualMuxAlarm<
              'static, nrf52::rtc::Rtc<'static>>,
    >,
    button: &'static
      capsules::button::Button<'static,
            nrf52::gpio::GPIOPin<'static>>,
    ipc: kernel::ipc::IPC<NUM_PROCS>,
    alarm: &'static capsules::alarm::AlarmDriver<
      'static,
      capsules::virtual_alarm::VirtualMuxAlarm<
        'static, nrf52::rtc::Rtc<'static>>,
    >,
      // ...
    digit_letter_display: &'static
     drivers::digit_letter_display::
       DigitLetterDisplay
          // 'a is set to 'static
          'static,
          // L is set to LedMatrixLed<...>
          LedMatrixLed<
              'static,
              nrf52::gpio::GPIOPin<'static>,
              capsules::virtual_alarm::
                  VirtualMuxAlarm<'static,
                  nrf52::rtc::Rtc<'static>>,
          >,
      >,
}
```

Since the structure DigitLetterDisplay has two parameters, we have to provide these. The lifetime is straightforward. We just use 'static. The second parameter is a data type that implements the Led trait. In our case, this is the LedMatrixLed structure presented in Listing 8-23. This structure is capable of interacting with the LedMatrix driver and controlling one of the LEDs. The tricky part is handling the generic arguments of this structure. First, it has a lifetime, followed by a data type that implements Pin, and a data type that implements Alarm.

Listing 8-23. The LedMatrixLed definition

```
pub struct LedMatrixLed<
    'a,
    L: Pin,
    A:  Alarm<'a>
> {
    matrix: &'a LedMatrixDriver<'a, L, A>,
    row: usize,
    col: usize,
}
```

When defining the actual data type of our driver, we have to supply all the concrete data types recursively. This is why the type definition is long. If we take a closer look, the structure that implements the Alarm trait also uses generics, which makes the data type even longer.

More precisely, for LedMatrixLed, L is replaced by nrf52::gpio::GPIOPin<'static> and A is replaced by capsules::virtual_alarm::VirtualMuxAlarm<'static, nrf52::rtc::Rtc<'static>>.

Note   The data type would have been much shorter if the DigitLetterDisplay used the Led trait object (&dyn Led). There is always a tradeoff between simplicity and performance.

Now that the data type is out of the way, an easy step is to register the capsule within the SyscallDriverLookup trait and implement the with_driver function as shown in Listing 8-24. All we have to do is to add another branch to the match statement. This is where we use the DRIVER_NUM constant defined earlier.

Listing 8-24. Registering the capsule with the kernel

```
impl SyscallDriverLookup for MicroBit {
    fn with_driver<F, R>(&self, driver_num: usize, f: F) -> R
    where
        F: FnOnce(Option<&dyn kernel::Driver>) -> R,
    {
        match driver_num {
            capsules::console::DRIVER_NUM => f(Some(self.console)),
            capsules::gpio::DRIVER_NUM => f(Some(self.gpio)),
            capsules::alarm::DRIVER_NUM => f(Some(self.alarm)),
            capsules::button::DRIVER_NUM => f(Some(self.button)),
            capsules::led_matrix::DRIVER_NUM => f(Some(self.led)),
            // ...
            drivers::digit_letter_display::DRIVER_NUM =>
            f(Some(self.digit_letter_display)),
            kernel::ipc::DRIVER_NUM => f(Some(&self.ipc)),
            _ => f(None),
        }
    }
}
```

The final step is to actually initialize the driver. This involves creating a new instance of the DigitLetterDisplay structure. As Listing 8-25 outlines, we define a variable called digit_letter_display and assign it a large and strange value that we analyze next.

Listing 8-25. The MicroBit structure initialization

```
let digit_letter_display = static_init!(
    DigitLetterDisplay<
        'static,
        LedMatrixLed<
            'static,
            nrf52::gpio::GPIOPin<'static>,
            capsules::virtual_alarm::VirtualMuxAlarm<'static,
            nrf52::rtc::Rtc<'static>>,
        >,
    >,
    DigitLetterDisplay::new(components::led_matrix_leds!(
        nrf52::gpio::GPIOPin<'static>,
        capsules::virtual_alarm::VirtualMuxAlarm<'static,
        nrf52::rtc::Rtc<'static>>,
        led,
        (0, 0),
            (1, 0),
            (2, 0),
            (3, 0),
            (4, 0),
            (0, 0),
            (1, 1),
            (2, 1),
            (3, 1),
            (4, 1),
            (0, 2),
            (1, 2),
            (2, 2),
            (3, 2),
            (4, 2),
```

```
        (0, 3),
        (1, 3),
        (2, 3),
        (3, 3),
        (4, 3),
        (0, 4),
        (1, 4),
        (2, 4),
        (3, 4),
        (4, 4)
    ))
);

let microbit = MicroBit {
    console,
    gpio,
    button,
    led,
    alarm,
     ipc: kernel::ipc::IPC::new(
        board_kernel,
        kernel::ipc::DRIVER_NUM,
        &memory_allocation_capability,
     ),
    digit_letter_display,
};
```

First of all, we need to provide the board's implementation a reference to a DigitLetterDisplay structure, not the structure itself. What's even more interesting is that this reference needs to have a 'static lifetime, in other words, a reference to a global variable.

Mutable global variables are unsafe in Rust, and sometimes the semantics of defining them and assigning them a value can be rather difficult. This is why Tock, and Rust, provide us with a macro called static_init that will do the trick for us. This macro receives two arguments: the data type and the initialization code for a value. Inside, the macro declares a static (global) variable and assigns it the desired value. It then returns a reference to it. In our particular case, the data type that the macro receives is the full type for the DigitLetterDisplay shown in Listing 8-26.

Listing 8-26. The full type for the DigitLetterDisplay structure

```
DigitLetterDisplay<
    'static,
    LedMatrixLed<
        'static,
        nrf52::gpio::GPIOPin<'static>,
        capsules::virtual_alarm::VirtualMuxAlarm<'static,
        nrf52::rtc::Rtc<'static>>,
    >,
>
```

The second parameter received by the static_init macro is the value with which it should initialize the static variable. In our case, it is the value returned by the DigitLetterDisplay::new function. Again, this seems to be a long line of code, even though the new function should only receive one single parameter, the reference to an array of Led references.

Obtaining a single Led from the LedMatrix is a very long line of code due to many generic parameters. To avoid this and streamline code writing, the LedMatrixLed driver provides a macro called led_matrix_leds (Listing 8-27) that receives three parameters followed by sets of Led coordinates.

The first two parameters are the data types that implement the Pin and Alarm traits. These are necessary as the macro needs to know the exact type of the LedMatrix (which in turn uses them). The third parameter, led, is a reference to the LedMatrix driver initialized in Listing 8-15. The macro takes a variable list of (column, row) coordinates for each LED that should be placed into the array that it returns.

Note   Rust macros are very different from the macros in C. They allow developers to extend the Rust language. For a better understanding of these Rust macros, we strongly recommend reading the *Little Book of Macros*[1].

Listing 8-27. The function call that creates a new DigitLetterDisplay structure

```
DigitLetterDisplay::new(components::
  led_matrix_leds!(
      nrf52::gpio::GPIOPin<'static>,
      capsules::virtual_alarm::VirtualMuxAlarm<'static,
      nrf52::rtc::Rtc<'static>>,
        led,
        (0, 0),
        (1, 0),
    // ...
```

Our driver is now complete. The next step is to write a userspace library that allows processes to interact with it.

---

[1] https://danielkeep.github.io/tlborm/book/index.html

Writing the Userspace Library

Each capsule has a corresponding userspace library. The primary purpose of this library is to encapsulate the system calls and export relevant functions for the processes that use it. In other words, instead of directly using the system call API, processes will use a set of functions exposed by this library. These functions will perform the actual system calls.

The header and source files for the library will be located in the **applications/drivers** folder.

For our `DigitLetterDisplay` Syscall capsule, we export the two functions described in Table 8-4.

Table 8-4. *The functions exposed by the DigitLetterDisplay userspace library*

Function	Parameters	Description
is_present	None	Returns true if the driver is present, false otherwise
show_ character	the ASCII character to display	Displays the ASCII character using the LED matrix. Returns true if the character could be displayed (it is either a digit either a letter) or false otherwise.

Note   As the C language does not provide namespacing, the function names are prefixed with the driver's name. The actual function names are `digit_letter_display_is_present` and `digit_letter_display_show_character`.

The Header File

The first step is to write a new header file called **digit_letter_display.h**
that contains the declaration of the two functions exposed by the library.
Listing 8-28 displays the header's contents. To make sure that the header
file is imported only once into a source file, we use the #pragma once tag.
As using numeric constants in favor of named constants is discouraged,
we will define the capsule number (0xa0001) using DRIVER_NUM_DIGIT_
LETTER_DISPLAY. This constant value will be used when issuing the
command system calls.

Listing 8-28. The userspace library API definition

```
// Digit Letter Display API

#pragma once
#include "tock.h"
#define DIGIT_LETTER_DISPLAY_DRIVER_NUM 0xa0001

#ifdef __cplusplus
extern "C" {
#endif

bool digit_letter_display_is_present (void);
bool digit_letter_display_show_character (
    char digit_or_letter);

#ifdef __cplusplus
}
#endif
```

The largest section of the header file is focused on the declaration of
the two exported functions. Since we use the C language, but part of the
libtock-c library is written in C++, we have to ensure that the two functions

314

declared here are seen as C functions, regardless if the header file is included into a C or C++ file. Surrounding the two function declarations by #ifdef __cplusplus ... #endif tags will do precisely this.

The Library

After defining the header for the library, the next step is to write the definition for the two functions. For this, we create a new source file called **digit_letter_display.c**. Listing 8-29 shows the complete source code.

Listing 8-29. The userspace library implementation for the DigitLetterDisplay API Capsule

```
// Digit Letter Display API

#include "digit_letter_display.h"
#include "tock.h"

bool digit_letter_display_is_present (void) {
 syscall_return_t ret = command
   (DIGIT_LETTER_DISPLAY_DRIVER_NUM, 0, 0, 0);
 if (ret.type == TOCK_SYSCALL_SUCCESS) {
   return true;
 } else {
   return false;
 }
}

bool digit_letter_display_show_character (char
     digit_or_letter) {
 syscall_return_t ret = command
     (DIGIT_LETTER_DISPLAY_DRIVER_NUM, 1,
      digit_or_letter, 0);
```

```
  if (ret.type == TOCK_SYSCALL_SUCCESS) {
    return true;
  } else {
    return false;
  }
}
```

We first include the previously created header file and **tock.h**. The ladder defines the system call functions and system call return types.

The first function that we write is digit_letter_display_is_present. This will issue a command system call towards the DigitLetterDisplay driver and verify its return value. Based on that, the function will return true if the driver is present and false otherwise. The command system call is sent using the library function with the same name. The first argument of the function represents the capsule number. In our case, it is the previously defined constant value DIGIT_LETTER_DISPLAY_DRIVER_NUM. The second argument is the command number, in other words, the action that we require the driver to perform. In our case, it is the value 0, which in Tock's convention means checking if the driver is present.

The command function returns a syscall_return_t type presented in Listing 8-30.

Listing 8-30. The system call return type

```
// Generic return structure from a system call.
typedef struct {
 syscall_rtype_t type;
 uint32_t data[3];
} syscall_return_t;
```

The structure contains the following fields:

- *type* - the return type of the system call having one of the values in Listing 8-31;

- *data* - an array of three 32 bits unsigned integers.

Listing 8-31. The possible values of the system call return type, corresponding to the CommandReturn::failure..(...) and CommandReturn::success..(...) functions in the kernel

```
typedef enum {
  TOCK_FAILURE                          =    0,
  TOCK_SYSCALL_FAILURE_U32              =    1,
  TOCK_SYSCALL_FAILURE_U32_U32          =    2,
  TOCK_SYSCALL_FAILURE_U64              =    3,
  TOCK_SYSCALL_SUCCESS                  = 128,
  TOCK_SYSCALL_SUCCESS_U32              = 129,
  TOCK_SYSCALL_SUCCESS_U32_U32          = 130,
  TOCK_SYSCALL_SUCCESS_U64              = 131,
  TOCK_SYSCALL_SUCCESS_U32_U32_U32      = 132,
  TOCK_SYSCALL_SUCCESS_U64_U32          = 133
} syscall_rtype_t;
```

The type field of the structure provides the type of the return value. The data field has to be interpreted differently based on the value of the type field. If type is set to one of the TOCK_SYSCALL_FAILURE... values, the first value of data (data[0]) represents the ErrorCode, while the rest of the values represent some additional data. Their encoding differs depending on what kind of a TOCK_SYSCALL_FAILURE... the result encodes. For instance, if it is TOCK_SYSCALL_FAILURE_U32, data[1] has a valid value. On the other hand, if we have TOCK_SYSCALL_FAILURE_U64, data[1] and data[2] have to be combined using the big endian encoding to extract the valid value (data[1] + data[2] << 32).

The same system applies in the case of success, the only difference being that success may have up to three 32 bits unsigned integers as there is no need to encode an ErrorCode.

The Tock C userspace provides two error types that encode errors differently:

- returncode_t - encodes an error using the C standard (Listing 8-32);

- statuscode_t - tries to encode it closer to what Rust does (Listing 8-33).

The actual system calls return statuscode_t.

Listing 8-32. The error codes that respect the usual C standard: positive numbers mean success, negative numbers mean errors

```
// ReturnCode type in libtock-c.
//
// 0 is success, and a negative value is an
// error (consistent with C
// conventions). The error cases are
// -1*ErrorCode values.
typedef enum {
  RETURNCODE_SUCCESS      = 0,
  RETURNCODE_FAIL         = -1,
  RETURNCODE_EBUSY        = -2,
  RETURNCODE_EALREADY     = -3,
  RETURNCODE_EOFF         = -4,
  RETURNCODE_ERESERVE     = -5,
  RETURNCODE_EINVAL       = -6,
  RETURNCODE_ESIZE        = -7,
  RETURNCODE_ECANCEL      = -8,
  RETURNCODE_ENOMEM       = -9,
  RETURNCODE_ENOSUPPORT   = -10,
  RETURNCODE_ENODEVICE    = -11,
  RETURNCODE_EUNINSTALLED = -12,
```

```
RETURNCODE_ENOACK      = -13,
RETURNCODE_EBADRVAL    = -1024
} returncode_t;
```

Listing 8-33. The status code represented in Tock style: 0 means success, anything else means a failure

```
// StatusCode from the kernel. Uses same mapping
// for errors as ErrorCode, but
// includes a success case with identifier 0.
typedef enum {
  TOCK_STATUSCODE_SUCCESS     = 0,
  TOCK_STATUSCODE_FAIL        = 1,
  TOCK_STATUSCODE_BUSY        = 2,
  TOCK_STATUSCODE_ALREADY     = 3,
  TOCK_STATUSCODE_OFF         = 4,
  TOCK_STATUSCODE_RESERVE     = 5,
  TOCK_STATUSCODE_INVAL       = 6,
  TOCK_STATUSCODE_SIZE        = 7,
  TOCK_STATUSCODE_CANCEL      = 8,
  TOCK_STATUSCODE_NOMEM       = 9,
  TOCK_STATUSCODE_NOSUPPORT   = 10,
  TOCK_STATUSCODE_NODEVICE    = 11,
  TOCK_STATUSCODE_UNINSTALLED = 12,
  TOCK_STATUSCODE_NOACK       = 13,
} statuscode_t;
```

Generally, Rust and Tock provide a clear difference between an error and success. Functions that might return errors usually use the Return<(), ErrorCode> or a similar return type. This is a problem when it must be encoded in C. The C language convention states that functions usually return integer numbers. A negative number represents failure, while a zero or positive value represents success.

To make the transformation easier, libtock-c provides a convenience function, `tock_status_to_returncode,` to convert the system call return status to a C style error.

In our case, the `command` function returns either `TOCK_SYSCALL_SUCCESS` if the driver is present (Listing 8-29) or `TOCK_SYSCALL_FAILURE` with `ErrorCode::NODEVICE` otherwise. For the library, we only care about the case when the function returns `TOCK_SYSCALL_SUCCESS`. Any other return type is treated as an error, and we consider that the driver does not exist or is not available for some other reason.

Next, we implement the actual character displaying function. The function called `digit_letter_display_show_charaters` takes one single parameter, the actual digit or letter to display. Similar to the previous function, it uses the `command` library function to issue a `command` system call. This time, it specifies command number 1, which represents the display character command (Listing 8-29), and uses the first of the two value arguments to send the digit's or letter's ASCII code. The second value argument is not used and is set to 0.

The `command` system call can only return either `TOCK_SYSCALL_SUCCESS` if the ASCII character is a digit or a letter and can be displayed, or `TOCK_SYSCALL_FAILURE` with `ErrorCode::INVAL` if the character cannot be displayed as it is not a digit or a letter. Our function verifies the return type and returns the result accordingly.

Using the Library Inside the Process

The final step is to write a process that uses the library that we have just created. For this, we create a new process called `display_text`. The easiest way to create a new process is to make a copy of the **example_app** folder inside the **applications** folder.

The source code for the process is now placed in **applications/ display_text/main.c**. Listing 8-34 shows the entire process source code. First, we include the new capsule's header file **digit_letter_display.h**.

Besides the normal standard input-output library (**stdio.h**), we also include **timer.h** from the Tock library. This will provide us with the declaration of the delay_ms function.

Listing 8-34. The process using the DigitLetterDisplay Syscall Capsule

```
#include "digit_letter_display.h"

#include <stdio.h>
#include <timer.h>

const char *DISPLAY_TEXT = "MicroBit";

int main(void) {
 // if(driver_exists(DIGIT_LETTER_DISPLAY...)) {
 if (digit_letter_display_is_present()) {
   for (unsigned int index = 0;
       index < strlen (DISPLAY_TEXT); index++) {
     digit_letter_display_show_character (DISPLAY_TEXT[index]);
     delay_ms (500);
   }
 } else {
   printf ("DigitLetterDisplay Syscall Capsule is not present\n");
 }
}
```

The first action that the process performs is to check if the display driver is present. If so, the process will iterate over the DISPLAY_TEXT variable and print it character by character, waiting 500ms in between.

If the driver is not present, it will show an error message in the console.

Tip   The Tock library exposes a function called `driver_exists` that takes as an argument a driver id and returns whether a driver is present or not. This is the standard way of verifying if a driver exists. We will use this from now on instead of a dedicated function that we define.

All there's left to do is build the kernel with the new driver and the `display_text` process and flash both of them to the micro:bit board.

Run the Project on the Raspberry Pi Pico

The advantage of using an embedded operating system like Tock is that processes and drivers become portable across boards. We have designed and tested the driver using a micro:bit. Now let's see how the driver works when using the Raspberry Pi Pico.

The Hardware Setup

The Raspberry Pi Pico does not have an integrated LED matrix, so we have to attach one to it. For this project, we use a KWM-R30881CUAB LED matrix shown in Figure 8-3. To determine the hardware pins, look at the sides of the LED matrix. One of the sides is printed with the name and type of the LED matrix. The pins closer to that side are pins 1 to 8.

Note   The LED matrix device that we use here is one without a controller. It has 16 pins that directly control the LEDs. Each LED's anode (positive) pin is connected directly to one of the pins. All LEDs from one row are connected to a common cathode (negative) pin.

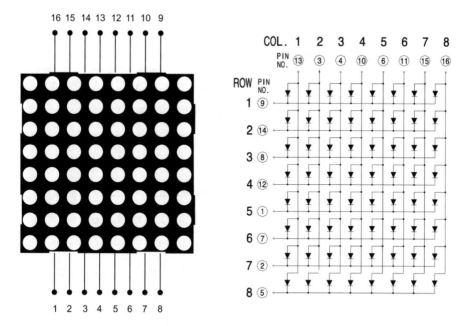

Usually printed on this side: KWM-R30881CUAB

Figure 8-3. *The datasheet of the KWM-R30881CUAB LED matrix*

Having the datasheet in mind, we connect the LED matrix to the Raspberry Pi Pico board. Figure 8-4 displays the complete schematics. We have to use two breadboards as the LED matrix does not fit otherwise. We connect pins GP2, GP3, GP4, GP5, and GP6 to the LED matrix columns 1 to 5 and pins GP7, GP8, GP9, GP10, and GP11 to the LED matrix rows. The exact pin mapping is shown in Table 8-5.

Table 8-5. *Raspberry Pi Pico pins mapping to the LED matrix*

Raspberry Pi Pico Pin	LED Matrix Pin	Description
GP2	13	Controls the anode of LEDs in column 1
GP3	3	Controls the anode of LEDs in column 2
GP4	4	Controls the anode of LEDs in column 3
GP5	10	Controls the anode of LEDs in column 4
GP6	6	Controls the anode of LEDs in column 5
GP7	9	Controls the cathode for LEDs within row 1
GP8	14	Controls the cathode for LEDs within row 2
GP9	8	Controls the cathode for LEDs within row 3
GP10	12	Controls the cathode for LEDs within row 4
GP11	1	Controls the cathode for LEDs within row 5
3V3 (via breadboard)	7	Always turns off row 6
3V3 (via breadboard)	2	Always turns off row 7
3V3 (via breadboard)	5	Always turns off row 8

Each cathode connection has a 220Ω resistor. This limits the current flow through the LEDs and prevents damage to the Raspberry Pi Pico board and the LED.

Note   The LED matrix pins 7, 2, and 5 are connected to the 3.3V pin. While this is not actually needed, it ensures that LEDs in rows 6 to 8 are not lighting up due to electrical interferences.

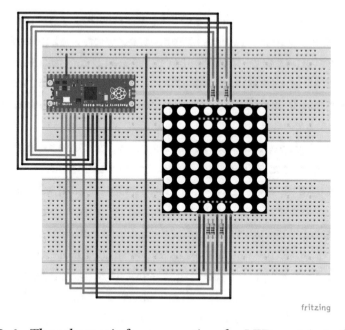

fritzing

Figure 8-4. *The schematic for connecting the LED matrix to the Raspberry Pi Pico*

To upload the firmware and view the console messages, we have to hook up the Raspberry Pi Pico to a regular Raspberry Pi using the instructions provided in chapter 5. This means connecting two serial TX and RX jumper wires between GP0, GP1, and the serial0 pins from the standard Raspberry Pi. We also connect the grounds of the two boards, GND to GND. Finally, we connect the SWD (side) pins of the Raspberry Pi Pico to the GPIO pins of the normal Raspberry Pi.

Setting Up the Driver

To use the LED matrix with the Raspberry Pi Pico and display digits and letters, we have to enable two drivers on the device. First, we have to set up the LED matrix driver, and secondly, set up the DigitLetterDisplay driver and connect it to the LED matrix.

The first action that we take is to copy the **raspberry_pi_pico** folder from **tock/boards** to our project in **kernel/raspberry_pi_pico**. Next, we have to modify the **Cargo.toml** file to reflect the correct paths to the **tock** folder and add the drivers capsule. Before building the kernel from our project, we have to modify the paths to the tock folder in **layout.ld** and **Makefile**.

All these steps are identical to the actions performed for the micro:bit. A detailed description of them was presented in chapter 6.

Now that we have set up the Raspberry Pi Pico board, we register the DigitLetterDisplay driver with the RaspberryPiPico board structure in the **main.rs** file as shown in Listing 8-35. First of all, we import the LedMatrixLed structure that allows us to use single LEDs from the LED matrix. Next, we declare the DigitLetterDisplay driver in the RaspberryPiPico board structure. The data type of the driver is very similar to the one for the micro:bit, just that the Pin and Alarm types are different and specific to the Raspberry Pi Pico.

Listing 8-35. Adding the TextDisplayDriver to the Raspberry Pi Pico board structure

```
use capsules::led_matrix::LedMatrixLed;
// ...
pub struct RaspberryPiPico {
    // ...
    digit_letter_display: &'static drivers::digit_letter_
    display::DigitLetterDisplay<
        'static,
        LedMatrixLed<'static, RPGpioPin<'static>,
        VirtualMuxAlarm<'static, RPTimer<'static>>>,
    >,
}
// ...
```

```
impl SyscallDriverLookup for RaspberryPiPico {
    fn with_driver<F, R>(&self, driver_num: usize, f: F) -> R
    where
        F: FnOnce(Option<&dyn SyscallDriver>) -> R,
    {
        match driver_num {
            // ...            drivers::digit_letter_
            display::DRIVER_NUM =>
        f(Some(self.digit_letter_display)),
            _ => f(None),
        }
    }
}
```

The next step is to add a branch in the match statement within the with_driver function from the SyscallDriverLookup trait. This is the actual registration of the driver with the kernel.

All that is left now is to initialize the driver. This requires three steps that modify the main function. First, we have to disable the GPIO pins that the LED matrix uses from the Gpio driver. This prevents the userspace processes from accidentally using the GPIO pins and overlapping with the functionality of the LED matrix. We simply comment in the pins 2 to 11 as presented in Listing 8-36.

Listing 8-36. Disabling pins 2 to 11 from the Gpio driver

```
let gpio = GpioComponent::new(
 board_kernel,
 components::gpio_component_helper!(
  RPGpioPin,
  // Used for serial communication.
  //Comment them in if you don't use serial.
```

```
//0=>&peripherals.pins.get_pin(RPGpio::GPIO0),
//1=>&peripherals.pins.get_pin(RPGpio::GPIO1),
//2=>&peripherals.pins.get_pin(RPGpio::GPIO2),
//3=>&peripherals.pins.get_pin(RPGpio::GPIO3),
//4=>&peripherals.pins.get_pin(RPGpio::GPIO4),
//5=>&peripherals.pins.get_pin(RPGpio::GPIO5),
//6=>&peripherals.pins.get_pin(RPGpio::GPIO6),
//7=>&peripherals.pins.get_pin(RPGpio::GPIO7),
//8=>&peripherals.pins.get_pin(RPGpio::GPIO8),
//9=>&peripherals.pins.get_pin(RPGpio::GPIO9),
//10=>&peripherals.pins.get_pin(RPGpio::GPIO10),
//11=>&peripherals.pins.get_pin(RPGpio::GPIO11),
 12=>&peripherals.pins.get_pin(RPGpio::GPIO12),
 // ...
 ),
).finalize(components::gpio_component_buf!(
RPGpioPin<'static>));
```

The second step is to initialize the LED matrix driver (Listing 8-37). The code is identical to the one used for the micro:bit, the only difference being the data types of GPIO pins and the Alarm and the activation of the LEDs. As the LED matrix that we use has a common cathode (ground), the columns are *ActiveHigh*, meaning that individual LEDs are lightened up by setting the pins to 1 (HIGH). The rows are *ActiveLow*, in other words, activated by setting the pins to 0 (LOW).

Note   The micro:bit uses a common anode. This means the LEDs are activated by writing 0 (LOW) to the GPIO pins controlling the LEDs and writing 1 (HIGH) to pins controlling the rows. This is the configuration that we would have to use if our LED matrix were KWM-R30881AUAB.

Listing 8-37. The LED Matrix driver initialization

```
// LED Matrix

let led_matrix_driver = components::led_matrix_component_
helper!(
    RPGpioPin<'static>,
    RPTimer<'static>,
    mux_alarm,
    @fps => 60,
    @cols => kernel::hil::gpio::ActivationMode::ActiveHigh,
    &peripherals.pins.get_pin(RPGpio::GPIO2),
    &peripherals.pins.get_pin(RPGpio::GPIO3),
    &peripherals.pins.get_pin(RPGpio::GPIO4),
    &peripherals.pins.get_pin(RPGpio::GPIO5),
    &peripherals.pins.get_pin(RPGpio::GPIO6),
    @rows => kernel::hil::gpio::ActivationMode::ActiveLow,
    &peripherals.pins.get_pin(RPGpio::GPIO7),
    &peripherals.pins.get_pin(RPGpio::GPIO8),
    &peripherals.pins.get_pin(RPGpio::GPIO9),
    &peripherals.pins.get_pin(RPGpio::GPIO10),
    &peripherals.pins.get_pin(RPGpio::GPIO11),
)
.finalize(components::led_matrix_component_buf!(
    RPGpioPin<'static>,
    RPTimer<'static>
));
```

Now that we have initialized the LED matrix driver, we can initialize the DigitLetterDisplay driver that uses the individual LEDs. The code presented in Listing 8-38 is the same as the one used for the micro:bit, except that the GPIO pins and alarm data types are different.

Listing 8-38. Setting up the DigitLetterDriver for the Raspberry
Pi Pico

```
let digit_letter_display = static_init!(
    drivers::digit_letter_display::
      DigitLetterDisplay<
        'static,
        LedMatrixLed<
         'static,
          RPGpioPin<'static>,
          capsules::virtual_alarm::
VirtualMuxAlarm<'static, RPTimer<'static>>,
        >,
      >,
    drivers::digit_letter_display::
DigitLetterDisplay::new(components::
led_matrix_leds!(
    RPGpioPin<'static>,
    capsules::virtual_alarm::VirtualMuxAlarm<'static,
    RPTimer<'static>>,
        led_matrix_driver,
        (0, 0),
        (1, 0),
        // ...
    ))
);
// ...
let raspberry_pi_pico = RaspberryPiPico {
    // ...
    digit_letter_display,
};
}
```

Using the Driver

We have successfully set up the *DigitLetterDisplay* driver for the Raspberry Pi Pico. Due to the fact that we have used an embedded operating system, the changes that we had to make were minimal. All that is left to do is connect the Raspberry Pi Pico to a regular Raspberry Pi board and upload the kernel and the example application. Chapter 5 describes in detail all the steps that are required to perform this action.

One key difference between the Raspberry Pi Pico and the micro:bit is the type of the ARM MCU. Raspberry Pi Pico uses an ARM Cortex-M0+ MCU, while micro:bit uses an ARM Cortex M4 MCU. Tock allows the distribution of binary applications in the format of a TBF file. Since the Raspberry Pi Pico has a different MCU than the micro:bit, we cannot use the same TBF file as the MCU would throw errors due to incompatible instructions. This is where the Tock Application Bundle (TAB) file comes into play. This is a tar archive that contains several TBF files, one for each MCU architecture. While tockloader knows how to use this file, gdb does not.

When loading processes to the Raspberry Pi Pico, we must be careful to select the correct ELF file. We must make sure that we use the file in the **build/cortex-m0** folder.

Note   From the process' point of view, Cortex-M0 and Cortex-M0+ architectures are the same.

Summary

Even though we wrote a relatively simple driver, we have covered a lot of ground in this chapter. We have identified the three types of capsules or drivers that the kernel works with, namely *Syscall capsules*, *service capsules*, and *drivers*.

For each of them, we detailed their meaning and their relevance in Tock's architecture. Furthermore, we presented the system call infrastructure and how system calls are dispatched from the userspace process to a syscall capsule.

Another important aspect we described is how Tock starts and how drivers are initialized and registered with the kernel. You should be familiar now with the API that the kernel provides for driver development.

Last but not least, we provided an example of how to build a library for a Syscall capsule and how to use it in a process.

As writing Tock capsules for the first time can be tricky, we have deliberately used only the command system call. In the following chapters, we will improve our drivers and use the other system calls.

Probably one of the most important takeaways from this chapter is the portability of the drivers and applications. We have two different boards, the micro:bit and the Raspberry Pi Pico that run the same drivers and applications, with no driver or application changes. The only changes that we had to make were in the board implementation. When it comes to the application, we did not even have to recompile it. We have directly used the binary that was previously compiled.

CHAPTER 9

Asynchronous Syscall Capsules

The previous chapter has covered all the details about Tock capsule types and how to develop a simple Syscall capsule. This chapter aims to extend the capsule from chapter 8 and allow it to write more than one character. While the previous capsule version received one character and displayed it, this version will receive a string of characters to display. The capsule will display a digit or letter, wait for a small amount of time, then display the next until it reaches the last character.

To get started, you will need the project built in the previous chapter.

Requirements

This chapter requires the following hardware components based on the device you use:

- **Micro:bit**
    - 1 x micro:bit v2 board
- **Raspberry Pi Pico**
    - 1 x Raspberry Pi Pico board;
    - 1 x KWM-R30881CUAB or KWM-R30881AUAB LED matrix;

© Alexandru Radovici and Ioana Culic 2022
A. Radovici and I. Culic, *Getting Started with Secure Embedded Systems*,
https://doi.org/10.1007/978-1-4842-7789-8_9

- 14 x jumper wires;

- 5 x 220Ω resistors;

- 2 x (or 1 x large) breadboards.

Extending the API

So far, for the first version of the *DigitLetterDisplay* capsule, we have used only the command system call. For the second version presented in this chapter, we make use of all the possible system calls. Table 9-1 illustrates the proposed API.

Table 9-1. *The system call API for the DigitLetterDisplay capsule*

Command			
No **Arg 1**	**Arg 2**	**Description**	**Return**
0 Not used	Not used	Verifies if the capsule is available.	*CommandReturn ::success()*
1 The number of characters that are to be displayed from the allowed buffer.	The inter-character delay value in milliseconds.	Start displaying all the characters from the allowed buffer.	*CommandReturn ::success()* *CommandReturn ::failure(ErrorCode::RESERVE)* *CommandReturn ::failure(ErrorCode::NOMEM)* *CommandReturn ::failure(ErrorCode::SIZE)*

Subscribe	
No **Description**	**Return**
0 Upcall issued when the whole buffer has been displayed.	The previous *Upcall* function that was registered

(continued)

Table 9-1. (*continued*)

Allow		
No	**Description**	**Return**
0	The buffer used to send the characters.	The previous *ProcessBuffer* that was shared

Instead of receiving simple command system calls, this version of the capsule will follow the steps described in Figure 9-1. The userspace has first to allow a buffer containing the text that should be displayed, subscribe for an upcall, send a command and wait for the upcall.

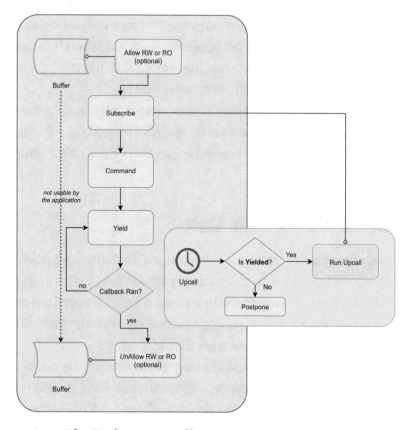

Figure 9-1. *The Tock system call pattern*

The *command* System Call

The first change to be made is to the command system call. This version of the capsule has to receive a string of characters, in other words, a buffer. This is not possible using the command system call, as it has only two 32 bits parameters, which is not enough. To be able to send a buffer, we have to use the allow system call, which we will detail later. The purpose of the command system call here is to ask the capsule to start displaying the digits or letters from the previously allowed buffer.

The two parameters supplied describe the way the text should be displayed. The first parameter tells the capsule how many valid characters are to be displayed from the buffer. Usually, the userspace will allow the same fixed-size buffer for multiple texts. The capsule has no way of knowing how many characters the application actually wants it to display. This parameter cannot be larger than the buffer's size. If this happens, the command system call will fail with ErrorCode::SIZE.

The second parameter that the command system call takes represents the speed at which the characters are displayed. The value represents the number of milliseconds that the capsule will wait between displaying two characters.

The *subscribe* System Call

The subscribe system call is handled automatically by the kernel. We do have to help the kernel a little to be able to perform the subscribe. Pointers to the callback functions registered by a process for each upcall are stored in a table within the grant data region. Before it can store the first callback pointer, the kernel needs the driver to allocate its grant.

When a process sends a subscribe request to a driver, the kernel verifies if the respective driver has an allocated grant. If not, it calls the allocate_grant function to ask the driver to allocate it. Details about this function will be presented in the *Writing the Capsule* section.

The *allow* System Call

Applications need a way to share more data with the drivers than the two 32-bit arguments of the command system call. This is where the allow pair of system calls comes into play. The two system calls, allow_readwrite and allow_readonly provide to the userspace process a mechanism to share buffers with drivers. Both allow system calls receive the same arguments displayed in Table 9-2.

Table 9-2. *The arguments of the allow system call*

Argument	Name	Description
1	*capsule number*	Uniquely identifies the capsule (destination) that the system call targets.
2	*allow number*	Specifies a use for the shared buffer.
3	*buffer*	A pointer to a buffer in the process' memory space.
4	len	The length of the shared buffer.

Similar to command and subscribe, the allow system calls receive the capsule number as the first parameter. This instructs the kernel to which driver to send the system call.

The second argument is the allow number. Based on this number, each driver knows what data should be read and written from and to the buffer. This number gives each buffer a semantic meaning. For instance, a driver that reads and writes information from and to a peripheral might have two allow numbers: number 1 for the output buffer, data sent to the peripheral, and number 2 for the input buffer, data read from the peripheral. The buffer for number 1 is shared using allow_readonly as the driver does not write to it, while the buffer for number 2 is shared using allow_readwrite as the driver has to write to it.

The allow system calls require a little more processing on the kernel side before they can be forwarded to a capsule. Figure 9-2 depicts the flow.

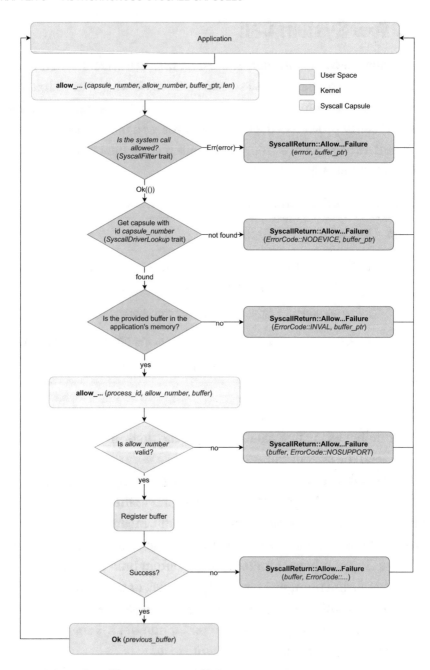

Figure 9-2. *The allow system call flow*

Similar to the command and subscribe system calls, the kernel first asks the board implementation whether it should forward or not the system call. Next, if the call should be sent to the driver, the kernel will request the driver in the board implementation. If it is found, the kernel has to build the shared buffer. This step is unique for the allow system call. It requires the kernel to perform some verifications and generate a Rust type starting from the pointer and length it received.

Before forwarding the system call to the driver, the kernel makes sure that the process has provided a valid buffer. It verifies that the buffer's pointer is within the process flash or memory limits and its length does not exceed the flash or memory allocated to the process. If the verification fails, the kernel will stop the system call and return ErrorCode::INVAL to the process. If the call can be forwarded, the kernel will construct an internal structure of type ReadOnlyAppBuffer or ReadWriteAppBuffer, based on the allow type. This structure, illustrated in Listing 9-1, ties the pointer and length to a process id.

Listing 9-1. The internal kernel application buffer

```
/// Read-only memory region of a process, shared
/// with the kernel
pub struct ReadOnlyProcessBuffer {
    ptr: *const u8,
    len: usize,
    process_id: Option<ProcessId>,
}

/// Read-writable memory region of a process,
/// shared with the kernel
pub struct ReadWriteAppSlice {
    ptr: *mut u8,
    len: usize,
    process_id: Option<ProcessId>,
}
```

The kernel's next step is to call one of the `allow` functions within the capsule's `SyscallDriver` trait. This function receives the calling process id, the allow number, and the buffer of type `ReadOnlyAppBuffer` or `ReadWriteAppBuffer`.

Upon receiving an `allow` system call, the capsule verifies the `allow` number. If it is valid, the capsule tries to store the received buffer and return the previous one. If the capsule does not validate the `allow` number or cannot store the received buffer, it returns an error together with the received buffer.

The `ReadOnlyAppBuffer` and `ReadWriteAppBuffer` structures have an optional `process id` parameter. This informs the kernel whether the buffer is valid or not. A buffer without a process id (value `None`) is considered invalid. This behavior is because `allow` system calls have to return the previously shared buffer. When no buffers are shared, the capsule uses `ReadOnlyAppBuffer::default()` or `ReadWriteAppBuffer::default()` buffers that have the process id set to `None`. Returning one of these buffers will make the kernel return a `null` value to the application.

Caution   Processes are not allowed to access buffers that are shared with a driver. To access any of these buffers, a process has to reclaim (`unallow`) them either by sharing another buffer or a `null` value. The kernel does not enforce this. Not respecting this rule might lead to strange behaviors.

Capsule Architecture

Once we have established all the necessary system calls, it is time to describe how the driver works. Figure 9-3 shows the flow necessary to display a piece of text from a process.

First of all, the process sends system calls to the TextDisplay driver. In turn, the driver uses the Led HIL to communicate with the LEDs in LedMatrix. This is identical to the previous capsule that we have created.

What is different about this new driver is that it cannot perform the printing task directly from within the command system call. In contrast, it needs to print one character, wait for an amount of time, print the next character, and so on. To be able to wait, the driver uses the Alarm trait.

First of all, the process shares with the driver the buffer containing the text. The buffer is shared using allow_readonly as the driver does not need to write to it, it only reads each character and prints it.

As the task of printing a text takes some time (each letter is printed individually, and a delay between letters is used), the action cannot be performed with the command system call. The process will subscribe to the capsule to be notified when the printing has finished.

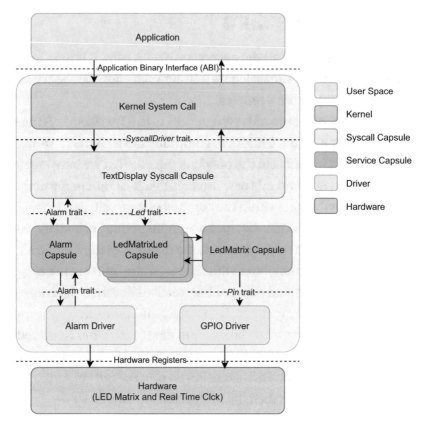

Figure 9-3. *The TextDisplay capsule architecture*

If allowing the buffer and subscribing to the done event are successful, the process issues a command system call to ask the driver to start printing the text. The driver receives the command system call, starts the printing, and immediately returns to the process. In the background, the driver performs the printing task. After the last letter or digit is printed, the driver schedules an upcall for the process.

In turn, the process has two possible ways to continue: it does something else in between and checks from time to time if the driver has scheduled an upcall, or it waits until it receives the upcall from the driver.

Asynchronous Tock Drivers

Tock drivers use a *split-phase* or *asynchronous* implementation when performing tasks. Figure 9-4 displays the functioning of the *TextDisplay* capsule that we detail in this section.

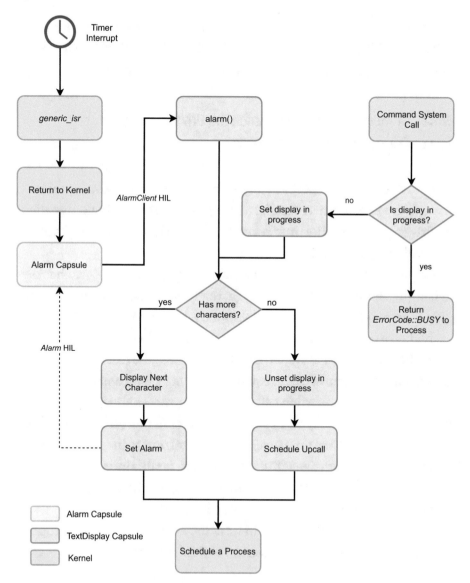

Figure 9-4. *The TextDisplay capsule's asynchronous flow*

The action starts when the process issues a command system call and asks the driver to start printing the text from the shared buffer. First of all, the driver verifies if it has another activity in progress. If so, the command returns ErrorCode::BUSY and the process will have to retry the command later.

If there is no other display in progress, the driver verifies that it has a buffer to display from and, if so, starts the displaying. It flags that it now has a displaying in progress and returns success to the process.

Note   If there is no allowed buffer, the driver will return ErrorCode::NOMEM to the process.

The driver does not perform any actions in the *background* as there is no way a driver can run in parallel with a process. Tock is single-threaded. The driver *splits* the action into several smaller actions and interleaves them with the processes.

Just before it returns from the command system call, the driver checks if it has any characters left to display (actually if the length of the supplied buffer is greater than 0). If so, it displays a character, and asks the Alarm to schedule a callback for the driver after several milliseconds. It then returns from the command system call. In a nutshell, the driver displays a character and asks the alarm to call the driver back after some time.

When the command system call returns, the process and the kernel resume their regular activity. At some point later in time, the alarm system, controlled by the MCU's timer, will send an interrupt to the MCU. The kernel has registered the generic_isr function for this interrupt. As soon as the interrupt fires, the MCU will execute the generic_isr function, suspending any running process, exiting the interrupt mode, and transferring control to the kernel. In turn, the kernel reads the interrupt information and forwards the interrupt to its alarm driver.

The alarm driver then calls the TextDisplay driver using the AlarmClient HIL. When the TextDisplay driver receives the alarm function call, it verifies if it has any characters left to display. If it does, it displays a new character and schedules another alarm. It then returns control to the kernel, which in turn returns control to the process that was running when the interrupt fired.

Note   The kernel might not transfer the control back to the same process that was running when the interrupt fired. It is the kernel's scheduler that will decide who gets the control back right away.

If all the text has been displayed, meaning that there are no more characters left to show, the driver schedules an *upcall* for the process and marks that it has no display action in progress.

The process that has requested the text display might not get notified immediately. Whenever a driver schedules an upcall, it actually asks the kernel to add an upcall to the queue. Each process has a queue of scheduled tasks. Whenever the process yields (uses the yield system call), the kernel verifies if there is any upcall in the processes' task queue. If so, that upcall is fired, and the process executes the function registered for it. Whenever that function returns, the control returns in the process right after the yield system call.

If no upcall is scheduled in the queue, the process is suspended (placed into the *Yielded* state) until an upcall is scheduled. When using the yield system call, the process can ask the kernel not to suspend it if there is no scheduled upcall. This is done using the yield's system call argument.

Writing the Capsule

Now that we have described how our capsule works, we can start writing the code. We create the new capsule, set up an alarm used for the delay between each character, store an upcall to the process, and signal the process when the display of the text is done.

Defining the Capsule's Data Structures

As this capsule is an improved version of the DigitLetterDisplay capsule described in the previous chapter, we use it as the starting point. First of all, we create a new file called **text_display.rs** in the **project/kernel/drivers** folder. The initial contents of the file is displayed in Listing 9-2.

Listing 9-2. The initial TextDisplay driver

```
use core::cell::Cell;
use core::mem;
use kernel::grant::Grant;
use kernel::hil::led::Led;
use kernel::hil::time::{
    Alarm, AlarmClient, ConvertTicks
};
use kernel::process::{Error, ProcessId};
use kernel::processbuffer::{
    ReadOnlyProcessBuffer,
    ReadableProcessBuffer
};
use kernel::syscall::{
    CommandReturn, SyscallDriver
};
use kernel::utilities::cells::OptionalCell;
use kernel::ErrorCode;

pub const DRIVER_NUM: usize = 0xa0002;

#[derive(Default)]
pub struct AppData {
    buffer: ReadOnlyProcessBuffer,
    position: usize,
```

```
    len: usize,
    delay_ms: usize,
}

pub struct TextDisplay<'a, L: Led, A: Alarm<'a>> {
    leds: &'a [&'a L; 25],
    alarm: &'a A,
    grant: Grant<AppData, 1>,
    in_progress: Cell<bool>,
    process_id: OptionalCell<ProcessId>,
}

impl<
      'a, L: Led, A: Alarm<'a>
> TextDisplay<'a, L, A> {
    pub fn new(
          leds: &'a [&'a L; 25],
          alarm: &'a A,
          grant: Grant<AppData, 1>
    ) -> Self {
     TextDisplay {
      leds,
      alarm,
      grant,
      in_progress: Cell::new(false),
      process_id: OptionalCell::empty(),
     }
    }
    // ...
}
```

Similar to the previous driver, we define a new structure called TextDisplay. In addition to the lifetime and L trait parameters, the structure receives another generic parameter A bound to the Alarm trait. This makes it possible for the driver to schedule a callback after a couple of milliseconds.

We declare the following fields within the structure: leds, alarm, grant, in_progress, and len. Further on, we detail each of them.

The *leds* Field

Similar to the previous driver, we define the leds reference to an array of LEDs. This allows the capsule to control each LED separately.

The *alarm* Field

The alarm field is a reference to a data type that implements the Alarm trait illustrated in Listing 9-3. This allows the capsule to schedule a callback from the underlying alarm system after a certain amount of time.

Listing 9-3. The Alarm and AlarmClient traits

```
/// Callback handler for when an Alarm fires (a
/// `Counter` reaches a specific value).
pub trait AlarmClient {
    fn alarm(&self);
}

pub trait Alarm<'a>: Time {
    /// Specify the callback for when the counter
    ///reaches the alarm value.
    fn set_alarm_client(&'a self, client: &'a dyn AlarmClient);
```

```
/// Specify when the callback should be
///called and enable it.
fn set_alarm(
  &self,
  reference: Self::Ticks,
  dt: Self::Ticks
);

/// Return the current alarm value.
fn get_alarm(&self) -> Self::Ticks;

/// Disable the alarm and stop it from firing
/// in the future.
fn disarm(&self) -> Result<(), ErrorCode>;

/// Returns whether the alarm is currently
/// armed.
fn is_armed(&self) -> bool;

/// Return the minimum dt value that is
/// supported.
fn minimum_dt(&self) -> Self::Ticks;
}
```

After each letter is displayed to the LED matrix, the driver uses the
alarm to ask for a callback after the *inter-character* time provided by the
process that has requested the display. Whenever the hardware alarm fires,
the underlying driver calls the alarm function from the AlarmClient trait.

The *grant* Field

Another important field is grant. We discussed in chapter 3 about the grants. These are memory regions that reside within a process' memory. Figure 9-5 describes the location of the grant in the process' memory, while Figure 9-6 shows the grant's format.

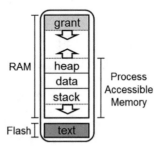

Figure 9-5. *The Tock 's' process memory layout*

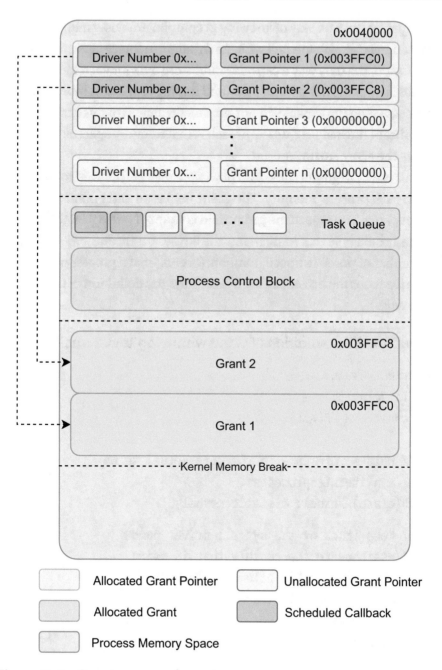

Figure 9-6. Grant memory layout

Capsules have no way of knowing at compile time how many applications they will interact with. As dynamic memory allocation is not allowed, the only way a capsule could store data for each individual process is by using a fixed-size array and hoping that the number of processes using the capsule do not surpass the length of this array. A significant downside of this approach is that memory space is wasted if parts of the array are never used.

This is where grants come into play. Capsules are allowed to store data in each process' memory. The grant field is an entry point to such a memory area. The type of the grant field is Grant<T, NUM_UPCALLS>, T being any data type that implements the Default trait, and NUM_UPCALLS the number of possible upcall numbers (events) that a process can subscribe to for the driver. Listing 9-4 displays the definition of the Grant type.

Listing 9-4. The definition of Grant within the Tock kernel

```
pub struct Grant<
    T: Default,
    const NUM_UPCALLS: usize
> {
    /// Hold a reference to the core kernel so we
    /// can iterate processes.
    pub(crate) kernel: &'static Kernel,

    /// Keep track of the syscall driver number
    /// assigned to the capsule that is using
    /// this grant. This allows us to uniquely
    /// identify upcalls stored in
    /// this grant.
    driver_num: usize,
```

```
    /// The identifier for this grant. Having an
    /// identifier allows the Process
    /// implementation to lookup the memory for
    /// this grant in the specific process.
    grant_num: usize,

    /// Used to keep the Rust type of the grant.
    ptr: PhantomData<T>,
}

impl<
    T: Default,
    const NUM_UPCALLS: usize
> Grant<T, NUM_UPCALLS> {
  /// Create a new `Grant` type which allows a
  /// capsule to store process-specific data for
  /// each process in the process's memory
  /// region.
    pub(crate) fn new(
      kernel: &'static Kernel,
      grant_index: usize
    ) -> Grant<T> {
        Grant {
            kernel: kernel,
            driver_num: driver_num,
            grant_num: grant_index,
            ptr: PhantomData,
        }
    }
```

```
/// Enter the grant for a specific process.
pub fn enter<F, R>(
  &self, processid: ProcessId,
  fun: F
) -> Result<R, Error>
where
    F: FnOnce(
        &mut GrantData<T>,
        &GrantUpcallTable
    ) -> R,
{
    // ...
}

/// Enter the grant for a specific process
/// with access to an allocator.
pub fn enter_with_allocator<F, R>(
  &self,
  processid: ProcessId,
  fun: F
) -> Result<R, Error>
where
    F: FnOnce(
        &mut GrantData<T>,
        &GrantUpcallTable,
        &mut GrantRegionAllocator
    ) -> R,
{
    // ...
}
```

```
/// Run a function on the grant for each
/// active process if the grant has been
/// allocated for that process.
pub fn each<F>(&self, fun: F)
where
    F: Fn(
        ProcessId,
        &mut GrantData<T>,
        &GrantUpcallTable
    ),
{
    // ...
}

/// Get an iterator over all processes and
/// their active grant regions for this
/// particular grant.
pub fn iter(&self) -> Iter<T> {
    // ...
}
}
```

By taking a look at its definition, we realize that the grant structure does not actually own or keep any reference to the data type T. PhantomData is just a placeholder for an empty data structure (size 0) that makes the structure behave as if it were storing a data type T. This allows the compiler to compute several safety properties. The compiler will complain about the type T not being used otherwise.

Note   The new function is defined as pub(crate), which means it can be called only from the same crate where Grant is defined. This is the kernel crate and means that only the kernel can create a new grant.

The grant field is just an entry point to the memory stored in the grant area. As shown in Listing 9-4, Grant exposes the enter and each functions, each of them receiving a closure as an argument. The actual grant data is shown in Figure 9-7. This stores a data type T, the generic type of Grant, and a list with NUM_UPCALLS pairs storing the callback pointer and user data for each possible upcall.

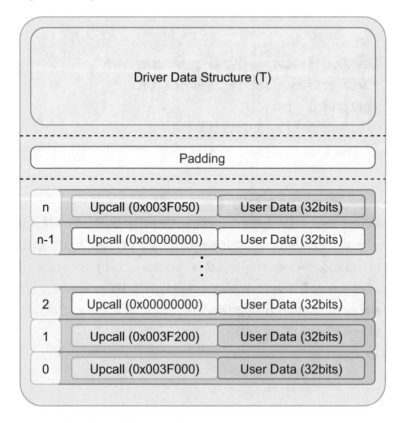

Figure 9-7. *The driver's grant layout*

When a capsule calls enter upon a grant, it has to provide a process_id and a closure as arguments. First, the kernel verifies if the process still exists. If not, the enter function returns an error. Suppose the process is valid, the kernel checks if the grant data is allocated within the respective process. If not, it tries to allocate it. Upon success, the kernel calls the closure and provides two arguments: the first one of type &mut GrantData<T> which is automatically dereferenced to &mut T and the second one of type &GrantUpcallTable. The lifetimes of these references are valid only within the closure.

Note   Each grant type is identified by a unique number and contains the grant data and the upcalls table. When we talk about the grant, we usually talk about a T type of memory space that might be present in a process' memory. Think of a grant as a data type. When we talk about an allocated grant, we talk about an actual memory space within a process (the *variable*).

The grant exposes another important function called each. This allows capsules to iterate over all the grants stored in every process and access the data. This driver is not making use of this function. Similar to each, the grant provides the iter function which returns an iterator performing the same task as each, but that allows the grant to be used within Rust standard iterations like a for statement.

Note   In theory, the generic data type that Grant expects as an argument may be anything with a compile-time size. The Default trait bound is necessary as grants are automatically initialized by the kernel and, without the Default trait, the kernel would not know how to do that.

For instance, [u8] does not have a size at compile-time, as the compiler has no way of knowing the length of the slice, in contrast with [u8; 5] that has a defined size of 5.

How *subscribe* Works

The subscribe system call is automatically implemented by the kernel. When allocating the grant, the kernel allocates an array of NUM_UPCALLS elements. Each element contains a function pointer and a usize user data.

Following the same flow as for the allow and command system calls, the kernel asks the board implementation if it should allow the subscribe. If the subscribe is allowed, the kernel searches for the requested driver. If the driver is registered, the system call is not actually forwarded to the driver, but the kernel tries to execute it.

Registering a callback function requires an allocated grant for the driver. For technical reasons, the kernel is not able to allocate the grant entirely itself. The problem is the size of the T data. The kernel has no way of knowing the actual size of a grant, as it does not have access to its generic data type. The grant is defined as Grant<T>, and while the kernel has access to the Grant structure, it has no way of knowing the actual data type that a driver has used for T. This is why the driver has to implement the allocate_grant function.

The kernel checks if the driver's grant for the requesting process has been allocated. If not, it calls the driver's allocate_grant function. All that the driver has to do within that function is to enter the grant. As the enter function is called with the actual Grant<AppData> type, the kernel now knows the exact size of the grant and is able to allocate it.

If the grant has been allocated, the kernel will try to register the callback. If not, it will report an error to the process. The complete flow is displayed in Figure 9-8. The kernel actually performs some additional verifications that have been omitted as they are not essential.

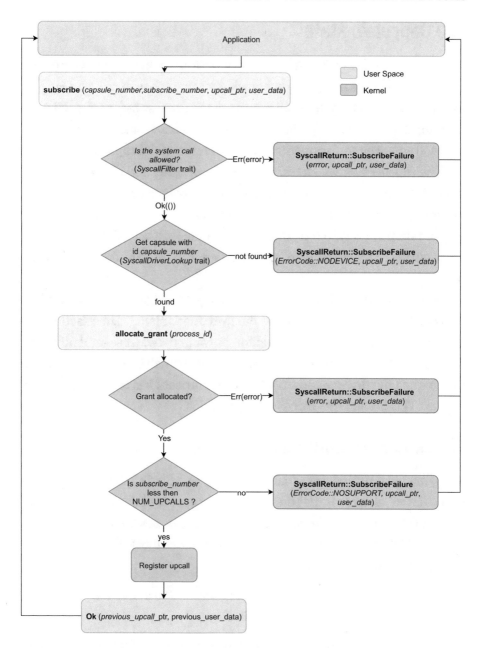

Figure 9-8. *The subscribe system call flow*

The Capsule's State

This capsule uses a *split-phase* system to perform actions. When a process issues a command, the capsule acknowledges that it has to perform an action. The command system call returns to the process before the action is performed. Unlike the previous capsule, which was stateless and any command was executed immediately, this version of the capsule has states.

The capsule has two states. Let's call them *ready* and *displaying*. The driver is in the *ready* state when there is no display in progress and the *displaying* state when a display is in progress.

The simplest way to represent the two states is a bool field named in_progress. This stores whether the driver is in the middle of displaying a text or not.

When the driver displays a text, it displays one digit or letter at a time, waits for an interval, then displays the next digit or letter. These actions are not performed within a single function but split between several function calls and callbacks. Due to technical reasons that will be described later in the chapter, the driver needs to store which process has requested the text display. This is what the process_id field does.

The Data Stored for Each Process

The grant used by this driver stores a data type called AppData. The first thing that we observe is that the compiler is capable of deriving the Default trait for this structure. This is possible out of the box as all the structure's fields are either primitive data types or implement the Default trait. For each process, the capsule stores:

- *buffer* - a buffer shared by the process that stores the characters that the driver displays;

- *upcall* - the upcall that the driver schedules when it has finished displaying all the characters;

- *position* - stores the current position within the buffer; whenever the process sends a `command` system call to ask the driver to start displaying characters, the driver resets the *position* to 0; after displaying each character, the driver increments the *position;*

- *len* - the number of characters in the buffer to display; the shared buffer might have a larger capacity than the actual number of characters that the process asks the driver to display;

- *delay_ms* - the number of milliseconds to wait between displaying two characters; the process provides this value as the second argument to the `command` system call.

When the capsule enters the grant the first time, the kernel will create a new grant data and initialize all the fields of `AppData` with their default value. For numbers, this value is 0. For upcall, it is a `null` function, and for buffers, it is a `null` buffer. Scheduling a `null` upcall results in no action from the kernel, so drivers can safely schedule it. The kernel simply does not schedule anything.

Using a `null` buffer will result in an error for the driver, so drivers have to ensure they have a valid buffer before using it. The way the buffer is accessed is similar to the `grant`, so there is no risk of invalid memory access.

Note   The name of the data type used by the grant is not relevant. Most drivers will name it `AppData`.

Storing the Buffer

The first action a process has to perform to display a text is to write it into a buffer and share it in a read-only manner with the capsule. This is where we use the allow_readonly function to define the SyscallDriver trait. Instead of using the default implementation that always returns an error, our capsule defines its custom implementation (Listing 9-5).

Listing 9-5. Storing the read-only shared buffer in the application's grant data

```
impl<
     'a, L: Led, A: Alarm<'a>
> Driver for TextDisplay<'a, L, A> {
 fn allow_readonly(
   &self,
   process_id: ProcessId,
   allow_number: usize,
   mut buffer: ReadOnlyProcessBuffer,
 ) -> Result<
         ReadOnlyProcessBuffer,
         (ReadOnlyProcessBuffer, ErrorCode)
     > {
     match allow_number {
      0 => {
        let res = self.grant.enter(
           process_id,
           |app, _| {
              mem::swap(
                  &mut app.buffer,
                  &mut buffer
              );
```

```
                app.len = 0;
                app.position = 0;
                app.delay_ms = 0;
            }
        );
        match res {
          Ok(()) => Ok(buffer),
          Err(err) => Err((buffer, err.into())),
          }
        }
        _ =>
Err((buffer, ErrorCode::NOSUPPORT)),
      }
    }
    // ...
}
```

The allow_readonly function returns a Result that contains the previously shared buffer in case the allow system call succeeds, or a tuple with the newly received buffer and an ErrorCode otherwise. In other words, this function swaps buffers. Whenever a process shares a new buffer with a capsule, it performs a swap. If the share is successful, the process gets back the previous buffer (that might be null). Otherwise, it receives the supplied buffer and an error.

The function receives three parameters: the *process id* of the process that has requested the allow, an *allow number* representing the meaning of the buffer (the driver needs to know how to use the data from the buffer), and the *buffer* wrapped in the kernel's ReadOnlyProcessBuffer type. The process_id is necessary as the capsule will have to enter the grant data of the calling process. The buffer is wrapped in a kernel's structure due to security reasons. Drivers are never allowed to access a process' memory directly.

First of all, the capsule will check the `allow` number. As described in Table 9-1, the only `allow` number recognized by this driver is 0. If the process supplied another number, the driver simply returns an error containing the buffer provided and `ErrorCode::NOSUPPORT`.

If the allow number is 0, the driver must store the provided buffer and return the previous one. This is where the grant data is used. To access the data stored for each process, we call the `enter` function for the grant with the received `process_id`. The kernel tries to access the grant for us and, if it succeeds, calls the closure that we supplied. Within the closure, we receive a parameter called `app`. This indirectly represents a mutable reference to the `AppData` structure stored within the calling process' memory.

Note   The memory inside the process' grant data can only be accessed from within the `enter` closure.

Upon accessing the grant, the driver swaps the previous buffer `app.buffer` with the newly provided `buffer`. The `swap` function defined in the `core::mem` module effectively swaps the memory contents stored at the locations provided by the two arguments.

Besides storing the buffer, the driver resets all the other data stored within the grant. This reset is a significant action as the driver might be right in the middle of writing another buffer to the display. The process might have shared another buffer earlier, might have issued a display command, and might have decided not to wait for the *upcall* before unsharing or sharing another buffer.

The driver's state, in this case, is waiting for the alarm in between characters. By resetting all the position and length values, whenever the alarm callback arrives, the driver will realize that it has finished displaying characters as `position` will have the same value as `len`. This will become more clear later in the chapter as we discuss the actual process of displaying characters.

The match statement following the enter function call is necessary as enter returns Result<(), Error> which is different from the return type that allow expects. If entering and accessing the grant data is possible, the enter function will return Ok(()). Otherwise, it will return Err(Error) with one of the variants shown in Listing 9-6.

By using match, we transform the returned value into what allow expects. In case of an error, we use the into function to transform the Error into an ErrorCode. This is possible as ErrorCode implements the From<Error> trait.

Listing 9-6. The process Error, the full error type is kernel::process::Error

```
pub enum Error {
    NoSuchApp,
    OutOfMemory,
    AddressOutOfBounds,
    /// The process is inactive (likely in a
    /// fault or exit state) and the attempted
    /// operation is therefore invalid.
    InactiveApp,
    /// This likely indicates a bug in the kernel
    /// and that some state is inconsistent in
    /// the kernel.
    KernelError,
    /// Indicates some process data, such as a
    /// Grant, is already borrowed.
    AlreadyInUse,
}
```

```
impl From<Error> for ErrorCode {
 fn from(err: Error) -> ErrorCode {
  match err {
    Error::OutOfMemory => ErrorCode::NOMEM,
    Error::AddressOutOfBounds => ErrorCode::INVAL,
    Error::NoSuchApp => ErrorCode::INVAL,
    Error::InactiveApp => ErrorCode::FAIL,
    Error::KernelError => ErrorCode::FAIL,
    Error::AlreadyInUse => ErrorCode::FAIL,
  }
 }
}
```

The compiler infers the Ok(()) return type for enter due to the last empty statement inside the closure. The last visible statement ends with ;.

Caution   Grants cannot be entered recursively. Any call to enter will fail with Error::AlreadyInUse if it is called directly or indirectly from another enter closure.

Executing the Commands

Once the process shares a buffer and subscribes for the upcall, it is time to send the actual command to the driver. This system call tries to start the display action (Listing 9-7).

Listing 9-7. The command system call that starts the displaying of the text

```
impl<
     'a, L: Led, A: Alarm<'a>
> Driver for TextDisplay<'a, L, A> {
 // ...
 fn command(
  &self,
  command_number: usize,
  r2: usize,
  r3: usize,
  process_id: ProcessId,
 ) ->
  CommandReturn {
   match command_number {
    0 => CommandReturn::success(),
    1 => {
        if !self.in_progress.get() {
         let res = self.grant.enter(
            process_id,
            |app, _| {
              if app.buffer.len() > 0 {
                if app.buffer.len() >= r2 {
                  app.position = 0;
                  app.len = r2;
                  app.delay_ms = r3;
                  Ok(())
                } else {
                  Err(ErrorCode::SIZE)
                }
```

```
            } else {
                Err(ErrorCode::NOMEM)
            }
        }
    );
    match res {
     Ok(Ok(())) => {
        self.process_id.set(process_id);
        self.in_progress.set(true);
        self.display_next();
        CommandReturn::success()
     }
     Ok(Err(err))=>
        CommandReturn::failure(err),
     Err(err) =>
        CommandReturn::failure(err.into()),
    }
   } else {
      CommandReturn::failure(ErrorCode::BUSY)
            }
   }
  _ =>  CommandReturn::failure(
ErrorCode::NOSUPPORT),
     }
   }
}
```

Like the previous version of the driver, the command number 0 signals the process of the driver's existence. It always returns CommandReturn::success().

Most of the action performed by this driver is within command number 1. First of all, we have to check whether there is another action in progress, which means that the driver has previously received a display command and is executing it right now. If so, we simply return an error to the process informing it that another displaying action is in progress.

If the road is clear and no other display is in progress, we can start a new display action. Before we dive into the code, let's detail the command's parameters.

As described in Table 9-1, the r2 parameter represents the text length that should be displayed. This must be smaller or equal to the length of the previously shared buffer. The r3 parameter represents the speed at which the text will be displayed. Technically speaking, it is the time that the driver has to wait in between characters.

Before we can start the actual displaying of characters, we have to make sure that we have a buffer and that it can store the number of characters that the application wants to display. We use the enter function to access the grant data. Within the closure supplied to enter, the first action is to check whether the buffer exists, in other words, if the process has shared one. The kernel data structure that provides access to a buffer, ReadOnlyProcessBuffer, does not have a None value. Just like the Grant, the data structure is just the entry point towards the buffer. As such, this data structure always exists. The question that we have to answer is whether it wraps a buffer or not. We do this by checking the buffer's length. If it is 0, that means the application has not shared anything, so we immediately return ErrorCode::NOMEM.

If we do have a shared buffer, the next action that we take is to check its length and compare it to the size the process has sent us via r2. If the length of the buffer is smaller than what the process has asked us to display, we cannot perform the display action and return ErrorCode::SIZE.

If the buffer is large enough, the displaying can be started. We reset the current position to 0, as the next character that should be displayed from the buffer is at position 0 (the first character), and memorize the length and speed within the AppData. As we are ready to display, we return Ok(()).

An important aspect here is the return type of the enter function, implicitly the return type of closure we have provided. The enter function returns Result<R, Error>. This means that if enter cannot access the grant data, it returns Err(Error), Error being one of the kernel errors. This is different from ErrorCode. On the other hand, the R data type is up to us. The compiler will replace it with whatever type is returned by the closure.

The enter function returns an error only if it cannot access the grant data. Otherwise, it considers that enter was successful. This is not enough for us, as the actual display action can fail due to other reasons, such as wrong parameters or an inexistent buffer. This is why the closure returns Result<(), ErrorCode>. Now, if we replace the R type with the actual return type, our enter function will return Result<Result<(), ErrorCode>, Error>.

The driver considers a success only the case when this value is Ok(Ok(())), in other words, if both Result types return Ok. We use a match statement to unwrap the return type and return a success or failure to the process. If the returned value is Ok(Ok(())), we can start the displaying of characters, all the data is in place.

First, we keep the process_id of the process that called the display action as we will need it in the future to access the grant data space. Next, we mark that the driver has a display in progress by setting the in_progress field to true. Before returning CommandReturn::success(), we ask the driver to display the next character using the display_next function presented in the next section.

If the returned value is Ok(Err(err)), err being an ErrorCode, we report the failure to the application together with the err value. If the enter function has failed, the returned value is Err(err), where err is of type Error. We return a failure to the process together with the err value converted to an ErrorCode.

The Text Display

The last section of this driver represents the actual display of characters to the LED matrix. We start from the implementation of the previous driver, to which we add the display_next function. Its purpose is to extract the next character from the process' buffer, send it to the display function, and set the alarm for the requested time interval. The code is presented in Listings 9-8, 9-9 and 9-12.

This function's first action is to check if the driver has a displaying action in progress. Technically, this function should never be called if no display action is in progress. But it's safer to do this check.

Listing 9-8. Displaying the characters using the LED matrix

```
impl<
    'a, L: Led, A: Alarm<'a>
> TextDisplay<'a, L, A> {
  pub fn new(
    leds: &'a [&'a L; 25],
    alarm: &'a A,
    grant: Grant<AppData>
) -> Self {
    /* ... */
  }
```

```
fn display_next(&self) {
  if self.in_progress.get() {
    self.process_id.map_or_else(
      || {
        self.in_progress.set(false);
        // panic!("..., no process id");
      },
      |process_id| {
        // ... display next character
        // shown in listing 9-9
      },
    );
  }
}

fn print(&self, glyph: u32) {
  /* ... */
}

fn clear(&self) {
  /* ... */
}

fn display(&self, character: char) ->
          Result<(), ErrorCode> {
  /* ... */
}
}
```

If we do have a display action in progress, we need to ensure we have
stored the process_id. This is the id of the process that has requested
the display of the text. We need it as all the information about the current
status of the displaying action is stored within the process' grant data.

We use the map_or_else function of the OptionalCell to unwrap the value of process id. Technically speaking, if we make no mistake, this value should always be present. In other words, the OptionalCell storing the process id should always have a value stored at this point.

To make sure our capsule returns an error in case it cannot perform the display action, we use map_or_else. The first parameter is a closure that gets called when the process id has no value. While this should happen only if we make a mistake, it is better to handle it than allow it to fail silently. First, we set the in_progress field to false as there is no way we can continue to display characters (we have no process id, so we cannot enter the grant data). Optionally, we could panic and stop the kernel and ask it to print some debug information. While this is allowed while debugging, in a production environment, the kernel should never stop. This is why we have commented in the panic line.

If we have a process id, we can continue. The map_or_else function will call the closure supplied as the second argument. The parameter that this closure receives is a reference to the process id owned by OptionalCell. We only borrow it for the time the closure executes.

The following actions are shown in Listing 9-9. First, we enter the grant data. One thing that is worth mentioning is the way we provide the process_id. While for the SyscallDriver functions, we used process_id directly, here we use a dereferenced value, *process_id. This is because we received a reference to it from the closure parameter.

Note   Even though we might encounter errors when we are outside (the closure function that allows us to access) the processes' grant data, we do not notify the process. While this seems to be a silent failure, there is no way to notify the process outside the closure that gives us access to the grant data and the upcalls table.

Once inside the grant data closure, we must check whether we still have some characters left to print. By comparing the current position and the length of the text, we establish if we have displayed the whole text or if there is still some processing to do. If there is still work to do, we need to extract another character from the buffer, increment the current position and display the character.

Listing 9-9. Displaying the next character

```
let res = self.grant.enter(
  *process_id,
  |app, upcalls| {
    if app.position < app.len {
      let res = app.buffer.enter(|buffer| {
        let _ = self.display(
                            buffer[app.position].get()
                              as char
        );
        self.alarm.set_alarm(
              self.alarm.now(),
              A::ticks_from_ms(app.delay_ms as u32),
        );
        true
      }).unwrap_or (false);
      // signal the process (listing 9-12)
    } else {
      self.in_progress.set(false);
      upcalls.schedule_upcall(0, (0, 0, 0));
    }
  }
);
```

```
match res {
  Ok(()) => {}
  Err(_) => self.in_progress.set(false),
}
```

If the displaying is done, meaning the current position is greater or equal to the length of the text, we set the in_progress field to false and schedule an upcall for the process.

Scheduling an upcall is done using the second parameter of the enter closure. This is the upcalls table. Just like for the command and allow system calls, a subscribe from a process maps a callback function pointer to a subscribe number. The upcalls table provides the schedule_upcall function to schedule an upcall. This function takes two arguments: the first is the subscribe number for which the driver wants to schedule the upcall. The second argument is a tuple of three values sent to the process.

Tock does not define the meaning of the three tuple values, it is left up to the capsule and its userspace library to decide. In our example, we use only the first value for reporting the status. A value of 0 means that the display is complete.

Note   The schedule_upcall function returns a Result<(), Error>. If scheduling the upcall fails, Error is the reason why the upcall could not be scheduled. To prevent the compiler from complaining that we do not verify the error, we store the error into an anonymous variable _. While silent failures are not a good way of doing things, for simplicity, this example will assume upcalls always get scheduled.

Accessing the buffer is not straightforward. The actual buffer is wrapped in a kernel's structure that gives us access to the actual byte array only within a closure supplied as an argument to the enter function.

This is so complicated for a reason. The driver performs all the actions asynchronously, meaning that the process can freely execute any code while the driver is displaying characters. Nothing stops a process from unallowing or swapping the buffer while the driver has a displaying action in progress. Suppose the driver had direct access to the buffer and could keep a reference to it while the action was carried out. There could be a situation where the process has swapped the buffer, and the driver still uses the older reference.

This is why the kernel enforces the use of the buffer only within the closure. As long as the closure executes, as Tock is running on a single-core, no other process can run in parallel. The reference to the buffer that the closure receives has an anonymous lifetime valid only for as long as the closure runs. In a nutshell, all the interaction with the buffer's bytes has to be done inside the closure.

As soon as we are inside the closure, we are ready to display the character. We get the character at the current position from the buffer and send it to the `display` function. The `display` function is the same as the one presented in the previous chapter. If the character is a valid digit or letter, the function will set up the LEDs to display it. If not, the function will turn off all the LEDs, displaying no character.

The buffer that stores the characters is defined as a slice of `Cell<u8>`. This is why we have to use the `get` function to access the u8 value. The decision to store the buffer as `[Cell<u8>]` instead of `mut [u8]` is because of Rust's borrowing rules. These rules state that there may be only one single mutable reference to a value at any given time. For shared process buffers, this is not true. While the kernel has one single reference to the mutable buffer, the process that shares the buffer keeps another mutable reference. Wrapping the u8 values into `Cell` solves the problem by using interior mutability.

For simplicity, we do not take into account if the character can be displayed or not. We will just assume that the process sends valid characters. To avoid a Rust warning, we store the `display`'s returned value in a variable called `_`. Without this, the compiler would complain that we do not use a value of type `Result`.

Note   The compiler complains about not using the `Result` type to force developers to handle errors.

Implementing the Delay

Now that we have displayed the character, all that we have to do is to ask the alarm driver to send us a callback after the amount of time that the application has requested. This is done using the `set_alarm` function from the `Alarm` driver. This function receives two parameters: the time reference and the time interval to send the callback. As the underlying alarm works in ticks rather than a time unit, we have some convenience functions like `tick_from_ms` that allow us to convert the time value. Ticks represents the number of increments that the hardware timer performs and is dependent on the hardware.

As the hardware implementation of the alarm is a timer, most probably, there will be a small, but sometimes significant, time delay from the moment we issue `set_alarm` until the function computes the absolute time for the callback by adding the time interval to the current time. This is why the function takes a time reference besides the time interval.

Another aspect that we have to detail is the `Client` trait, which is the mechanism through which an underlying driver can signal another driver. Our driver is using the `Alarm` HIL to get a service from an `alarm` driver. Most of the HILs come in pairs, `HILName` and `HILNameClient`. As such, the `Alarm` HIL has its counterpart `AlarmClient`.

Each service capsule, like the `Alarm`, has one single client that it can signal. If you are familiar with Java, this is the observer pattern, but with one single observer. This means that the `Alarm` HIL provides several functions that can be called to control the alarm. In contrast, any response from the Alarm is sent asynchronously to any data structure that implements the AlarmClient HIL. In our case, it is our driver that implements the AlarmClient HIL. The implementation is presented in Listing 9-10.

Listing 9-10. The TextDisplay driver Implementation of the AlarmClient HIL

```
impl<
    'a, L: Led, A: Alarm<'a>
> AlarmClient for TextDisplay<'a, L, A> {
  fn alarm(&self) {
      self.display_next();
  }
}
```

The AlarmClient HIL provides one single function named alarm. This function is called by the alarm driver when an alarm that was previously set expires. When the TextDisplay driver receives this function call, it tries to display the next character using the display_next function that we presented above.

Note   Implementing the AlarmClient HIL is not enough for getting the actual alarm call. The underlying alarm driver has to be connected to our driver. This is done within the main function in the board implementation (**main.rs**).

Signaling the Application

A particular topic that we have to detail is how we signal the application when the job is done or if there is an error. Tock provides the upcall mechanism. Just as discussed before, processes can subscribe to events from drivers. These events are called *upcalls*.

> **Note** The name *upcall* is inspired from the Tock stack. The processes live above the kernel, and as such, the kernel sends a call upwards to the process.

Each upcall has three arguments of type u32. The actual meaning of these arguments is not defined by Tock itself, but rather it is left up to each capsule and its corresponding userspace library to agree upon some rules. The unwritten rule of Tock that most capsules use is to provide a StatusCode via the first argument. The data type StatusCode does not exist, it is a transformation from Result<(), ErrorCode> to usize (Listing 9-11). In other words, 0 means success. Any other number different from 0 is the corresponding ErrorCode.

Listing 9-11. The implementation of the From<ErrorCode> trait for usize

```
impl From<ErrorCode> for usize {
    fn from(err: ErrorCode) -> usize {
        err as usize
    }
}
```

> **Note** usize implements the From<ErrorCode> trait, making it possible to use the into function on an ErrorCode to convert it to a usize.

In our case, if we have finished displaying all the characters from the buffer, we schedule an upcall to the process with the first argument 0. This is shown in Listing 9-12. The only error we could encounter and that we could send back to the process is the lack of a buffer. This can happen only if the process has swapped the buffer while the driver is still displaying characters. This is why we use enter(...).unwrap_or when accessing the buffer. If the buffer is missing, the enter function will return Err(...). If the buffer is accessible, it will execute the closure that has the last expression true wrapped within a Result.

If the value returned by enter is Err(...), unwrap_or returns its argument (in this case false). If the value is Ok(value) it returns value.

Listing 9-12. Scheduling the upcall

```
if res {
  app.position = app.position + 1;
} else {
  self.in_progress.set(false);
  let _ = upcalls.schedule_upcall(0,
                (
                    ErrorCode::NOMEM.into(), 0, 0
                );
}
```

We use an if statement upon the returned value of unwrap_or to verify if we had an error or not. If the returned value is true, we had no error, and another character was displayed. We simply increment the current position. If there was an error, we report ErrorCode:NOMEM to the process and set the in_progress field to false, as we cannot continue to display characters having no buffer.

The Capsule Registration

The final step in setting up the TextDisplay is to register it within the board implementation. Similarly, with the previous version of the driver, we have to declare it as a field in the MicroBit board structure. Listing 9-13 shows the declaration.

Note   If you are using a Raspberry Pi Pico device, the driver needs to be declared in the RaspberryPiPico structure, as shown at the end of this chapter.

Listing 9-13. Declaring the TextDisplay driver field in the board implementation structure

```
pub struct MicroBit {
    console: &'static capsules::console::Console
        <'static>,
    ipc: kernel::ipc::IPC<NUM_PROCS>,
    gpio: &'static capsules::gpio::GPIO<'static,
        nrf52::gpio::GPIOPin<'static>>,
    led: &'static capsules::led_matrix::
        LedMatrixDriver<
          'static,
          nrf52::gpio::GPIOPin<'static>,
          capsules::virtual_alarm::
              VirtualMuxAlarm<'static,nrf52::rtc::
              Rtc<'static>>,
        >,
    button: &'static capsules::button::Button
```

```
        <'static, nrf52::gpio::GPIOPin<'static>>,
    alarm: &'static capsules::alarm::AlarmDriver<
        'static,
        capsules::virtual_alarm::VirtualMuxAlarm
          <'static, nrf52::rtc::Rtc<'static>>,
    >,
    // ...
    text_display: &'static drivers::text_display
        ::TextDisplay<
          'static,
          LedMatrixLed<
            'static,
            nrf52::gpio::GPIOPin<'static>,
            capsules::virtual_alarm::
                VirtualMuxAlarm<'static,
                  nrf52::rtc::Rtc<'static>>,
        >,
capsules::virtual_alarm::VirtualMuxAlarm
  <'static, nrf52833::rtc::Rtc<'static>>,
    >,
}
```

The next step is to register the driver in the with_driver function so that the kernel can find it when a system call is sent out, as shown in Listing 9-14.

Listing 9-14. Registering the TextDisplay driver in the with_driver function

```
impl Platform for MicroBit {
 fn with_driver<F, R>(&self, driver_num:
    usize, f: F) -> R
  where
```

```
  F: FnOnce(Option<&dyn kernel::Driver>) -> R,
  {
    match driver_num {
      capsules::console::DRIVER_NUM => f(Some(self.console)),
      capsules::gpio::DRIVER_NUM => f(Some(self.gpio)),
      capsules::alarm::DRIVER_NUM => f(Some(self.alarm)),
      capsules::button::DRIVER_NUM => f(Some(self.button)),
      capsules::led_matrix::DRIVER_NUM => f(Some(self.led)),
      // ...
      drivers::text_display::DRIVER_NUM => f(Some(self.text_
      display)),
      kernel::ipc::DRIVER_NUM => f(Some(&self.ipc)),
      _ => f(None),
    }
  }
}
```

Note   The `driver` type is a little longer than its previous version
since it has an extra `Alarm` trait argument.

Now that we have declared the driver and registered it so that the
kernel can call its functions, we have to initialize it. This part is slightly
different from the previous version, as we have to add an alarm to it.

First of all, we have to create an `alarm` driver. As most of the drivers are
asynchronous, they receive a `command` request, either through a system call,
or a HIL function call, then start the action and return immediately. To be
able to signal the completion of the requested action, drivers need a client.
This is an entity that implements the driver's `Client` HIL. For example, the
`Alarm` HIL has a counterpart `AlarmClient` HIL that the alarm's client has to
implement.

In Tock, most of the drivers can have one single client. This means that even if several other drivers were to have a reference to it, and all these drivers can request actions from this driver, the driver itself can only signal one single driver about the completion of a requested action. This is an important limitation for the alarm, as many drivers rely on the alarm driver.

To solve this issue, Tock provides virtual devices. Figure 9-9 illustrates a comparison between using a virtual device and directly accessing the actual device. The actual device drivers always talk to the hardware device. As we have seen before, this device driver is able to report to one single client. When using virtual devices, the device driver reports back to a multiplexer (Mux).

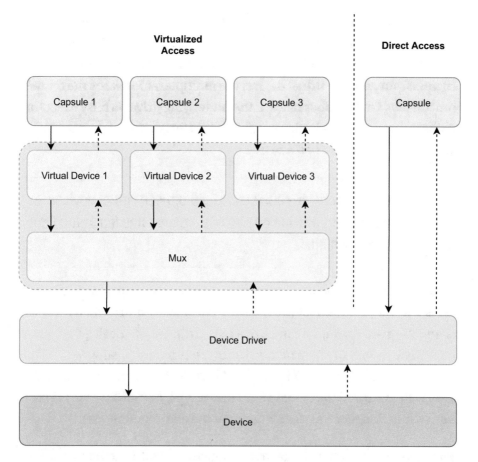

Figure 9-9. *Using a virtual device versus directly accessing the device*

The multiplexer provides a set of virtual devices that implement the same HIL as the actual device driver. Instead of talking to the hardware, the virtual devices ask the mux to talk to the actual device driver. The mux queues all requests and executes them one at a time. Each virtual device may have a maximum of one pending request. When the underlying device driver completes a request, it informs the multiplexer. In turn, the multiplexer informs the current virtual device and starts handling a request from another virtual device.

There is one caveat when using virtual devices. The HILs that are used in virtual devices are not able to provide synchronous functions. This is because the multiplexer queues requests. If there is no request in progress from another virtual device, the multiplexer forwards the request immediately. On the other hand, if the underlying driver is busy executing another request, the multiplexer will delay the execution of the request waiting for the driver to become free.

Note   While in theory, all capsules should provide virtual devices, in reality not all of them provide one as this was not needed at the time of the capsule's writing.

Just like many of the other drivers, our driver, too, requires the alarm. This is why the alarm driver provides the virtualizing functionality. Before instantiating our driver, we initialize a new virtual alarm device that our driver will use with the help of the static_init macro (Listing 9-15). The type for the virtual alarm is VirtualMuxAlarm. This is parametrized with a 'static lifetime and the actual alarm driver type, nrf52833::rtc::Rtc. The new function receives as an argument the alarm multiplexer.

Listing 9-15. Initializing the virtual alarm for the TextDisplay driver

```
let virtual_alarm_text_display = static_init!(
    capsules::virtual_alarm::VirtualMuxAlarm
        <'static, nrf52833::rtc::Rtc>,
    capsules::virtual_alarm::VirtualMuxAlarm::
    new(mux_alarm)
);
```

Now that we have initialized the virtual alarm, we can instantiate the driver (Listing 9-16). We use the same code as for the previous version of the driver. First, the driver type is changed to include the virtual alarm type in its generic arguments. The second change is in the arguments supplied to the new function. Besides the array of LEDs, the function receives a reference to the virtual alarm and the grant.

As mentioned before, the grant argument is just an entry point towards the grant data allocated within each process. The kernel is the one that can create this entry point for us through its create_grant function.

Listing 9-16. Initializing the TextDisplay driver with the board implementation

```
let text_display = static_init!(
drivers::text_display::TextDisplay<
  'static,
  LedMatrixLed<
  'static,
  nrf52::gpio::GPIOPin<'static>,
  capsules::virtual_alarm::VirtualMuxAlarm
    <'static, nrf52::rtc::Rtc<'static>>,
  >,
  capsules::virtual_alarm::VirtualMuxAlarm
    <'static, nrf52::rtc::Rtc<'static>>,
  >,
  drivers::text_display::TextDisplay::new(
    components::led_matrix_leds!(
      nrf52::gpio::GPIOPin<'static>,
      capsules::virtual_alarm::VirtualMuxAlarm
        <'static, nrf52::rtc::Rtc<'static>>,
      led,
      (0, 0),
      (1, 0),
      (2, 0),
      (3, 0),
```

```
        (4, 0),
        (0, 0),
        (1, 1),
        (2, 1),
        (3, 1),
        (4, 1),
        (0, 2),
        (1, 2),
        (2, 2),
        (3, 2),
        (4, 2),
        (0, 3),
        (1, 3),
        (2, 3),
        (3, 3),
        (4, 3),
        (0, 4),
        (1, 4),
        (2, 4),
        (3, 4),
            (4, 4)
        ),
        virtual_alarm_text_display,
        board_kernel.create_grant(
          &memory_allocation_capability)
      ),
);
```

Before using the driver, we still have to perform one more step shown in Listing 9-17. We have to connect the virtual alarm to the driver. This means setting the driver as the alarm's client by using the set_alarm_client function. This step is essential, and failing to do so will render the driver unusable. The driver will never receive the callback from the alarm when the timeout expires. In other words, the driver will wait forever for the alarm's callback.

Listing 9-17. Connecting the virtual alarm to the TextDisplay driver by setting the driver as the alarm's driver

```
virtual_alarm_text_display.set_alarm_client
  (text_display);
```

The Userspace Library Implementation

Once the driver is in place and registered with the kernel, we have to write a userspace library to access it. Just like for its previous version, we create two files in the **applications/drivers** folder. The function declarations go into the **text_display.h** header file while their definition goes into **text_display.c**.

The Userspace API

The header file displayed in Listing 9-18 is very similar to the one used for the previous driver. It defines the driver number and the API functions. One important difference is the definition of the text_display_ status_t structure. This is used when waiting for the driver to finish the asynchronous action. We will discuss this structure in detail further on in this chapter.

Listing 9-18. The TextDisplay userspace API function definitions

```
// Text Display API

#pragma once

#include "tock.h"

#define DRIVER_NUM_TEXT_DISPLAY 0xa0002

#ifdef __cplusplus
extern "C" {
#endif

typedef void (text_display_done_t) (
    returncode_t, void *user_data
);

// Asynchronous API
void text_display_set_done_callback (
    text_display_done_t callback,
    void *callback_args
);

returncode_t text_display_show_text (
    const char* text, unsigned int display_ms
);

// Synchronous API
returncode_t text_display_show_text_sync (
    const char* text, unsigned int display_ms
);

#ifdef __cplusplus
}
#endif
```

The driver's userspace API exposes two categories of functions. The first category provides the functions to display a text asynchronously. First, we have the text_display_set_done_callback function that allows us to register a callback function for when the displaying of a text is done. The function's prototype is defined as void (text_display_done_t) (returncode_t, void *user_data). The callback function receives two parameters: the displaying action's return code and the pointer sent as the second argument to text_display_set_done_callback.

Next, we have the text_display_show_text function that starts the displaying of the text. It receives two parameters, the text to be displayed and the milliseconds delay between characters. The function returns immediately before the text is displayed. If the function returns RETURNCODE_SUCCESS, it means that the driver started displaying the text and will notify the process upon completion by calling the callback set using the text_display_set_done_callback function.

The second category consists of a single function called text_display_show_text_sync. This is more of a wrapper function that uses the asynchronous function to display the text. This function returns only when there is an error, or the text is fully displayed.

The API Implementation

Once we define each function required and its behavior, we can move forward to implementing them in the **text_display.c** file.

Definitions

The userspace library implementation starts with the data type definitions illustrated in Listing 9-19.

Listing 9-19. Data type definition for the API

```
// asynchronous
static text_display_done_t *done_callback =
  NULL;
static void * done_callback_args = NULL;

// synchronous
typedef struct {
 bool done;
 statuscode_t status;
} text_display_status_t;
```

The first definition in the C source code is for the asynchronous function. The done_callback variable stores a pointer towards a callback function provided by the user of the library. Initially, its value is NULL as there is no default callback. The done_callback_args variable stores a pointer that is supplied by the user of the library. This pointer will be sent as an argument to the done_callback function. Both of these two values are set by the text_display_set_done_callback function.

The second declared data type is used for the synchronous API. The text_display_status_t structure is used as the callback user data by the text_display_show_text_sync function. The callback function that it registers will fill in the structure with the status code and the done flag.

Next, we define a wrapper function for the system calls (Listing 9-20). As we use allow, subscribe, and command several times with the same driver number, we defined these wrappers to reduce one of the arguments and make sure we make no mistake when passing the driver number. Now, instead of using the standard system calls, we will use these from within our functions.

Listing 9-20. Wrapper functions for system calls

```
static syscall_return_t text_display_command (
    uint32_t command_number, int arg1, int arg2
) {
    return command (
      TEXT_DISPLAY_DRIVER_NUM, command_number,
      arg1,
      arg2
    );
}

static allow_ro_return_t text_display_allow (
    uint32_t allow_number,
    const void* ptr,
    size_t size
) {
    return allow_readonly (
      TEXT_DISPLAY_DRIVER_NUM,
      allow_number,
      ptr,
      size
    );
}

static subscribe_return_t text_display_subscribe (
    uint32_t subscribe_number,
    subscribe_upcall upcall,
    void* userdata
) {
    return subscribe (
      TEXT_DISPLAY_DRIVER_NUM,
      subscribe_number,
```

```
    upcall,
    userdata
  );
}
```

Asynchronous API

The driver that we have created in this chapter performs the displaying of the text in an asynchronous way. From the process's point of view, this means that it can issue a request to the driver to display a text, do some other work, and later on, check if the text displaying has been done. This is what an *asynchronous API* means.

Our driver's asynchronous API is represented by two functions and a private callback. First we have the text_display_set_done_callback function. This allows the user of the driver library to register a callback to be called upon the completion of the text display process. Besides the callback pointer, the function takes an additional pointer parameter that will be sent as an argument when the driver calls the callback. As Tock processes are single-threaded, we can safely store these two parameters in global variables. Listing 9-21 presents the function.

Listing 9-21. The function that sets the driver callback

```
void text_display_set_done_callback
  (text_display_done_t callback, void
  *callback_args) {
    done_callback      = callback;
    done_callback_args = callback_args;
}
```

The function that sends the display command to the driver is text_display_show_text, illustrated in Listing 9-22. At the beginning of the function, we make sure that we have a valid pointer towards a string. If this pointer is NULL, we return an INVALID error.

Listing 9-22. The text display function and its associated callback

```
static void text_displayed (
    int status,
    __attribute__ ((unused)) int unused2,
    __attribute__ ((unused)) int unused3,
    __attribute__ ((unused)) void *user_data
) {
  text_display_allow (0, NULL, 0);
  text_display_subscribe (0, NULL, NULL);
  if (done_callback != NULL) {
    (*done_callback)(
        tock_status_to_returncode(status),
        done_callback_args
    );
  }
}

returncode_t text_display_show_text (
    const char* text,
    unsigned int display_ms
) {
  if (text == NULL) {
    return RETURNCODE_EINVAL;
  }
  // allow the buffer
  allow_ro_return_t allow_ret =
    text_display_allow (
        0, text, strlen (text)
    );
  if (allow_ret.success) {
    // subscribe to the display finished event
```

```
subscribe_return_t subscribe_ret =
    text_display_subscribe (
        0, text_displayed, NULL
);
if (subscribe_ret.success) {
  // execute command
    syscall_return_t ret =
      text_display_command (
        1, strlen (text), display_ms
      );
  if (ret.type == TOCK_SYSCALL_SUCCESS) {
    return RETURNCODE_SUCCESS;
  } else {
    // unallow the buffer
    text_display_allow (0, NULL, 0);

    // unsubscribe
    text_display_subscribe (0, NULL, NULL);

    return
      tock_status_to_returncode(
            ret.data[0]
      );
  }
} else {
  // unallow the buffer
  text_display_allow (0, NULL, 0);
  return tock_status_to_returncode(
        subscribe_ret.status
  );
}
```

```
  } else {
    return tock_status_to_returncode(
        allow_ret.status
    );
  }
}
```

Once we ensure that we have a valid string, we must share it with the driver. This is done using the allow_readonly system call. The driver receives read-only access to the text, as it only needs to read it, it never modifies the text. Instead of using the allow_readonly system call directly, we use the wrapper function defined earlier. We use the allow number is 0, the text is the pointer for the buffer, and the length of the text is for the buffer size. This function returns an allow_ro_return_t data type with two fields: a boolean success field and an integer status representing the error code in case of an error. If allow_readonly is successful, we can continue. Otherwise, we just return the error status. If we cannot share the buffer, the driver will have no way of reading and displaying the text.

Note   The system call will return a statuscode_t which is the standard of errors that Tock uses. As this is a C library, we convert the returned statuscode_t to the C style returncode_t to follow the C type of errors.

The next step after sharing the buffer is to subscribe for an upcall from the driver that will notify us when the text has been fully displayed. In userspace, an upcall is represented by a function pointer and a pointer to custom user data. The upcall API provided by Tock is generic and requires a callback function that receives four parameters.

Caution   If a callback function is expected to be called upon a sucessful command system call, it is important to **subscribe** the callback function **before** the **command** system call is issued. The Tock kernel clears all the previous scheduled upcalls for a subscribe number when a new subscribe system call for it is received. This means that if a capsule's command system call schedules an upcall immediately and the user space process subscribes a callback after the command system call, the previously scheduled upcall will be cleared.

We do not want to expose this directly to the users of our API. The reason is twofold. First, the standard callback function has four parameters, and we only need two: the status of the text display and a user-supplied custom pointer.

Second, Tock firmly states that processes cannot access buffers while they are shared with a driver. Having this in mind, whenever the driver makes the upcall, we have to unallow the buffer containing the text so that the process can safely modify and reuse the buffer.

Note   The kernel will consider a NULL buffer to be an *unallow* request.

Within our code, we define a function called text_displayed. This is the actual callback function that we use to subscribe to number 0. In other words, the driver will call this function when the text is fully displayed or when an error is encountered. The function is a standard Tock callback and, as such, takes four parameters. The first three are the values supplied by the driver via the upcall, while the last one is the the custom user data pointer sent as the last argument to the subscribe system call. For this driver, the user data pointer is NULL as we do not need it.

Note   Optimization is important due to the restricted hardware that the process will run on. We mark the unused parameters of the callback accordingly (__attribute__ ((unused))) to hint to the compiler so that it can better optimize the code.

If the subscribe works and returns success, we can send the display command to the driver. On the other hand, if an error is returned, we have to clean up. This means that we have to unallow the buffer that we shared previously with the driver. Tock does not have the concept of unallowing a buffer, it only knows how to allow one. As long as we share another buffer for the same allow number (we actually swap the buffer), we can use the buffer that we have previously shared. The new buffer can be NULL, and this is precisely what we do.

If both actions of sharing a buffer and subscribing are successful, we send command number 1 to the driver to start displaying the text. The first argument the command receives is the length of the text. The second one is the time it should display each character expressed in milliseconds. If the command is successful, the driver has started displaying the text and will notify us using the text_displayed callback function. We can safely return RETURNCODE_SUCCESS. The driver will eventually call our callback when it finishes displaying the text or if it encounters an error.

In case of an error, the driver is not able to display the text, and we have to clean up again. This means unsubscribing the callback function and unallowing the buffer. Similar to allow, Tock does not provide a way of unsubscribing a callback but instead uses the idea of swapping a callback. Just like for buffers, providing a NULL function pointer for the callback does the trick.

For command system calls, the actual error value is stored in the first data item returned, data[0]. We return this value to report the error.

The text_displayed function is called when the text is displayed or if there is an error. Within this function, we perform two actions. First, no matter whether the text was displayed successfully or not, we have to clean up by unsubscribing the callback and unallowing the buffer. Next, we verify if the user of the library has registered a callback and if so, we call it with the status and stored user data as arguments.

Synchronous API

So far, we have shown the asynchronous API that is very similar to how drivers work. Many times, though, using an asynchronous API is difficult for application developers. This is why most of the userspace libraries provide synchronous APIs for the drivers. That is to say, the library implements all the code necessary to wait for the callback.

Before we dive in deeper, we have to describe the yield system call briefly.

Drivers may schedule upcalls anytime, regardless of what userspace processes do. When a driver schedules an upcall, the kernel, instead of immediately calling the registered function from userspace, enqueues the upcall. Unlike Linux, which interrupts processes to deliver signals, Tock never interrupts processes due to upcalls. The kernel will call the function callback only when processes are in the Yielded state.

Note   Each process has a limited queue of tasks that can be scheduled. Upcalls are among these tasks. By default, the size of the queue is 10. If the queue is full, the upcall scheduling fails.

Processes ask the kernel to place them in the Yielded state by using the yield system call. When the kernel receives a yield system call, it tries to unqueue the process' first upcall and call the callback function. If the task queue is empty, the process is placed into the Yielded state until an upcall is scheduled. Namely, callback functions can only be called as a result of a yield system call.

A process can ask for several asynchronous actions from several drivers. Each time the process uses the yield system call, one of the callbacks will be called. The order in which these are called depends on the order that drivers have scheduled the upcalls. No assumption should be made about this order.

The libtock library provides an additional variant of the yield system call, yield_no_wait. This works similarly but returns immediately if there is no upcall scheduled. Unlike the yield function, which returns void, yield_no_wait returns an integer. If the value is 1, it means that a callback has been executed. A 0 value means that the task queue had no scheduled upcalls.

The synchronous API shown in Listing 9-23 provides a function and a private callback. The text_display_show_text_sync function works similarly to its asynchronous counterpart, except that it returns only after the whole text has been displayed.

First, it defines a text_display_status structure that contains two fields. Its first field, done, is a boolean value that memorizes whether the text has been fully displayed or not. Its second field, status, stores the status value returned by the driver through the callback function when the text has been fully displayed. The default values for the field are false and TOCK_STATUSCODE_SUCCESS.

Listing 9-23. The synchronous API

```
static void text_displayed_sync (
    statuscode_t status, void *user_data
) {
  text_display_status_t *display_status =
          (text_display_status_t*)user_data;
```

```
  display_status->done   = true;
  display_status->status = status;
}

returncode_t text_display_show_text_sync (
    const char* text, unsigned int display_ms
) {
  text_display_status_t display_status;
  display_status.done   = false;
  display_status.status = TOCK_STATUS_SUCCESS;

  text_display_set_done_callback
      (text_displayed_sync, &display_status);
  returncode_t ret = text_display_show_text (
    text, display_ms
  );

  if (ret == RETURNCODE_SUCCESS) {
    yield_for (&display_status.done);
    return tock_status_to_returncode(
        display_status.status
    );
  } else {
    return ret;
  }
}
```

Note   The default value of the status field is not relevant as it is overwritten in the callback function.

Next, using `text_display_set_done_callback`, we subscribe to the completion callback function `text_displayed_sync`, and call the asynchronous API to display the text. If this is successful, we wait for the driver to call the `text_displayed_sync`. If an error is encountered, we return the error code.

Special attention has to be paid to the user data pointer supplied to the subscribed callback. Instead of setting it to `NULL`, in the synchronous API we set it as a pointer to the `text_display_status` structure. This way, the subscribed callback function will have access to this structure. This is important due to how we wait for the completion of the text display.

A detailed description of how we wait for the callback is necessary. Technically, we could simply use `yield` and assume that the callback has been called as soon as `yield` returns. This assumption is not valid as `yield` returns if any scheduled callback is called. There is no guarantee that the callback that we wait for is the only callback that might be called. In other words, we should `yield` and use a way of signaling that the specific callback that we are waiting for has been called. If `yield` returns, but the callback we wait for has not been called, we should `yield` again. Listing 9-24 illustrates an example of this kind of implementation.

Listing 9-24. An example of waiting for a callback to be called

```
while (expected_function_has_not_been_called) {
  yield ();
}
```

Note   Signaling that a particular callback has been called can be done using a global variable or the user data sent as an argument to the callback.

To streamline the development process, the libtock library provides us with a convenience function called yield_for. This receives as an argument a pointer towards a boolean variable and yields until this variable becomes true. This is the function the synchronous API uses to wait.

In the synchronous API, we use the yield_for function with a reference to the done field of the display_status structure that we have previously defined. The process will be yielded as long as the value of done remains false.

When the driver schedules the upcall to inform the process that it has finished displaying the text, the kernel will eventually call the text_displayed_sync function. This function converts the user data received as an argument to a text_display_status_t structure and sets the done field to true. Additionally, it sets the status filed to the value sent by the driver. When the function returns, the yield_for function finds the done field set to true and allows us to continue in the synchronous API. All that is left to do is to return the stored status from the display_status variable.

Writing an Example Application

To test our driver and library, we have to write a single process application that displays text using the LED matrix. The application will be located in the **applications/example_app** folder. It will use both the asynchronous and the synchronous API.

The Synchronous Application

The synchronous API is the easiest one to use as it actually mimics the exact flow of the program. First of all, we verify if the driver is present using the driver_exists function. If so, we display a text at a speed of about three characters per second (300 ms for each digit or letter) using the text_display_show_text_sync function. Listing 9-25 displays the complete source code.

Listing 9-25. The synchronous application using the TextDriver driver

```
#include <stdio.h>
#include "timer.h"
#include "text_display.h"
int main(void) {
 if (driver_exists(DRIVER_NUM_TEXT_DISPLAY)) {
   text_display_show_text_sync (
     "Hello World from the Microbit", 300
   );
 } else {
        printf ("Error: the text_display driver
                   is not present\n");
 }
 return 0;
}
```

The Asynchronous Application

When displaying a text, we might want to perform another task while the text is being displayed instead of just waiting. This is what the asynchronous API is for, and this application showcases the real power of Tock (Listing 9-26).

Listing 9-26. The asynchronous application using the
TextDriver driver

```
#include <stdio.h>
#include "timer.h"
#include "text_display.h"

static void job_done (
   __attribute__ ((unused)) returncode_t status,
   void *user_data
) {
   bool *done = (bool*)user_data;
   *done = true;
}

int main(void) {
 if (text_display_is_present()) {
   bool done = false;
   text_display_set_done_callback (
     job_done, &done
   );
   text_display_show_text (
     "Hello World from the Microbit", 300
   );
   if (text_display_show_text (
     "Hello World from the Microbit", 300
   ) == RETURNCODE_SUCCESS)
   {
     while (
         yield_no_wait() == 0 && done == false
     ) {
```

```
    printf (".");
    fflush (stdout);
    delay_ms (1000);
  }
 }
} else {
  printf ("Error: the text_display driver is
                          not present\n");
}
 return 0;
}
```

As this example performs an asynchronous action, we have to define a function that will be called when the action is done. We define the job_ done function that takes as an argument the status code returned by the driver and an optional user data pointer.

Just like for the synchronous API, we first verify if the driver is present. Next, we set the job_done function to be called when the text has been fully displayed using the text_display_set_done_callback function. Besides the callback function pointer, this function takes an extra argument that is sent to the callback function when it is called. We use this argument to determine when the text has been displayed inside our main function.

We define a bool variable named done and set its value to false. The value of this variable is helpful to let us know when the text has been fully displayed. We send a pointer to the done variable to the callback function. Whenever the kernel calls the callback function, the function will take the user data, convert it into a pointer to our done variable and set its value to true. In the main function, this would be equivalent to setting done to true.

We then instruct the driver to display a text using the text_display_ show_text function. We use the same speed of about three digits or letters per second. When the function returns success, it means that the driver has started displaying the text. In the meantime, we do not wait for it to finish. Within a while loop, we use `yield_no_wait` to ask the kernel to call a scheduled callback if one exists. Eventually, this will make the kernel call the `job_done` function when the driver finishes displaying the text.

The `yield_no_wait` function returns 0 if the kernel had no scheduled callback to run and 1 otherwise. If there is no callback to run, our driver is still working, and we can do something else in the meanwhile. In this example, we print a dot, flush the print buffer so that it actually displays the dot, and wait for one second. We then ask the kernel again to call one of the scheduled callbacks.

Whenever `yield_no_wait` returns 1, the kernel has called a callback. This might be `job_done` or another callback scheduled by another driver. The kernel simply calls the first scheduled callback, regardless if it is the callback that our driver sent or not. We use the done variable to verify if our callback was called. Whenever the kernel calls our callback `job_done`, this callback will set the done variable to true.

Using the asynchronous API gives us a significant advantage. We can perform several actions in parallel. We do not have to wait for an action to finish before starting another one. This is a key concept that has become more and more important in standard computer applications.

Using the Raspberry Pi Pico

Using the driver with the Raspberry Pi Pico is straightforward. We use the same hardware setup from chapter 8. The only change that we have to make is the driver's initialization in the board implementation. This is the **main.rs** file inside the **project/kernel/raspberry_pi_pico folder**.

The steps that we have to follow are:

- define the *TextDisplay* driver in the *RaspberryPiPico* structure;

- add a `match` branch in the `with_driver` function from the `SyscallDriverLookup`'s trait implementation that returns the *TextDisplay* driver;

- disable the GPIO pins 2 to 11 from the GPIO driver;

- initialize a virtual alarm for the driver;

- initialize the *TextDisplay* driver;

- set the *TextDisplay* driver as the *alarm*'s client.

Listing 9-27 shows all the changes to the **main.rs** file, highlighting the differences between the micro:bit and the Raspberry Pi Pico implementations.

Listing 9-27. Initializing the TextDisplay driver for the Raspberry Pi Pico

```
use capsules::led_matrix::LedMatrixLed;
// ...
pub struct RaspberryPiPico {
    // ...
    text_display: &'static drivers::text_display::TextDisplay<
        'static,
        LedMatrixLed<
            'static,
            RPGpioPin<'static>,
            VirtualMuxAlarm<
                'static,
                RPTimer<'static>
            >
        >,
```

```rust
        VirtualMuxAlarm<
            'static,
            RPTimer<'static>
        >,
    >,
}

impl SyscallDriverLookup for RaspberryPiPico {
    fn with_driver<F, R>(
        &self, driver_num: usize, f: F
    ) -> R
      where
      F: FnOnce(Option<&dyn kernel::Driver>) -> R,
      {
          match driver_num {
              // ...
              drivers::text_display::DRIVER_NUM =>
                          f(Some(self.text_display)),
              _ => f(None),
          }
      }
}
// ...
pub unsafe fn main() {
    // ...
    let gpio = GpioComponent::new(
        board_kernel,
        components::gpio_component_helper!(
            RPGpioPin,
          // Used for serial communication.
          //Comment them in if you don't use serial.
```

```
//0 => &peripherals.pins.get_pin(RPGpio::GPIO0),
//1 => &peripherals.pins.get_pin(RPGpio::GPIO1),
//2 => &peripherals.pins.get_pin(RPGpio::GPIO2),
//3 => &peripherals.pins.get_pin(RPGpio::GPIO3),
//4 => &peripherals.pins.get_pin(RPGpio::GPIO4),
//5 => &peripherals.pins.get_pin(RPGpio::GPIO5),
//6 => &peripherals.pins.get_pin(RPGpio::GPIO6),
//7 => &peripherals.pins.get_pin(RPGpio::GPIO7),
//8 => &peripherals.pins.get_pin(RPGpio::GPIO8),
//9 => &peripherals.pins.get_pin(RPGpio::GPIO9),
//10=>&peripherals.pins.get_pin(RPGpio::GPIO10),
//11=>&peripherals.pins.get_pin(RPGpio::GPIO11),
12 => &peripherals.pins.get_pin(RPGpio::GPIO12),
    ),
  )
  .finalize(
    components::gpio_component_buf!(
        RPGpioPin<'static>
    )
  );
  // ...
  // LED Matrix

  let led_matrix_driver = components::led_matrix_component_
  helper!(
      RPGpioPin<'static>,
      RPTimer<'static>,
      mux_alarm,
      @fps => 60,
      @cols => kernel::hil::gpio::ActivationMode::ActiveHigh,
      &peripherals.pins.get_pin(RPGpio::GPIO2),
      &peripherals.pins.get_pin(RPGpio::GPIO3),
```

```
        &peripherals.pins.get_pin(RPGpio::GPIO4),
        &peripherals.pins.get_pin(RPGpio::GPIO5),
        &peripherals.pins.get_pin(RPGpio::GPIO6),
        @rows => kernel::hil::gpio::ActivationMode::ActiveLow,
        &peripherals.pins.get_pin(RPGpio::GPIO7),
        &peripherals.pins.get_pin(RPGpio::GPIO8),
        &peripherals.pins.get_pin(RPGpio::GPIO9),
        &peripherals.pins.get_pin(RPGpio::GPIO10),
        &peripherals.pins.get_pin(RPGpio::GPIO11),
    )
    .finalize(
        components::led_matrix_component_buf!(
          RPGpioPin<'static>,
          RPTimer<'static>
        )
    );

    let virtual_alarm_text_display =
       static_init!(
       capsules::virtual_alarm::VirtualMuxAlarm<
           'static, RPTimer<'static>
       >,
       capsules::virtual_alarm::VirtualMuxAlarm::new(mux_alarm)
    );

    let text_display = static_init!(
       drivers::text_display::TextDisplay<
           'static,
           LedMatrixLed<
               'static,
               RPGpioPin<'static>,
```

```
            capsules::virtual_alarm::VirtualMuxAlarm<'static,
            RPTimer<'static>>,
        >,
        capsules::virtual_alarm::VirtualMuxAlarm<'static,
        RPTimer<'static>>,
    >,
    drivers::text_display::TextDisplay::new(
        components::led_matrix_leds!(
            RPGpioPin<'static>,
            capsules::virtual_alarm::VirtualMuxAlarm<'static,
            RPTimer<'static>>,
            led_matrix_driver,
            (0, 0),
            (1, 0),
            // ...
        ),
        virtual_alarm_text_display,
        board_kernel.create_grant(
            &memory_allocation_capability
        )
    )
);

virtual_alarm_text_display.set_alarm_client(
    text_display
);
// ...
let raspberry_pi_pico = RaspberryPiPico {
    // ...
    text_display: text_display,
};
// ...
}
```

Summary

In this chapter, we have presented how capsules exposing asynchronous API should be written. This is the fundamental way in which capsules work in Tock. Instead of blocking the execution while an action finishes, Tock takes an asynchronous approach. Drivers start the first action of a task and hand back the execution control to the kernel. Whenever the action is done, the kernel is signaled and hands back control to the capsule to continue with the next task action.

While this approach makes driver writing more complex, it has several advantages. First of all, it allows concurrency by efficiently using the hardware resources. Most of the actions that hardware components execute are asynchronous. The hardware device receives a command, executes it completely separated from the main MCU, and signals the MCU through an interrupt upon completion. In the meanwhile, the MCU can perform several tasks that are not related to this particular device.

The second advantage of this approach is that it makes the kernel's code simpler. Modern operating systems have mechanisms to interrupt a driver that is performing an action that takes a longer time. In other words, drivers become a kind of *kernel processes* that have to be preempted and scheduled. This adds a lot of complexity to the kernel's source code. Linux takes this approach.

Most modern software, programming languages, and libraries take this asynchronous or collaborative approach in favor of using the classical threads. This uses the hardware resources more efficiently. All the time used for context switches is not used to perform valuable work. Nginx, NodeJS and Swift are examples of software that encourage the asynchronous model.

A downside of the asynchronous approach is that any driver can delay the kernel by performing a long-running synchronous task. An infinite loop in any of the drivers will block the kernel. This is why developers have to be extra careful not to perform long-running tasks in the drivers.

Even though writing drivers in an asynchronous way requires more effort, the benefits in efficiency gain make up for it, especially in embedded systems where resources are limited.

CHAPTER 10

Service Capsules

Tock has three types of capsules: syscall capsules, service capsules, and low-level drivers. Syscall capsules extend the kernel's functionality and expose an API towards the userspace while service capsules and low-level capsules interact with hardware. So far, we have discussed, designed, and implemented synchronous and asynchronous syscall capsules. This chapter presents an adaptation of the *TextDisplay* syscall capsules to function as a service driver.

Requirements

This chapter requires the following hardware components based on the device you use:

- **Micro:bit**
  - 1 x micro:bit v2 board
- **Raspberry Pi Pico**
  - 1 x Raspberry Pi Pico board;
  - 1 x KWM-R30881CUAB or KWM-R30881AUAB LED matrix;
  - 14 x jumper wires;
  - 5 x 220Ω resistors;
  - 2 x (or 1 x large) breadboards.

© Alexandru Radovici and Ioana Culic 2022
A. Radovici and I. Culic, *Getting Started with Secure Embedded Systems*,
https://doi.org/10.1007/978-1-4842-7789-8_10

The Separation Between Syscall and Service Capsules

Syscall capsules expose an API towards the userspace. While nothing stops a driver from providing a specific API, good practice rules state that separating the API and the actual implementation is very important. Let us take the example of a display driver. There are many types of displays available, every single one of them functioning differently and requiring a different kind of interfacing. If there were a driver for every display, application developers would have a different API for each of them. This would render applications less portable, as an application would depend on the exact display type.

Tock solves this issue by providing generic Syscall drivers such as *TextScreen, NineDoF,* or *Humidity*. All these drivers provide a standard API towards the userspace and require the services of an actual driver to perform the requested actions. For instance, the `NideDoF` (9 Degrees of Freedom) driver exposes a standard Syscall API towards the applications, allowing them to request information about the system's motion (accelerometer, gyroscope, and magnetometer). Underneath, it does not actually know how to retrieve this data from sensors and requires an actual service driver that can do just that. This can be any sensor driver that implements the `NineDofF` trait that is shown in Listing 10-1.

Listing 10-1. The NineDoF and the NineDoFClient traits

```
pub trait NineDof<'a> {
    /// Set the client to be notified when the
    /// capsule has data ready or has finished
    /// some command. This is likely called in a
    /// board's main.rs and is set to the
    /// virtual_ninedof.rs driver.
    fn set_client(&self,client:&'a NineDofClient);
```

```
/// Get a single instantaneous reading of the
///acceleration in the X,Y,Z directions.
fn read_accelerometer(&self) -> Result<(), ErrorCode> {
  Err(ErrorCode::NODEVICE)
}

/// Get a single instantaneous reading from
/// the magnetometer in all three directions.
fn read_magnetometer(&self) -> Result<(), ErrorCode> {
  Err(ErrorCode::NODEVICE)
}

/// Get a single instantaneous reading from
/// the gyroscope of the rotation around all
/// three axes.
fn read_gyroscope(&self) -> Result<(), ErrorCode> {
  Err(ErrorCode::NODEVICE)
}
}

/// Client for receiving done events from the
/// chip.
pub trait NineDofClient {
  /// Signals a command has finished. The
  /// arguments will most likely be passed over
  /// the syscall interface to an application.
  fn callback(&self,x: usize,y: usize,z: usize);
}
```

This separation between the API and the service allows developers to use the same API with different drivers. In other words, an application can use the *NineDoF API* with any motion sensor, regardless of the hardware it uses, as long as the sensor service driver implements the *NineDoF HIL*. Figure 10-1 illustrates the relationship between the *NineDoF Syscal Driver* and the *Fxos8700 Driver*.

419

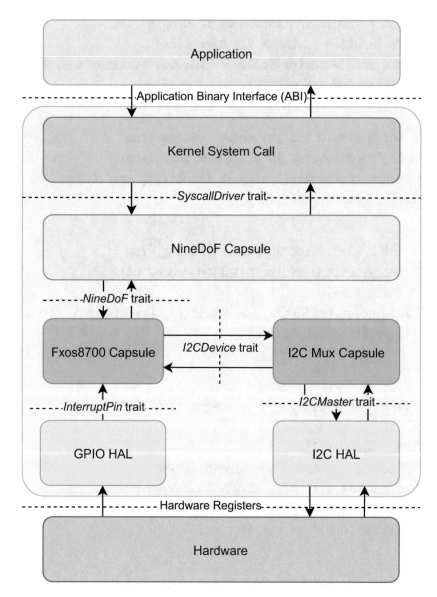

Figure 10-1. *Capsule architecture using the NineDof example*

In this chapter, we will design and implement a *TextScreen* service capsule that uses the LED matrix as its screen. In other words, we are writing a driver that links the generic *TextScreen* syscall driver to the LED matrix hardware.

The TextScreen Driver

Before we dive into how the *TextScreen* driver works, we have to define the text screen hardware. Just as its name suggests, the text screen is a display that can print only text and sometimes a few special characters, like text emoticons. Figure 10-2 illustrates two of the most used LCD text displays.

Figure 10-2. *The most popular LCD text screens*

These displays have an internal data buffer, an MCU, and a ROM memory with a font. The MCU, or display controller, reads the text data from the buffer and uses the font definition to turn the LCD crystals on and off to display the corresponding text. This is done in a very similar way to what we did for each character using the LED matrix, just that the display, compared to the LED matrix, can display more than 25 dots.

A Tock service driver controlling a text display has to copy the text data it receives to the display's buffer and send the display a few commands to make the new data visible.

To access the text screen, processes have to interact with the *TextScreen* driver. Its purpose is to provide a standard system call API to the userspace and forward requests further to the actual service driver that directly controls the hardware. Figure 10-3 shows how the *TextScreen* driver works. The driver keeps an internal buffer, called an intermediate text frame buffer. Its purpose is to store the data received from a process through a read-only allowed buffer and send it to the hardware driver. As its name says, it intermediates the data transfer between the process and the hardware.

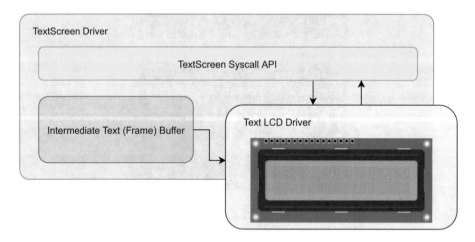

Figure 10-3. *The TextScreen driver's architecture*

All processes that want to display some text to the screen have to send data to the screen driver using a read-only allowed buffer. In turn, the *TextScreen* driver will copy the data to its intermediate buffer and send it to the hardware.

The *TextScreen*'s intermediate buffer might be smaller than the actual display's buffer and smaller than the buffer that the process has allowed. In this case, the *TextScreen* driver will split the data in several *packets* that fit into its buffer and send them one at a time.

The Architecture of the Capsule

In this chapter, we are building a *software* text screen using an LED matrix. Instead of having a separate MCU controlling the display, we use the system's MCU. Figure 10-4 shows this architecture. The hardware display is emulated by the driver that we are writing. Just like the asynchronous text display driver that we have presented in chapter 9, this driver uses an alarm to schedule callbacks at a specific interval. During each callback, it displays the next character stored in its frame buffer. Whenever it gets to the end of the frame buffer, it starts over.

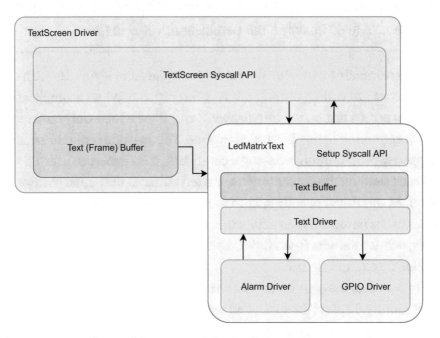

Figure 10-4. *The architecture of the LedMatrixText capsule*

To provide the service to the *TextScreen* driver, our driver has to conform to the TextScreen HIL (Hardware Interface Layer). In other words, it has to implement the TextScreen trait. As some of the driver's parameters, like the speed at which it should display characters, are not configurable through the *TextScreen* driver, our driver will expose a small set of syscall APIs for these. In this way, processes that only want to display text can use the standard text screen API. In contrast, processes that require a greater level of control can additionally call our specific setup API.

Note   Processes that use the TextScreen API will be able to display text regardless of the type of hardware that is present. It does not matter if there is an actual text screen attached or if our driver simulates a screen using an LED matrix. On the other hand, processes that try to use the configuration API provided by our driver will be able to do so only if our particular driver is in use.

The complete interaction flow chart is displayed in Figure 10-5. The part that we are writing is the *LedMatrixText* capsule. When an application wants to print a text on the text display, it will allow a read-only buffer and send a command to the *TextScreen* capsule. This capsule is part of Tock's shipped capsules. Upon receiving a command, the *TextScreen* capsule will start sending the contents of the shared buffer to the actual hardware driver. As this driver usually talks to some real hardware, sending the buffer to the hardware is an action that takes longer to perform and thus an asynchronous one. Upon finishing, the *TextScreen* driver will notify the process through an upcall.

In our case, the capsule that we write is the hardware driver. This continuously displays the digits and letters from its buffer, one by one, using the LED Matrix. It uses the *alarm* driver to set a timeout between prints.

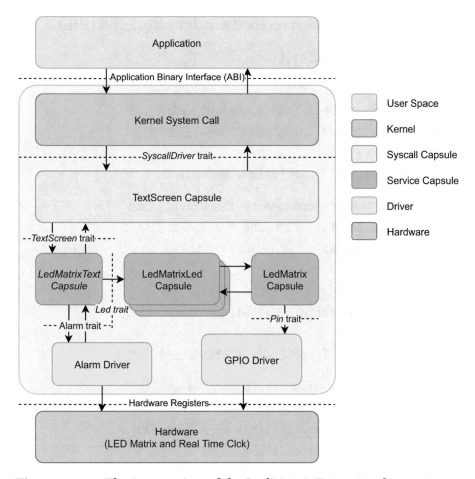

Figure 10-5. *The integration of the LedMatrixText capsule*

The Text Screen API

Before we start writing the capsule, we have to take a look at the
TextScreen and TextScreenClient traits presented in Listing 10-2.
The TextScreen trait's functions are divided into three categories:
synchronous functions, command functions, and the print function.

Listing 10-2. The TextScreen Hardware Interface Layer (HIL)

```
pub trait TextScreen<'a> {
    fn set_client(&self, client: Option<&'a dyn TextScreenClient>);

    /// Returns a tuple (width, height) with the
    /// resolution of the screen that is being
    /// used.
    fn get_size(&self) -> (usize, usize);

    /// Sends a write command to the driver. The
    /// buffer to write from and the len are sent
    /// as arguments.
    fn print(
        &self,
        buffer: &'static mut [u8],
        len: usize,
    ) -> Result<(), (ErrorCode, &'static mut [u8])>;

    /// Sends to the driver a command to set the
    /// cursor at a given position
    /// (x_position, y_position). When finished,
    /// the driver will call the
    /// `command_complete()` callback.
    fn set_cursor(&self, x_position: usize, y_position: usize)
    -> Result<(), ErrorCode>;

    /// Sends to the driver a command to hide the
    /// cursor. When finished, the driver will
    /// call the `command_complete()` callback.
    fn hide_cursor(&self) -> Result<(), ErrorCode>;

    /// Sends to the driver a command to show the
    /// cursor. When finished, the driver will
```

```rust
    /// call the `command_complete()` callback.
    fn show_cursor(&self) -> Result<(), ErrorCode>;

    /// Sends to the driver a command to turn on
    /// the blinking cursor. When finished, the
    /// driver will call the `command_complete()`
    /// callback.
    fn blink_cursor_on(&self) -> Result<(), ErrorCode>;

    /// Sends to the driver a command to turn off
    /// the blinking cursor. When finished, the
    /// driver will call the `command_complete()`
    /// callback.
    fn blink_cursor_off(&self) -> Result<(), ErrorCode>;

    /// Sends to the driver a command to turn on
    /// the display of the screen. When finished,
    /// the driver will call the
    /// `command_complete()` callback.
    fn display_on(&self) -> Result<(), ErrorCode>;

    /// Sends to the driver a command to turn off
    /// the display of the screen. When finished,
    /// the driver will call the
    /// `command_complete()` callback.
    fn display_off(&self) -> Result<(), ErrorCode>;

    /// Sends to the driver a command to clear
    /// the display of the screen. When finished,
    /// the driver will call the
    /// `command_complete()` callback.
    fn clear(&self) -> Result<(), ErrorCode>;
}
```

```
pub trait TextScreenClient {
    /// The driver calls this function when any
    /// command (but a write one) finishes
    /// executing.
    fn command_complete(&self, r: Result<(), ErrorCode>);

    /// The driver calls this function when a
    /// write command finishes executing.
    fn write_complete(&self, buffer: &'static mut [u8], len:
    usize, r: Result<(), ErrorCode>);
}
```

Most of the trait's functions are asynchronous. This means that upon the successful return, the caller will receive another callback function when the requested action is finished. In other words, if the function returns Ok(...), that means that the requested action will be performed, and one of the TextScreenClient trait's functions will be called when the action is done.

The set_client and get_size functions are synchronous. The first one sets the HIL's client. This is any data structure that implements the TextScreenClient trait, and that will be notified when actions are finished. The second one returns the size of the screen in the (columns, rows) format. This function is synchronous as text screens usually have a fixed size, and drivers do not need to read or request it from the hardware.

All the other functions, except print, are considered command functions. Upon completion of their action, they will call the TextScreenClient's command_complete function.

The print function is the one that copies the received buffer to the hardware buffer. Upon completion, this function calls the TextScreenClient's write_complete function. This distinction is necessary as the print function, in contrast with the other functions from the trait, has to return the buffer it has received.

We will discuss all the functions in detail while we implement the driver.

The Driver Implementation

Not that we have all discussed all the required principles, we can start implementing the driver. Our driver comprises three parts: the initialization, the implementation of the TextScreen HIL, and the implementation of the setup syscall API.

Driver Initialization

The first step in the driver's implementation is to define the structure together with all the necessary fields. Similar to the previous two drivers that we wrote, we define the LedMatrixText structure. It takes three arguments: a generic lifetime used for annotating the structure's references, a data type that implements the Led trait, and a data type that implements the Alarm trait (Listing 10-3).

Listing 10-3. The definition of the LedMatrixText driver structure

```
#[derive(Copy, Clone, PartialEq)]
enum Status {
    Idle,
    ExecutesCommand,
    ExecutesPrint,
}

pub struct LedMatrixText<
    'a, L: Led, A: Alarm<'a>
> {
    leds: &'a [&'a L; 25],
    alarm: &'a A,
```

```
client: OptionalCell<
  &'a dyn TextScreenClient
>,

buffer: TakeCell<'a, [u8]>,
position: Cell<usize>,
len: Cell<usize>,

client_buffer: TakeCell<'static, [u8]>,
client_len: Cell<usize>,

speed: Cell<u32>,

status: Cell<Status>,
is_enabled: Cell<bool>,

deferred_caller: &'a DynamicDeferredCall,
deferred_call_handle: OptionalCell<
  DeferredCallHandle
>,
}
```

The led and alarm fields should be familiar as we used them for the previous drivers we wrote. The first one is a reference to an array of references to LEDs and the second one is a reference to a virtual alarm.

Next, we have the client field that references a data structure that implements the TextScreenClient trait. This is used to inform TextScreen when the requested actions are done.

Buffers and Parameters

The buffer field represents our internal buffer. If this were an actual hardware component, buffer would be the part of the display's memory where the displayable data is stored. Its type, TakeCell<'a, T>, is worth some explanation. Similar to OptionalCell<T>, it wraps a value that may or may not exist. The difference is in how that value is placed, used, and taken out from the wrapper. When using OptionalCell, the value wrapped has to be of Copy type. This means that each time the wrapped value is used, Rust makes a copy of it. This is fine for primitive data types like numbers or immutable references but is a problem for mutable references, like our buffers.

As TakeCell does not require the interior data to be Copy, users have to either modify the internal data within the map closure function or move out the data from the TakeCell, making it empty.

Note   Tock provides MapCell for large buffers. This type is identical in API to TakeCell but is optimized for large buffers.

The position field is used to store the current position within the buffer. In other words, it is the index of the letter or digit that will be the next one displayed. The len field shows us the useful length of the data stored in the buffer. For instance, while the buffer may hold up to 100 letters or digits, the actual useful length is given by the amount of data TextScreen sends us. The initial value of len is 0, as the buffer is initially empty.

The following two fields, client_buffer and client_len, are used to store and represent the useful length of the buffer supplied by TextScreen's *print* function. These two fields will store useful data during the interval between the call to the print function and the write_complete callback.

The speed at which the digits and letters are being displayed is stored in the speed field as the number of milliseconds that each character should be visible on the screen.

Our capsule has to implement several asynchronous functions. This means that whenever it receives a function call from the TextScreen, it needs to perform an action, return from the function, and at a certain later time continue the action that it started. This will become more obvious when we start implementing the capsule. To *continue* an action that was previously started, our capsule will have the status field to store its current state. For our capsule, we have the following three states presented in Table 10-1.

Table 10-1. *The states of the LedMatrixText capsule*

State	Description
Idle	The capsule is not executing any action and can take new commands.
ExecutesCommand	The capsule executes a command that requires at completion a call of the client's command_complete function.
ExecutesPrint	The capsule executes a command that requires at completion a call of the client's write_complete function (this happens when the print function is called).

Hardware text screens can be enabled or disabled. Our capsule will simulate this behavior using the is_enabled field. When enabled, the capsule will display digits or letters. When disabled, the capsule will not display anything.

Deferred Calls

To simulate the hardware's asynchronous behavior, we need to use deferred calls. This is a mechanism that the Tock kernel provides to capsules to be able to simulate hardware interrupts. Whenever a driver receives a function call to instruct a piece of hardware to perform an action, it sends a command to the hardware and then returns from the function call. Whenever the hardware completes the task, it sends an interrupt to the Tock kernel. In turn, the Tock kernel executes the interrupt handler of the capsule that has requested the action. The Tock's kernel event loop is presented in Figure 10-6.

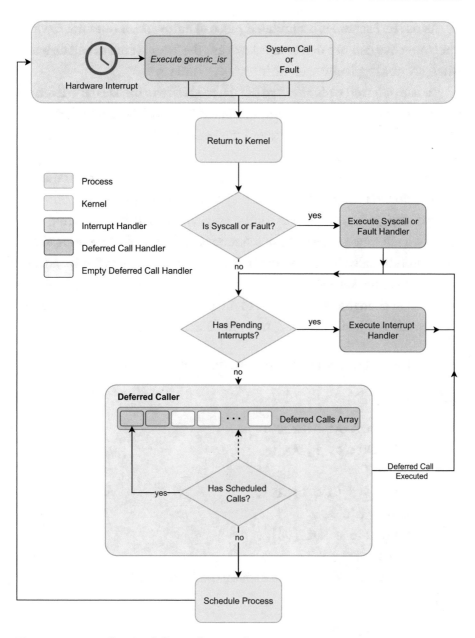

Figure 10-6. *The Tock kernel event loop*

As our text screen is a simulated piece of hardware, it does not have interrupts. We can use deferred calls to ask the Tock kernel to call us back when it would typically execute interrupt handlers.

To use deferred callbacks, we need a reference to the kernel's deferred caller and a handle to our deferred callback. The Tock kernel has an array of registered deferred callbacks, and the handle is the index of our callback function in that array.

Following the definition of the driver's structure, we implement the initialization of the capsule displayed by Listing 10-4. The new function is pretty straightforward. Just as for the previous capsule that we wrote, it receives a reference to an array of references of LEDs and a reference to an alarm. Additionally, it receives the buffer to store data, the initial speed, and a reference to the kernel's deferred caller. The client_buffer does not exist, as no actual client has sent a buffer to the capsule, so the wrapper is empty. The capsule is initially disabled, meaning that it will not display anything.

Listing 10-4. The initialization functions of the LedMatrixText driver

```
impl<
    'a, L: Led, A: Alarm<'a>
> LedMatrixText<'a, L, A> {
    pub fn new(
        leds: &'a [&'a L; 25],
        alarm: &'a A,
        buffer: &'a mut [u8],
        speed: u32,
        deferred_caller: &'a DynamicDeferredCall,
    ) -> Self {

        LedMatrixText {
            leds: leds,
            alarm: alarm,
```

```
            buffer: TakeCell::new(buffer),
            client_buffer: TakeCell::empty(),
            client_len: Cell::new(0),
            position: Cell::new(0),
            speed: Cell::new(speed),
            len: Cell::new(0),
            status: Cell::new(Status::Idle),
            is_enabled: Cell::new(false),
            deferred_caller: deferred_caller,
            deferred_call_handle:
                            OptionalCell::empty(),
            client: OptionalCell::empty(),
        }
    }

    pub fn initialize_callback_handle(
      &self,
      deferred_call_handle: DeferredCallHandle
    ) {
        self.deferred_call_handle.replace(
            deferred_call_handle
        );
    }

    fn schedule_deferred_callback(&self) {
        self.deferred_call_handle
            .map(|handle|
                self.deferred_caller.set(*handle)
        );
    }

    /* ... */
}
```

The following two functions are used by the deferred callbacks: `initialize_callback_handle` and `schedule_deferred_callback`. The first one receives the deferred call handle as an argument. This is what the capsule can use to schedule a call. As we described before, this is a number representing the index within the kernel's deferred calls array.

The second function, `schedule_deferred_callback`, asks the kernel to call the capsule back as soon as it (the kernel) can execute interrupt handlers.

The TextScreen HIL Implementation

Now that we have written the initialization of our capsule, we can implement the TextScreen trait. This allows us to connect our capsule to the generic *TextScreen* driver supplied by Tock. Listing 10-5 presents the source code. First, we add the get_buffer_length function to the driver's implementation. This returns the length of the buffer that we have received to simulate the hardware buffer.

Listing 10-5. The implementation of TextScreen for LedMatrixText

```
impl<
    'a, L: Led, A: Alarm<'a>
> LedMatrixText<'a, L, A> {
  /* ... */
  fn get_buffer_len(&self) -> usize {
      self.buffer.map_or(
          0, |buffer| buffer.len()
      )
  }
}
```

```rust
impl<
    'a, L: Led, A: Alarm<'a>
> TextScreen<'a> for LedMatrixText<'a, L, A> {
  fn set_client(
    &self,
    client: Option<&'a dyn TextScreenClient>
  ) {
      if let Some(client) = client {
          self.client.set(client);
      } else {
          self.client.clear();
      }
  }

  fn get_size(&self) -> (usize, usize) {
      (self.get_buffer_len(), 1)
  }

  fn print(
      &self,
      buffer: &'static mut [u8],
      len: usize,
  ) -> Result<
          (), (ErrorCode, &'static mut [u8])
  > { /* ... */ }

  fn set_cursor(
    &self,
    _x_position: usize,
    _y_position: usize
  ) -> Result<(), ErrorCode> {
      Err(ErrorCode::NOSUPPORT)
  }
```

```
fn hide_cursor(&self) -> Result<(), ErrorCode> {
    Err(ErrorCode::NOSUPPORT)
}

fn show_cursor(&self) -> Result<(), ErrorCode> {
    Err(ErrorCode::NOSUPPORT)
}

fn blink_cursor_on(&self) -> Result<(), ErrorCode> {
    Err(ErrorCode::NOSUPPORT)
}

fn blink_cursor_off(&self) -> Result<(), ErrorCode> {
    Err(ErrorCode::NOSUPPORT)
}

fn display_on(&self) -> Result<(), ErrorCode>
{
    if self.status.get() == Status::Idle {
        self.status.set(
                Status::ExecutesCommand
        );
        self.is_enabled.set(true);
        self.schedule_deferred_callback();
        Ok(())
    } else {
        Err(ErrorCode::BUSY)
    }
}

fn display_off(&self) -> Result<(), ErrorCode> {
    if self.status.get() == Status::Idle {
        self.status.set(
                Status::ExecutesCommand
        );
```

```
        self.is_enabled.set(false);
        self.schedule_deferred_callback();
        Ok(())
    } else {
        Err(ErrorCode::BUSY)
    }
}

fn clear(&self) -> Result<(), ErrorCode> {
    if self.status.get() == Status::Idle {
        self.status.set(
                Status::ExecutesCommand
        );
        self.position.set(0);
        self.len.set(0);
        self.clear();
        self.schedule_deferred_callback();
        Ok(())
    } else {
        Err(ErrorCode::BUSY)
    }
  }
}
```

The first function that we implement is set_client. This receives as an argument the client upon which we have to call the two functions, command_complete and write_complete, when a requested action is done. The function's code is pretty straightforward: if we receive a reference to a client, we unwrap it and store it. If we have no reference, we clear our previous reference to the client.

The *TextScreen* capsule will have to know the resolution of our screen, meaning the number of columns and rows that our screen can display. For this, it will call the get_size function. Within this function, we have to return a tuple of two usize variables synchronously: the first is the number of columns, and the second is the number of rows. The number of columns that we can display is the size of our buffer, and the number of rows is 1.

Note   The get_size function is synchronous as most screens have a fixed hardware resolution. Due to this, the capsules usually return constant values.

Asynchronous Functions

The following functions that we implement are display_on and display_ off. Just as their names suggest, these functions turn the display on and off. In our case, all that they need to do is to set the value of the is_enabled field. In the case of actual hardware, these functions send a command to the display hardware and immediately return. Whenever the display finishes performing the action, it notifies its driver using an interrupt, and the driver, in turn, calls the command_complete function. We need to take a close look at the two.

These are asynchronous functions, meaning that the function's caller, Tock's *TextScreen* capsule, expects them to either fail or to start an action and return and notify the capsule when the action is done. The functions return Result<(), ErrorCode>. If the called function returns an error, the caller understands that the requested action cannot be done and expects nothing else from the driver. If the called function returns Ok(()), the requested action can be done, or at least the capsule will try to do it. The caller now must wait for a call of the command_complete function before it can request another command.

Now let's take a look at the code. First of all, in both functions we check if the current status of the capsule is Idle. This means that the capsule has no action in progress and can accept a new request. If the status is not Idle, we have an action in progress and should not accept a new one. In this case, we simply return ErrorCode::BUSY. If the current status is Idle, we can start a new action.

First of all, we set the status to ExecuteCommand as we have started to perform an action. Secondly, we set the is_enabled field to the corresponding value. As our driver is not controlling an actual hardware display, setting the display on or off is the synchronous action of setting the is_enabled field. At this point, we have finished our action. If this were hardware, we would schedule a data transmission towards the device.

As we have completed the requested action, we are tempted to call the command_complete function right away. However, we cannot do this. Our caller expects to receive a call to command_complete **after** our function has returned. This means that before we can call command_complete, we have to return Ok(()), which is obviously not possible. This is where deferred calls come into play. Instead of directly calling command_complete, we ask the kernel to schedule a deferred call for us. In other words, we ask the kernel to call a function for us, after we have returned to our caller. To do this, we use the schedule_deferred_callback function defined in Listing 10-4.

Caution   Calling a client's callback function synchronously is an error and should not be attempted. This can lead to kernel errors and even panics. The source code presented in Listing 10-6 is incorrect and should not be used.

Listing 10-6. The incorrect way of calling the callback function

```
fn display_on(&self) -> Result<(), ErrorCode> {
    if self.status.get() == Status::Idle {
        self.status.set(Status::ExecutesCommand);
        self.is_enabled.set(true);
        /* error, do not use it like this */
        self.client.map(|client|
            client.command_complete(Ok(())));
        Ok(())
    } else {
        Err(ErrorCode::BUSY)
    }
}
```

To be able to call the deferred function, we still have to perform one more step, which is implementing the DynamicDeferredCallClient trait. Its implementation is illustrated in Listing 10-7. The call function is invoked by the kernel as if it were an interrupt handler. In this function, we verify the status of the driver. If it is Idle, we most probably made a mistake when writing the capsule. We shouldn't have scheduled a deferred call if we had no action in progress.

Listing 10-7. The implementation of the DynamicDeferredCallClient trait

```
impl<
        'a, L: Led, A: Alarm<'a>
>
DynamicDeferredCallClient for
                    LedMatrixText<'a, L, A> {
    fn call(&self, _handle: DeferredCallHandle) {
        match self.status.get() {
```

```
Status::Idle => {
  // panic! ("Error, callback Idle");
}
Status::ExecutesCommand => {
  self.client.map(|client|
      client.command_complete(Ok(()))));
}
Status::ExecutesPrint => {
    self.client.map(|client| {
      self.client_buffer.take()
        .map(|buffer|
            client.write_complete(
              buffer,
              self.client_len.get(),
              Ok(())
            )
        );
    });
  }
}
self.status.set(Status::Idle);
  }
}
```

Note   While in development, we can panic to signal an error. In
production environments, it is advised not to panic the kernel but
rather log the error.

If the status is ExecuteCommand, we call the command_complete
function. If the status is ExecutePrint, we call the write_complete
function and return the buffer received from the client. We will discuss
more about this as we describe the print function.

In the same way that we have implemented the display_on and
display_off functions, we now implement the clear function. By calling
clear, the *TextScreen* driver asks us to clean the display. In our case, we
set the current position and the useful buffer data length to 0. We then
schedule the deferred callback and return Ok(()).

Note   As you can notice, our capsule implements two functions
called clear. One is from the inherent implementation (impl
LedMatrixText) and the other one from the *TextScreen*
implementation (impl TextScreen for LedMatrixText). When
using self.clear() Rust looks for the function in the inherent
implementation, and only if it does not find one there, it calls the
one from the trait implementation. To call clear from the trait
implementation, we must write TextScreen::clear(self).

Printing the Text

The most important function that we have to implement is print. This
receives two arguments: a buffer and the number of useful characters
that the buffer stores. The function, displayed in Listing 10-8, copies the
useful data from the buffer to the driver's internal buffer. Just like the other
functions that we have implemented, it is asynchronous, which means that
it either returns an error or success followed by a call to the client's write_
complete function.

Listing 10-8. The implementation of the print function

```
impl<
    'a, L: Led, A: Alarm<'a>
> TextScreen<'a> for LedMatrixText<'a, L, A> {
  /* ... */

  fn print(
    &self,
    buffer: &'static mut [u8],
    len: usize,
  ) -> Result<(), (ErrorCode, &'static mut [u8])> {
    if self.status.get() == Status::Idle {
      if len <= buffer.len() {
        self.status.set(Status::ExecutesPrint);
        let previous_len = self.len.get();
        let printed_len = self.buffer.map_or(
                0, |buf| {
          let max_len = cmp::min
                      len, buf.len()
          );
          for position in 0..max_len {
            buf[position] = buffer[position];
          }
          self.len.set(cmp::max(
              max_len, self.len.get()
          ));
          max_len
        });
        self.client_buffer.replace(buffer);
        self.client_len.set(printed_len);
        self.schedule_deferred_callback();
```

```
        if previous_len == 0 && printed_len!=0 {
          self.display_next();
        }
        Ok(())
      } else {
        Err((ErrorCode::SIZE, buffer))
      }
    } else {
      Err((ErrorCode::BUSY, buffer))
    }
  }
}

/* ... */
}
```

Let's analyze step by step what the function does. First of all, it checks if there is any other action in progress by reading the value of the status field. If this is not Idle, another action is in progress, so the function returns ErrorCode::BUSY together with the buffer. If the driver's status is Idle, the function proceeds and verifies if the received arguments are valid. More specifically, it makes sure that the provided length of the useful data, len, is less or equal to the size of the received buffer. If this is not the case, the function stops and returns ErrorCode::INVALID and the buffer. With this, the function signals the caller that the received arguments are invalid.

If there is no other action in progress and the arguments are valid, the print function can start a new action by setting the value of the status field to ExecutePrint. Next, it stores the size of the useful data, len, in the previous_len variable so it can later make a power consumption optimization.

Note   We use a different status value for the `print` action as we have to call a different deferred callback when the action is done. Instead of calling `command_complete`, we have to call `write_complete`.

The following action is to copy the data from the received buffer to the capsules's buffer. For that, we have to access the internal buffer using the `map_or` function. This function will return the number of characters that have been copied.

If the `TakeCell` that wraps the capsule's buffer is storing a buffer, it will call the closure function, putting a reference to the buffer in `buf` argument. If there is no buffer stored, it will return 0 as no characters could be copied. For this capsule, this should never happen, as we never take away the buffer. On the other hand, if real hardware were involved, the driver would probably take away the buffer from its wrapper and send it to the transport (I2C, SPI, etc.) driver.

The actual size of the data being copied, stored in `max_len`, is the minimum between the requested data size, `len`, and the size of the driver's buffer, `buf.len()`. This makes sure that the capsule's buffer does not overflow. There can be two approaches to copying the data from the received buffer to the capsule's. We can either verify that the data we need to copy fits into the buffer and return an error if it does not or simply copy as much data as possible. The second solution is valid only if we can inform the caller that only a part of the data has been copied. As `write_complete` requires us to notify the caller of how much data has been copied, we chose the second approach.

The new length of the useful data stored into the capsule's buffer is the maximum between the size that we received as an argument, `len`, and the current size of the data within the buffer, `buf.len()`.

This requires a bit of explanation. Our capsule starts with an empty buffer, a buffer that contains 0 bytes of useful data. Whenever the *TextScreen* capsule asks us to write some data to our buffer, we copy that data starting at position 0. Now the useful data that the capsule's buffer stores is the amount that we have just written. When we get another print call, we again write the received data starting at position 0. The amount of data that we have just written might be longer than the one we previously stored.

Upon copying the data, the closure function returns the number of copied bytes, max_len. This concludes the print action. If this were actual hardware, the driver would have sent the received data buffer to the underlying hardware, returned Ok(()) to TextScreen, and waited for an interrupt. Within the interrupt, it would have called write_complete to return the received buffer and inform TextScreen about the amount of data that it had just transferred to the hardware device.

Our driver is a simulated one, so it does not have to send the buffer, it simply copies the data synchronously. As TextScreen requires an asynchronous response, the print function uses the client_buffer and client_len fields to store the received buffer and the written length of the data. It schedules a deferred callback and returns Ok(()).

Within the deferred callback, if the current action is ExecutePrint, the capsule takes back the stored buffer and written data length and returns them to the caller using the write_complete function.

Note   As we do not actually interface a hardware device, some of the actions defined in the TextScreen trait cannot be performed. All the actions that handle the cursor position, its blinking and displaying, return ErrorCode::NOSUPPORT.

The Text Displaying Process

Our capsule is now ready to interact with the *TextScreen* driver, but it is still missing the part that displays digits and letters. The print, clear, and display functions are almost identical to what we have written for our previous capsules. The display function verifies if the display is enabled and only then displays the character to the LED matrix. If the display is disabled, it turns off the matrix LEDs (Listing 10-9).

Listing 10-9. Displaying the digits and letters

```
impl<
    'a, L: Led, A: Alarm<'a>
> LedMatrixText<'a, L, A> {
  /* ... */
  fn display_next(&self) {
    if self.position.get() >= self.len.get() {
      self.position.set(0);
    }
    if self.position.get() < self.len.get() {
      if !self.buffer.map_or(false, |buffer| {
        if self.position.get() < buffer.len() {
          let _ = self.display(
            buffer[self.position.get()] as char
          );
          self.position.set(
            self.position.get() + 1
          );
          true
        } else {
          false
        }
      }) {
```

449

```
            self.clear();
          }
        } else {
            self.clear();
        }
        if self.len.get() > 0 {
          self.alarm.set_alarm(
            self.alarm.now(), self.alarm.ticks_from_ms(
                 self.speed.get()
            )
          );
        }
    }

    fn print(&self, glyph: u32) { /* ... */ }

    fn clear(&self) { /* ... */ }

    fn display(&self, character: char) -> Result<(), ErrorCode> {
      if self.is_enabled.get() {
        /* ... */
      } else {
        self.clear();
        Ok(())
      }
    }
    /* ... */
}

impl<
    'a, L: Led, A: Alarm<'a>
> AlarmClient for LedMatrixText<'a, L, A> {
    fn alarm(&self) {
```

```
      self.display_next();
  }
}
```

The core function that does the heavy lifting is display_text. This function is called whenever the alarm fires. Its purpose is to display the next character from the capsule's buffer. Within the capsule's structure, we have defined a field called position that stores the following position within the buffer that has to be displayed, and a field called len that stores the size of the actual data within the buffer. Before printing anything, display_next has to determine if it can actually display the digit or letter stored at position. The capsule might have already displayed the last digit or letter from the buffer. If position is larger than len, position is reset to 0.

Now, position should be less than len. The function still checks this condition before continuing, as the buffer might be empty as a result of a call to TextScreen::clear, and therefore it should not display anything and just turn off the LEDs. If position is valid, the function tries to access the buffer using the map_or function. In this case, this function returns whether a digit or letter has been displayed or not. Suppose there is no buffer, map_or returns false. If there is a buffer, the closure function is executed. Just to be on the safe side, the closure function verifies that the position is within the buffer's size, asks the display function to display the digit or letter, and increments position.

If there is no buffer available or the position is out of the buffer's size, the LEDs are turned off using the clear function.

This driver tries to perform a small power consumption optimization. Tock will do its best to put the MCU into low power mode if there is no task to perform. If the buffer is empty, there is no point in scheduling the next alarm until there is data to display. This is why display_next schedules the alarm only if there is data in the driver's buffer. This is why the print function in Listing 10-8 verifies if the previous length of the buffer was empty and the current length is different from 0 and calls `display_next` immediately. If the previous length was 0, there is no alarm scheduled to call `display_next`. If the current buffer size is 0, there is no point in calling `display_next` as there is nothing to display.

The Setup Syscall API Implementation

We currently have a fully working text screen service capsule that uses the LEDs matrix to display digits and letters. Processes that require a text screen to display text will be able to use Tock's text screen API without any modifications. On the other hand, our driver is not an actual text screen but instead displays one digit or letter at a time. Userspace processes might want to set the speed at which the text is being displayed.

The text screen API does not expose any configuration functions as it does not know anything about the underlying hardware. To solve this, we can expose a specific API for our driver that will enable processes to set the speed. Table 10-2 shows the proposed API.

Table 10-2. *The setup system call API for the LedMatrixText capsule.*

Command				
No	**Arg 1**	**Arg 2**	**Description**	**Return**
0	Not used	Not used	Verifies if the capsule is available.	*CommandReturn::success()*
1	speed	Not used	The time in milliseconds during which each digit or letter is displayed.	*CommandReturn::success()*

Subscribe (not used)

Allow (not used)

Our capsule exposes a single command number, 1, that uses one parameter, the time in milliseconds between each character.

The implementation, presented in Listing 10-10, is very basic. We implement the command function from the SyscallDriver trait. It recognizes command 0 to signal that the capsule is available, and command 1 that sets the speed field.

The allocate_grant function returns Ok(()) as our driver does not use a grant, and we have nothing to allocate.

As we provide a syscall API to the userspace processes, we have to assign a unique ID to our driver. For this driver, we choose 0xa0003.

Listing 10-10. The implementation of the setup system call API for the LedMatrixText driver

```
pub const DRIVER_NUM: usize = 0xa0003;

impl<
    'a, L: Led, A: Alarm<'a>
> SyscallDriver for LedMatrixText<'a, L, A> {
    fn allocate_grant(&self, _: ProcessId) -> Result<(), Error> {
        Ok(())
    }

    fn command(
        &self,
        command_number: usize,
        r2: usize,
        _r3: usize,
        _process_id: ProcessId,
    ) -> CommandReturn {
        match command_number {
            0 => CommandReturn::success(),
```

```
    1 => {
        self.speed.set(r2 as u32);
        CommandReturn::success()
    }
    _ => CommandReturn::failure(
            ErrorCode::NOSUPPORT
        ),
    }
  }
}
```

Capsule Registration

In the previous chapters, we implemented syscall capsules, which provide an API to the user space processes. All syscall capsules have to be registered with the kernel using the SyscallDriverLookup trait. On the other hand, service capsules provide services to other capsules and do not usually interact with the userspace directly. These capsules have to be connected to other capsules, in most cases through a reference passed as an argument to the other capsule's new function.

In our case, the capsule that uses our services is *TextScreen*. First, we register *TextScreen* with the kernel as illustrated in Listing 10-11 by adding the text_screen field to the MicroBit structure. Next, we connect its ID with this field within the with_driver function of the SyscallDriverLookup trait implementation. This is required only if we want to be able to use the setup syscall API.

Listing 10-11. The definition and registration of the TextScreen and
the LedMatrixText drivers

```
pub struct MicroBit {
  /* ... */

    text_screen: &'static capsules::text_screen::TextScreen<
    'static>,
    led_matrix_text: &'static drivers::led_matrix_text::
    LedMatrixText<
        'static,
        LedMatrixLed<
            'static,
            nrf52::gpio::GPIOPin<'static>,
            capsules::virtual_alarm::VirtualMuxAlarm<'static,
            nrf52::rtc::Rtc<'static>>,
        >,
        capsules::virtual_alarm::VirtualMuxAlarm<
            'static, nrf52833::rtc::Rtc<'static>
        >,
    >,
}

impl SyscallDriverLookup for MicroBit {
   fn with_driver<F, R>(
     &self, driver_num: usize, f: F
 ) -> R
   where
       F: FnOnce(Option<
           &dyn kernel::syscall::SyscallDriver
       >) -> R,
   {
```

```
match driver_num {
    /* ... */

    capsules::text_screen::DRIVER_NUM => f(Some(
    self.text_screen)),
     /* required only is the setup API
        is used */
    drivers::led_matrix_text::DRIVER_NUM => f(Some(
    self.led_matrix_text)),
    /* ... */
    _ => f(None),
    }
  }
}
```

All that is left to do is to initialize *TextScreen* and *LedMatrixText*. The first step is to make room for a deferred callback handler for our driver. micro:bit's board implementation defines the kernel's array of dynamic deferred clients called dynamic_deferred_call_clients. Originally, it has three positions. We have to add one for our capsule, so we will replace the number 3 with 4. Listing 10-12 presents in bold the line where we have to make the replacement.

The second step is to define a buffer that our driver will use. As *LedMatrixText* requires a buffer with a static lifetime, we use static_init to initialize an array of 50 u8 elements called led_matrix_buffer.

Listing 10-12. The initialization of the TextScreen and the LedMatrixText drivers

```
pub unsafe fn main() {
    /* ... */
```

```
let dynamic_deferred_call_clients =
static_init!(
    [DynamicDeferredCallClientState; 4],
    Default::default()
);

/* ... */

let led_matrix_buffer = static_init!(
  [u8; 50], [0; 50]
);

/* ... */

let virtual_alarm_led_matrix_text = static_init!(
    capsules::virtual_alarm::VirtualMuxAlarm<
        'static, nrf52833::rtc::Rtc
    >,
    capsules::virtual_alarm::VirtualMuxAlarm
            ::new(mux_alarm)
);

let led_matrix_text = static_init!(
    drivers::led_matrix_text::LedMatrixText<
        'static,
        LedMatrixLed<
            'static,
            nrf52::gpio::GPIOPin<'static>,
            capsules::virtual_alarm::VirtualMuxAlarm<'static,
            nrf52::rtc::Rtc<'static>>,
        >,
        capsules::virtual_alarm::VirtualMuxAlarm<'static,
        nrf52::rtc::Rtc<'static>>,
    >,
```

```
drivers::led_matrix_text::LedMatrixText::new(
    components::led_matrix_leds!(
        nrf52::gpio::GPIOPin<'static>,
        capsules::virtual_alarm::VirtualMuxAlarm<'static,
        nrf52::rtc::Rtc<'static>>,
        led,
        (0, 0),
        (1, 0),
        // ...
    ),
    virtual_alarm_led_matrix_text,
    led_matrix_buffer,
    300,
    dynamic_deferred_caller
    ),
);

virtual_alarm_led_matrix_text
        .set_alarm_client(led_matrix_text);
led_matrix_text.initialize_callback_handle(
    dynamic_deferred_caller
        .register(led_matrix_text)
        .expect("no deferred call slot available for led
        matrix text"),
);

let text_screen = components::text_screen::
TextScreenComponent:: new(
    board_kernel,
    capsules::text_screen::DRIVER_NUM,
    led_matrix_text,
)
.finalize(components::screen_buffer_size!(50));
```

```
/* ... */

let microbit = MicroBit {
    /* ... */

    text_screen,
    led_matrix_text,
};

/* ... */
}
```

Now that we have an allocated buffer, we can initialize the *LedMatrixText* driver. The initialization is similar to the initialization of the capsules from the previous chapters. We have to construct a new virtual alarm and an array of LEDs. The new arguments that we have to provide are the buffer and the kernel's deferred caller. These are displayed in bold in Listing 10-12.

Besides setting the virtual alarm's client, we have to register the actual deferred callback handle. To obtain it, we use the `register` function provided by the kernel's deferred caller, `dynamic_deferred_caller`. This function receives a data structure that implements the `DynamicDeferredCallClient` trait, in our case the capsule itself, and returns the position at which the kernel has registered it into its deferred callback clients array. This position is the handle. This handle is sent to the capsule using the `initialize_callback_handle` function.

With our capsule initialized, we can now create the *TextScreen* capsule and connect our capsule to it. As *TextScreen*'s initialization requires several steps that are similar to every board, Tock provides a component structure that simplifies the initialization by abstracting the boilerplate code. The component provides a new function that receives the kernel, *TextScreen*'s driver number, and a reference to a driver that implements the `TextScreen` trait. In this case, this is our driver.

The `finalize` function returns a reference to an initialized *TextScreen* capsule. It receives the return of the `screen_buffer_size` macro as an argument. In turn, the macro's argument is the size of the *TextScreen's* buffer.

Note   The two capsules that we have initialized use two different buffers of the same length. The *TextScreen* capsule has a buffer to copy the data from processes, data stored in allowed buffers, and send it to the hardware driver. This buffer is called the *frame buffer*. The hardware drivers that *TextScreen* uses do not usually contain a buffer but rather receives a reference to the *frame buffer* of *TextScreen*. On the other hand, our driver is not an actual hardware screen and simulates the screen's internal screen buffer. This is why we have two identically sized buffers, one for each driver.

Capsule Usage

So far, we have designed and implemented an LED matrix text screen service capsule. A service capsule means that it offers services to other capsules, in our case, Tock's T*extScreen* capsule. This means that a process that wants to use our capsule can do so by using Tock's text screen API. Listing 10-13 shows an example.

Listing 10-13. Usage example for the text screen driver API

```
#include "text_screen.h"
#include "timer.h"
#include <stdio.h>

#define SCREEN_BUFFER_SIZE 50
```

```
int main(void) {
 if (driver_exists(DRIVER_NUM_TEXT_SCREEN)) {
   if (text_screen_init(SCREEN_BUFFER_SIZE) == RETURNCODE_
   SUCCESS) {
    char *buffer = (char*)text_screen_buffer ();
    strcpy (
      buffer, "Hello World from the Microbit"
    );
    text_screen_set_cursor (0, 0);
    text_screen_write (strlen (buffer));
   } else {
     printf ("Error: failed to initialize text screen\n");
   }
 } else {
   printf ("Error: text screen driver is not present\n");
 }
 return 0;
}
```

The Text Screen API

First, we make sure that Tock's text screen driver is present in the kernel using the driver_exists function. Next up, we can use the text screen API to display messages. The text screen API is a relatively low-level API that should be used by other higher-level libraries and functions specialized in displaying text. Such an example might be the printf family of functions.

Note   At least for now, Tock does not provide such higher-level APIs for text screens. The printf function uses the serial console to display text.

461

The text screen API is specialized in sending buffers of data to the text screen driver. The text screen library allocates a buffer that holds the text that will be sent to the text screen driver. A process that wants to display a message has to copy the message's characters into this buffer, then ask the library to send the buffer over to the driver.

The text_screen_init function receives a number as an argument and allocates an internal text buffer of that size. To access that buffer, developers have to use the text_screen_buffer function, which returns a pointer to it. The next step is to copy the desired message to the buffer.

Before sending the text to the driver, processes usually inform the driver about the position where that text should be displayed using the text_screen_set_cursor function. In our specific case, this function returns an error as our driver does not have support for it. We can safely ignore the error. The buffer is sent to the driver using the text_screen_ write function.

Note   This example will work without any modifications on any device that has a text screen driver present, regardless of the display hardware that it uses.

The Setup API

Besides the text screen API, our driver provides some additional API for setting up the LED Matrix text screen. This setup API is specific to the driver that we wrote and will not be available for other hardware platforms. As with previous drivers, we have to write a library that exposes this API. We create two files in the **applications/drivers** folder called *led_matrix_text.h* and *led_matrix_text.c* (Listing 10-14). These files expose and implement the led_matrix_text_set_speed function that allows processes to set the delay between two displayed letters or digits.

Listing 10-14. The led_matrix_text.c library file

```c
#include "led_matrix_text.h"
#include "tock.h"

bool led_matrix_text_is_present (void) {
 syscall_return_t ret = command (
          DRIVER_NUM_LED_MATRIX_TEXT, 0, 0, 0
 );
 if (ret.type == TOCK_SYSCALL_SUCCESS) {
   return true;
 } else {
   return false;
 }
}

bool led_matrix_text_set_speed (
     unsigned int speed
) {
 syscall_return_t ret = command (
     DRIVER_NUM_LED_MATRIX_TEXT, 1, speed, 0
 );
 if (ret.type == TOCK_SYSCALL_SUCCESS) {
   return true;
 } else {
   return false;
 }
}
```

We can modify the application displayed in Listing 10-13 to use the setup API. The differences are shown in Listing 10-15 highlighted in bold. First of all, we verify if the underlying screen driver is *LedMatrixText*. If this is the case, we set the display speed using the led_matrix_text_ set_speed function from Listing 10-14.

Listing 10-15. Using the setup API to set the speed at which digits and letters are displayed

```c
#include "led_matrix_text.h"
#include "text_screen.h"
#include "timer.h"
#include <stdio.h>

#define SCREEN_BUFFER_SIZE 50

int main(void) {
 if (driver_exists(DRIVER_NUM_TEXT_SCREEN)) {
   if (text_screen_init(SCREEN_BUFFER_SIZE) == RETURNCODE_SUCCESS) {
     char *buffer=(char*)text_screen_buffer ();
     strcpy (
         buffer, "Hello World from the Microbit"
     );
     text_screen_set_cursor (0, 0);
     text_screen_write (strlen (buffer));
     if (driver_exists (
         DRIVER_NUM_LED_MATRIX_TEXT
     )) {
       printf ("Setting speed to 500\n");
       led_matrix_text_set_speed (500);
     }
   } else {
     printf ("Error: failed to initialize text screen\n");
   }
 } else {
   printf ("Error: text screen driver is not present\n");
 }
 return 0;
}
```

Use the Raspberry Pi Pico

Using the driver with the Raspberry Pi Pico is straightforward. We use the same hardware setup from chapters 8 and 9. The only changes that we have to make are the driver's initialization in the board implementation. This is the **main.rs** file inside the **project/kernel/raspberry_pi_pico folder**.

The steps that we have to follow are:

- define the *TextScreen* and *LedMatrixText* drivers in the RaspberryPiPico structure;

- add two match arms in the with_driver function from the SyscallDriverLookup's trait implementation that return the *TextScreen* and *LedMatrixText* drivers;

- disable the GPIO pins 2 to 11 from the GPIO driver;

- initialize a virtual alarm for the *LedMatrixText* driver;

- register a new deferred call handler;

- initialize the *TextScreen* and *LedMatrixText* drivers;

- set the *LedMatrixText* driver as the alarm's client.

Listing 10-16 shows all the changes to the **main.rs** file, highlighting the differences between the micro:bit and the Raspberry Pi Pico implementations.

Listing 10-16. The definition and setup of the TextScreen and LedMatrixText drivers for the Raspberry Pi Pico

```
pub struct RaspberryPiPico {
    /* ... */

    text_screen: &'static capsules::text_screen::
    TextScreen<'static>,
```

```
    led_matrix_text: &'static drivers::led_matrix_text::
    LedMatrixText<
        'static,
        LedMatrixLed<
            'static,
            RPGpioPin<'static>,
            capsules::virtual_alarm::VirtualMuxAlarm<'static,
            RPTimer<'static>>,
        >,
        capsules::virtual_alarm::VirtualMuxAlarm<
            'static, RPTimer<'static>
        >,
    >,
}

impl SyscallDriverLookup for RaspberryPiPico {
    fn with_driver<F, R>(
        &self, driver_num: usize, f: F
    ) -> R
    where
        F: FnOnce(
            Option<&dyn SyscallDriver>
        ) -> R,
    {
        match driver_num {
            /* ... */

            capsules::text_screen::DRIVER_NUM => f(Some(
            self.text_screen)),
            drivers::led_matrix_text::DRIVER_NUM => f(Some(
            self.led_matrix_text)),
            _ => f(None),
```

```
        }
    }
}

pub unsafe fn main() {
    /* ... */

    let led_matrix_driver = components::led_matrix_component_
    helper!(
        RPGpioPin<'static>,
        RPTimer<'static>,
        mux_alarm,
        @fps => 60,
        @cols => kernel::hil::gpio::ActivationMode::ActiveHigh,
        &peripherals.pins.get_pin(RPGpio::GPIO2),
        &peripherals.pins.get_pin(RPGpio::GPIO3),
        &peripherals.pins.get_pin(RPGpio::GPIO4),
        &peripherals.pins.get_pin(RPGpio::GPIO5),
        &peripherals.pins.get_pin(RPGpio::GPIO6),
        @rows => kernel::hil::gpio::ActivationMode::ActiveLow,
        &peripherals.pins.get_pin(RPGpio::GPIO7),
        &peripherals.pins.get_pin(RPGpio::GPIO8),
        &peripherals.pins.get_pin(RPGpio::GPIO9),
        &peripherals.pins.get_pin(RPGpio::GPIO10),
        &peripherals.pins.get_pin(RPGpio::GPIO11),
    )
.finalize(components::led_matrix_component_buf!(
        RPGpioPin<'static>,
        RPTimer<'static>
    ));
    let virtual_alarm_led_matrix_text = static_init!(
        capsules::virtual_alarm::VirtualMuxAlarm<'static,
        RPTimer<'static>>,
```

467

```
        capsules::virtual_alarm::VirtualMuxAlarm
                ::new(mux_alarm)
    );
    let led_matrix_buffer = static_init!(
        [u8; 50], [0; 50]
    );

    let led_matrix_text = static_init!(
        drivers::led_matrix_text::LedMatrixText<
            'static,
            LedMatrixLed<
                'static,
                RPGpioPin<'static>,
                capsules::virtual_alarm::VirtualMuxAlarm<'static,
                RPTimer<'static>>,
            >,
            capsules::virtual_alarm::VirtualMuxAlarm<'static,
            RPTimer<'static>>,
        >,
        drivers::led_matrix_text::LedMatrixText::new(
            components::led_matrix_leds!(
                RPGpioPin<'static>,
                capsules::virtual_alarm::VirtualMuxAlarm<'static,
                RPTimer<'static>>,
                led_matrix_driver,
                (0, 0),
                (1, 0),
                //...
            ),
            virtual_alarm_led_matrix_text,
            led_matrix_buffer,
            300,
```

```
            dynamic_deferred_caller
        )
    );
    virtual_alarm_led_matrix_text
            .set_alarm_client(led_matrix_text);
    led_matrix_text.initialize_callback_handle(
        dynamic_deferred_caller
            .register(led_matrix_text)
            .expect("no deferred call slot available for led
            matrix text"),
    );

    let text_screen = components::text_screen::
    TextScreenComponent::
new(
        board_kernel,
        capsules::text_screen::DRIVER_NUM,
        led_matrix_text,
    )
    .finalize(components::screen_buffer_size!(50));
    /* ... */
    let raspberry_pi_pico = RaspberryPiPico {
        /* ... */
        text_screen,
        led_matrix_text,
    };
    /* ... */
}
```

Summary

In this chapter, we have presented an example of how to design and implement a service capsule. Tock ships a series of *standard* capsules that provide different high-level APIs to the userspace. Such capsules are sensors, like *temperature, humidity, motion*, devices like *screen* and *text screen*, *touch* panels, *storage*, etc. All these *standard* syscall drivers need one or several underlying service capsules that interact with the actual hardware. This separation is important as processes in the user space can use a standard API, regardless of the underlying hardware. These standard syscall capsules are similar to Android's Hardware Abstraction Layer[1] or HAL.

Another important aspect discussed in this chapter is *deferred calls*. As Tock has an asynchronous design, most Hardware Interface Layers or HILs, like *TextScreen*, expect actions to be performed asynchronously. In other words, a request either returns an error or starts an action and immediately returns success. Upon the action's completion, the requester is notified through a callback. There are cases, though, where such behavior is not possible. The driver that we presented in this chapter simulates a hardware screen, and as such, all actions are synchronous. Tock provides the mechanism of deferred calls that allows developers to ask the kernel to run a callback during the next interrupt handling step. Another word for deferred calls is *software interrupts*.

Standard drivers provide a limited set of setup APIs. The underlying hardware might expose an extended set of setup possibilities that are not covered by the standard API. In this case, service drivers can add a small setup syscall API that processes can use. There is a downside to this: processes using the setup API become dependent on the specific hardware.

---

[1] Android Architecture, https://source.android.com/devices/architecture#hidl

Tip   With time, if several pieces of hardware expose similar sets of setup APIs, it is a good idea to start defining a new standard setup HIL that the standard driver can implement. This will make processes using these setup APIs hardware independent.

Last but not least, we have exemplified the usage of the text screen userspace API to display a text via our driver.

CHAPTER 11

Tock Userspace Drivers

In the previous chapters, we focused on building a kernel capsule to interface an LED matrix. This capsule is part of the Tock kernel and is registered as a new driver. However, the Tock architecture allows us to build drivers that run in the userspace.

The userspace drivers are deployed as regular processes that run on the system. They leverage Tock's inter-process communication mechanism so other processes can interact with them and ask them to perform various actions.

Requirements

This chapter requires the following hardware components based on the device you use:

- **Micro:bit**

  - 1 x micro:bit v2 board

- **Raspberry Pi Pico**

  - 1 x Raspberry Pi Pico board;

  - 1 x KWM-R30881CUAB or KWM-R30881AUAB LED matrix;

© Alexandru Radovici and Ioana Culic 2022
A. Radovici and I. Culic, *Getting Started with Secure Embedded Systems*,
https://doi.org/10.1007/978-1-4842-7789-8_11

- 14 x jumper wires;

- 5 x 220Ω resistors;

- 2 x (or 1 x large) breadboards.

The Tock Inter-Process Communication Library

As Tock is designed to support multiple processes running simultaneously, it also implements a way for these processes to communicate. The Inter-Process Communication, or IPC, mechanism in Tock relies on callback functions and notifications, which are described in the **ipc.h** file in **libtock-c**.

Some of the processes running on the system are designed to listen for commands and execute them. These are called services that the regular processes (clients) can access. A successful request from a client means that the kernel has acknowledged the notification and will send it to the service. Since the moment of the notification's delivery is not deterministic, the clients can subscribe a callback that the service can call once the request was performed. The two functions used to register the callbacks are:

- `int ipc_register_service_callback (subscribe_upcall callback, void *ud)` – registers the callback function that will be called within the service when a client makes a request;

- `int ipc_register_client_callback(int svc_id, subscribe_upcall callback, void *ud)` – registers the callback function that will be called within the client when the service notifies it.

To notify the service or the client, applications need to use other two functions:

- `int ipc_notify_client(int pid)` – sends a notification to the client with the specified process id;

- `int ipc_notify_service(int pid)` – sends a notification to the service with the specified process id.

To call the above functions, the client needs to identify the service process id (pid). The function that does this is `int ipc_discover(const char* pkg_name, int* svc_id)`. It receives the service's process name as a parameter and stores its pid in the `svc_id` variable. If no such service is found, `svc_id` will store a negative value.

Finally, the ipc library exposes a function that allows processes to share a buffer: `int ipc_share(int pid, void* base, int len)`. This is how processes can share information. The `base` parameter specifies the starting point of the buffer. For the micro:bit and Raspberry Pi Pico, it must be aligned to the value of `len`, while `len` must be a power-of-two value that is larger than 32, and 256 respectively. These constraints are due to the way the memory is shared on the ARM microcontrollers. Both the client or the service can call this function.

Note   The buffer length restrictions are determined by the memory protection of the MCU. For the micro:bit, the buffer has to be a minimum of 32 bytes and a power of two. For the Raspberry Pi Pico, the length has to be a minimum of 256 bytes and a power of two.

Use IPC to Implement a Userspace Driver

The IPC mechanism in Tock enables the development of userspace drivers. These are processes that are similar to the syscall drivers exposing APIs. For instance, we can replace the *LedMatrixText* capsule built in the previous chapters with a service that does the same actions. The service is a process that makes system calls to the *led* capsule and exposes IPC functions for displaying characters using the LED matrix.

The main advantage of creating a service instead of building a new capsule is that we do not have to alter the Tock kernel. In this case, we do all the development in the userspace while the kernel remains unchanged. The downside is that it usually occupies more space and runs a little slower than a capsule.

To exemplify how such a driver can be built, we will take the *LedMatrixText* capsule that we previously built and adapt it to run in userspace. In this case, we call the service *text_display*.

The *TextDisplay* Service

The *TextDisplay* service is designed to implement the functions necessary for lighting up LEDs to print characters on the matrix. To create the service files, we start with a new tock-project structure where the kernel setup is made for the device you choose to use: micro:bit or Raspberry Pi Pico. From there, we navigate to the **tock-project/applications** directory and create a new folder called **text_display**, together with a **main.c** file. This is where we place the service's code (Listing 11-1).

To implement the service, we first have to define the buffer where we store the text to be displayed, and similar to the capsule, we define the LEDs state for all letters and numbers. This is a 25-bit long binary code that identifies the state of each of the 25 LEDs of the matrix. The code is then interpreted by the display_code (uint32_t code) function, which turns on or off each LED according to the binary value.

Listing 11-1. The definitions in the text_display application

```
#include <stdio.h>
#include <ctype.h>
#include <timer.h>
#include <led.h>
#include <ipc.h>

#define NUM_LEDS 25
#define BUFFER_LEN 50

static char BUFFER[BUFFER_LEN];

#define MIN(a,b) (a<b?a:b)

const uint32_t DIGITS[] = {
    // 0
    0b11111100111101011100111111,
    // 1
    0b00100011000010000010001110,
    //...
};
const uint32_t LETTERS[] = {
    // A
    0b01110100011111111000110001,
    // B
    0b11111100011111101000111111,
    // ...
};

static void display_code (uint32_t code) {
 int led_index = 0;
```

```
for(led_index=0;led_index<NUM_LEDS;led_index++)
{
   if((((code>>(NUM_LEDS-1-led_index))&0x1)==1)
   {
     led_on(led_index);
   }
   else
   {
     led_off(led_index);
   }
 }
}
```

Further on, we implement the main functions necessary for writing the characters: display and clear, as illustrated in Listing 11-2. While clear simply turns off all the LEDs, display transforms the received character to uppercase, then calls display_code to light up the matrix LEDs accordingly. We clear the display if the character passed as a parameter is neither a letter nor a digit.

Note   The display function prints only one character.

Listing 11-2. The implementation of the display and clear functions

```
static void clear(void) {
 int led_index = 0;
 for(led_index=0;led_index<NUM_LEDS;led_index++)
 {
    led_off(led_index);
  }
}
```

```
static void display(char digit_or_letter) {
  digit_or_letter = toupper(digit_or_letter);
  if (digit_or_letter >= '0' && digit_or_letter <= '9') {
    display_code(DIGITS[digit_or_letter - '0']);
  }
  else if (digit_or_letter >= 'A' && digit_or_letter <= 'Z') {
    display_code(LETTERS[digit_or_letter-'A']);
  }
  else {
    clear();
  }
}
```

Next, we need to define a communication protocol between the clients and the service. For this service, the protocol is fairly simple. The client shares a buffer that contains a NULL-terminated string and notifies the service. The service receives the notification and copies the received bytes from the shared buffer to its own buffer. The number of copied bytes is the minimum between the length of the string stored within the buffer and the length of the service's own buffer. In this way, we make sure that the service does not access memory outside the buffer.

Note   Tock's inter-process communication mechanism does not define any communication protocol between processes. It only allows processes to share buffers and notify each other. It is up to the processes' developers to establish communication rules and data formats to interpret the data from the shared buffer. This is similar to Linux's shared memory.

Finally, we need to implement the `main` function, where we tell the service to listen for requests from other processes, retrieve the incoming text and display it character by character.

To do this, we first register a service callback function which is called each time a client sends a notification to the service. The callback function receives the buffer containing the text to be displayed as a parameter. When called, it copies the data in the local buffer and notifies the client when it's done (Listing 11-3).

Listing 11-3. The service callback function

```
static void ipc_callback(
     int pid,
     int len,
     int buf,
     __attribute__((unused)) void* ud
) {
  // update the buffer with data from an app
  const char *buffer = (const char *)buf;

  if (buffer != NULL) {
    strncpy (
       BUFFER, buffer, MIN(BUFFER_LEN, len)
    );
  }
  // notify the app that the service has copied
  // the data from the shared buffer
  // use while to make sure we notify the
  // application
  while (
     ipc_notify_client(pid)!=RETURNCODE_SUCCESS
  ) {};
}
```

An important aspect is the use of while when notifying the client. Notifications are sent using scheduled upcalls. If the client's task queue is full when the service tries to notify it, the ipc_notify_client function returns an error. The service should try to resend the notification. This is useful as the client might be stuck while waiting for it. An improvement is to try to send it a few times with an incremental delay between several retries and then give up.

After registering the service callback, the main function keeps iterating the buffer and displaying each character every 300 milliseconds. When the callback function is called and the buffer is changed, the characters displayed will be the new ones (Listing 11-4).

Listing 11-4. The service's main function

```
int main(void) {
  int leds;
  int position = 0;
  int len = 0;
  bool should_clear = true;
  strcpy (BUFFER, "");

  if (led_count (&leds) == RETURNCODE_SUCCESS){
    if (leds >= 25){
      // register text_display.service
      ipc_register_service_callback(
          ipc_callback, NULL
      );
      // run the service
      while (true){
        len = strnlen (BUFFER, BUFFER_LEN);
        if (len == 0) {
          position = 0;
```

```
         if (should_clear){
           should_clear = false;
           clear ();
         }
       }
       else if (position < len) {
         display (BUFFER[position]);
         should_clear = true;
         position = (position + 1) % len;
       }
       else{
           position = 0;
         display (BUFFER[position]);
         should_clear = true;
         position = (position + 1) % len;
       }
       delay_ms(300);
     }
   }
   else{
     printf ("text_display: Expected 25 LEDs, available
     %d\n", leds);
   }
 }
 else{
   printf ("text_display: LEDs driver is not available\n");
 }
 return 0;
}
```

Finally, we create the Makefile for the service (Listing 11-5). Because we want to identify the process under the name *text_display.service*, we use the PACKAGE_NAME variable to call the package like that.

Listing 11-5. The Makefile for the service

```
PACKAGE_NAME = text_display.service

# Specify this directory relative to the current #application.
TOCK_USERLAND_BASE_DIR = ../../../libtock-c

# External libraries used
# EXTERN_LIBS += ../drivers

# Which files to compile.
C_SRCS := $(wildcard *.c)

# Include path for drivers library
override CFLAGS += -I../drivers

# Include userland master makefile. Contains
# rules and flags for actually building the
# application.
include $(TOCK_USERLAND_BASE_DIR)/AppMakefile.mk

# Build the drivers
../drivers/build/cortex-m0/drivers.a:
	make -f ../drivers/Makefile

# Clean drivers folder
clean::
	rm -rf ../drivers/build
```

The Service API

Similarly to building a capsule API, we can create an interface for accessing the service. To be more specific, we create a local library that exposes two generic functions that the other processes can call. Therefore, we abstract the service interface and the callback functions specific to the IPC mechanism.

In our case, we call that library *text_display* and place it in the **tock-project/applications/drivers** folder.

We first define the two functions inside text_display.h (Listing 11-6). These are:

- bool text_display_is_present (void) - returns true if the process associated to text_display.service exists and has registered as a service;

- int text_display_print (const char *buffer) - asks the service to display a text.

Listing 11-6. The contents of text_display.h

```
#pragma once
#include <tock.h>
#define DISPLAY_BUFFER_LEN 64

#ifdef __cplusplus
extern "C" {
#endif

// verify if the service is present
bool text_display_is_present (void);

// display a test
int text_display_print (const char *buffer);
```

```
#ifdef __cplusplus
}
#endif
```

For the implementation, after importing the necessary libraries, we define the buffer that stores the text that will be shared with the service. According to the sharing mechanism constraints, we declare the buffer as 64 bytes and align it accordingly (Listing 11-7). We also store the pid of the service in the text_display_service variable. If this equals -1, the service does not exist.

Listing 11-7. The buffer and service status variables declaration

```
#include "text_display.h"
#include <tock.h>
#include <ipc.h>

char display_buffer[DISPLAY_BUFFER_LEN] __attribute__
((aligned(64)));
int text_display_service = -1;
```

The first function that we need to implement is designed to search for the *text_display* service, store its pid into the text_display_service variable and return true if found, as shown in Listing 11-8.

Listing 11-8. The function that searches for the text_display service

```
bool text_display_is_present (void) {
  // verifies if the service is present and
  // and registers its id
  return ipc_discover ("text_display.service", &text_display_
  service) == RETURNCODE_SUCCESS;
}
```

The second function the library exposes is designed to receive a text as a parameter and pass it to the service. This is done using the ipc_share function. Once the buffer is shared, the process registers a callback that the service calls when it has saved the data from the buffer. The process yields until that notification is emitted by the service. Once the service is done copying the contents of the buffer, the process stops sharing it, as illustrated in Listing 11-9.

Caution   The client has to register the service callback before it issues a notification to the service, otherwise the service might schedule a notification that the client will not receive.

Listing 11-9. The implementation of the text_display function

```
static void ipc_callback(
  __attribute__((unused)) int pid,
  __attribute__((unused)) int len,
  __attribute__((unused)) int buf,
  void* ud) {
  bool *done = (bool*)ud;
  *done = true;
}

int text_display_print (const char *buffer) {
  int ret = RETURNCODE_SUCCESS;
  bool done = false;

  // if the service ID has not yet been
  // registered, try to register it
  if (text_display_service == -1){
   text_display_is_present();
  }
```

```
// if the service is present, display the text
if (text_display_service){
 // copy the text into the shared buffer
 strncpy (
   display_buffer, buffer, DISPLAY_BUFFER_LEN
 );

 // share the buffer with the service
 // the buffer should not be accessed anymore
 ret = ipc_share(
   text_display_service,
   display_buffer,
   DISPLAY_BUFFER_LEN
 );
 if (ret == RETURNCODE_SUCCESS) {
  // register the service client callback to
  // get notified when the service buffer has
  // finished copying the data
  ret = ipc_register_client_callback (
   text_display_service,
   ipc_callback,
   &done
  );
  if (ret == RETURNCODE_SUCCESS){
    // notify the service to display the text
   ret = ipc_notify_service (
     text_display_service
   );
   if (ret == RETURNCODE_SUCCESS) {
     // wait for the service to copy the text
     // from the shared buffer to its own
     yield_for(&done);
```

```
    }
  }
  // stop sharing the buffer so that it becomes
  // accesible to the application
  ipc_share(text_display_service, NULL, 0);
  }
 }
 return ret;
}
```

The **Makefile** for the library is fairly simple and includes the necessary dependencies (Listing 11-10).

Listing 11-10. The library Makefile

```
# Base folder definitions
TOCK_USERLAND_BASE_DIR ?= ../../../libtock-c
LIBNAME := drivers
$(LIBNAME)_DIR := $(TOCK_USERLAND_BASE_DIR)/../chapter_11/
applications/$(LIBNAME)

# List all C and Assembly files
$(LIBNAME)_SRCS  := $(wildcard $($(LIBNAME)_DIR)/*.c)

override CFLAGS += -I$(TOCK_USERLAND_BASE_DIR)/libtock

include $(TOCK_USERLAND_BASE_DIR)/TockLibrary.mk
```

The Client Process

Now that the service and its API are defined, we can create a regular application that accesses the service to print a string to the matrix.

We create the application in the **tock-project/applications/example_ app** folder. Here, we need to change the **main.c** file so it includes the *text_display* library, then we check if the *text_display* service is running. If so, we ask it to display a character sequence by calling the text_display_ print function, as shown in Listing 11-11.

Listing 11-11. The client process implementation

```
#include <stdio.h>
#include <timer.h>
#include "text_display.h"

int main(void) {
  if (text_display_is_present()){
   text_display_print ("Hello World from the Microbit");
  } else {
    printf ("Error: the text_display.service service is not
    present\n");
  }
  return 0;
}
```

By compiling the two applications, the service and the client, and deploying them, we can notice the text being displayed on the matrix.

Summary

Tock's implementation supports a mechanism that enables processes to exchange information. This is done using a client-server architecture, where a process waits for others to issue commands. That process is called a service, while the others are the clients. However, in contrast to the classical client-server architecture, the service can also send notifications to the clients, independently from their requests. Data sharing between the clients and the service is implemented in a similar way to Linux's shared memory mechanism.

By leveraging the inter-process communication (IPC) mechanism, we can create userspace services that function like, and replace the kernel capsules. This way, we can limit our contribution to the userspace without interfering with the kernel.

To exemplify this, we have translated the *LedMatrixText* capsule created in the previous chapter to a userspace service together with an API that other processes can access.

CHAPTER 12

Tock Systems Management

So far, the chapters in this book have focused on application and system development using Tock. In a development environment, deploying a custom Tock system involves building the source code, bundling the applications with the kernel, and finally deploying the binaries in an easy to debug and monitor manner. We use tools such as OpenOCD and gdb to achieve this.

However, in the *Getting Started with Tock* chapter, we installed the tockloader utility as an alternative tool for deploying the Tock kernel and applications. Tockloader is best used in production environments for managing Tock systems. It is a command-line tool that supports various operations for inspecting and controlling the applications running on top of the Tock operating system.

Running Tockloader

The instructions in chapter 5: *Getting Started with Tock* include the installation of tockloader. To ensure that you have it installed on your system, either a Raspberry Pi device or your computer, based on your development setup, you need to open a terminal and run the following command: `tockloader --v`. This will display the tockloader version.

© Alexandru Radovici and Ioana Culic 2022
A. Radovici and I. Culic, *Getting Started with Secure Embedded Systems*,
https://doi.org/10.1007/978-1-4842-7789-8_12

In case you cannot run the command, tockloader is not installed on the system. To install it, run the first command in Listing 12-1. The second command is optional and is only used to enable tab completion in the shell.

Caution   Python3 and pip3 are required to install tockloader.

Listing 12-1. Install tockloader

```
$ pip3 install tockloader –user
$ register-python-argcomplete tockloader >> ~/.bashrc
```

Caution   Please make sure to use the tockloader version 1.8.0 or newer. Use `tockloader --version` to verify the version that you have installed.

Tockloader can be used both with the micro:bit and the Raspberry Pi Pico, but each device requires some specific operations beforehand. Further on, we will detail each of these necessary steps.

Note   Because the Raspberry Pi Pico does not use tock-bootloader (yet) and has no USB support (yet), the only way to control the Raspberry Pi Pico using the tockloader is directly from a Raspberry Pi.

Use tockloader with the micro:bit

The micro:bit can be controlled using tockloader as long as a custom Tock bootloader is flashed on the device or if OpenOCD is installed on your system. In general, the bootloader is a piece of software that runs first when the device is powered on. This is the software that launches the operating system. The tock-bootloader loads the Tock operating system. Before starting Tock, the tock-bootloader is capable of interacting with the tockloader utility. It can receive and execute commands coming via tockloader.

There are two ways of flashing the Tock bootloader on the device:

- By drag-and-drop via USB;

- Using openocd over the USB connection.

The first approach relies on connecting the micro:bit to the computer as an external USB device. This happens automatically when any micro:bit is connected to a computer. The next step is to copy the bootloader binary on the device. The easiest way to obtain the binary is to download it directly.[1] However, we can also choose to download and compile the source code (Listing 12-2).

Listing 12-2. Compile the Tock bootloader

```
$ git clone https://github.com/tock/tock-bootloader.git
$ cd tock-bootloader
$ cd boards/microbit_v2-bootloader
$ make
```

After the compilation, the tock-bootloader binary is found under the following path: **tock-bootloader/target/thumbv7em-none-eabi/release/microbit_v2-bootloader.bin**.

To flash the binary on the device, we just drag and drop the binary on the *MICROBIT* flash drive that appears when you connect the device.

If we use OpenOCD to flash the bootloader, the straightforward solution is to navigate to the **tock/boards/microbit_v2** folder and run the make flash-bootloader command.

---

[1] https://github.com/tock/tock-bootloader/releases/download/microbit_
v2-vv1.1.1/tock-bootloader.microbit_v2.vv1.1.1.bin

On the other hand, we can continue from the last step of Listing 12-2 and run make flash inside the **tock-bootloader/boards/microbit_v2-bootloader** folder. This will deploy the generated binary on the device.

To verify if the Tock bootloader was correctly flashed on the device, we press and hold the A button while pressing and releasing the reset button. This will reset the device and start the bootloader. When this happens, the microphone LED lights up.

Caution   If you try to enter the bootloader mode and the microphone LED does not light up, there is a problem, and you cannot proceed to the next step. A possible solution is to try to flash the Tock bootloader again.

Once the Tock bootloader is flashed on the device, we can run tockloader commands to control the micro:bit as long as the bootloader is running.

To test this, we open a terminal and run the command in Listing 12-3. This will display information about the device.

Listing 12-3. Run tockloader listen for the micro:bit

```
$ tockloader info [--serial]
[INFO   ] No device name specified. Using default name "tock".
[INFO   ] No serial port with device name "tock" found.
[INFO   ] Found 3 serial ports.
Multiple serial port options found. Which would you like to use?
[0]  /dev/cu.SOC - n/a
[1]  /dev/cu.MALS - n/a
[2]  /dev/cu.usbmodem1462302 - "BBC micro:bit CMSIS-DAP" - mbed
Serial Port
```

```
Which option? [0] 2
[INFO   ] Using "/dev/cu.usbmodem1462302 - "BBC micro:bit
CMSIS-DAP" - mbed Serial Port".
tockloader version: 1.8.0
[STATUS ] Showing all properties of the board...
Apps:
[INFO   ] No found apps.
Attributes:
00:     board = microbit_v2
01:      arch = cortex-m4
02:   appaddr = 0x40000
03: boothash = d07821e78b75d811de62f997de51808a50c38395
```

Caution   Before running any of tockloader commands, make sure you are in the bootloader mode by checking the microphone LED.

Troubleshooting

When using the micro:bit, tockloader is able to communicate with the device using two channels. It can either communicate with tock-bootloader through what is called the serial channel, or it can use openocd directly. The second way is faster as it allows tockloader to access the flash directly but does require OpenOCD to be installed.

As speed might be critical, tockloader will always try to use the fastest channel that is available. This means that it will first verify if OpenOCD is installed, and if so, it will try to use it. Another advantage of using OpenOCD is that the micro:bit does not need to run tock-bootloader.

While openocd has several versions available, depending on your operating system, tockloader might encounter some errors. At the time of writing, tockloader is not able to fallback to another channel if OpenOCD fails. It will simply exit with an error. Add --serial to the command line to force tockloader to use the serial channel. Make sure that the micro:bit is in bootloader mode, meaning that the microphone LED is lightened up.

Depending on the size of the apps that you load, tockloader might fail to write them correctly when using openocd. If your device does not seem to function properly, make sure to verify the installed apps using `tockloader list`. If some apps are not present, upload them again using tockloader and adding --bundle-apps to the command line.

Use tockloader with the Raspberry Pi Pico

Running tockloader to control the Raspberry Pi Pico is possible only by using a Raspberry Pi as a control center since tockloader can only use the OpenOCD channel to communicate with the Pico board. This implies that tockloader and OpenOCD need to be installed on the Raspberry Pi to which the Pico is connected via the SWD pins. Once tockloader is installed, we can open a terminal on the Raspberry Pi and run the desired tockloader commands. No special bootloader is required.

In contrast to the micro:bit, where the serial connection is enough, for the Raspberry Pi Pico, we need to use OpenOCD as means of communication. What is more, tockloader cannot automatically identify the device that it needs to communicate with, so we have to specify this. As a result, all tockloader commands will be suffixed by --board `raspberry_pi_pico -openocd` (e.g., `tockloader flash img.bin --board raspberry_pi_pico -openocd`).

Flash the Kernel

The first operation we can make using tockloader is to flash the kernel on the device. This is appropriate for a production environment with a stable kernel version that needs to be flashed on many devices.

The first step in doing this is to obtain the binary kernel image to be flashed on the device. To get it, we navigate to the device folder and run the make command. In the case of the micro:bit, the generated image is **tock/target/thumbv7em-none-eabi/release/microbit_v2.bin**, and for the Raspberry Pi Pico, it is **tock/target/thumbv6m-none-eabi/release/ raspberry_pi_pico. .bin**.

Once we have the binary file, to flash it on the micro:bit, we run the command in Listing 12-4.

Listing 12-4. Flash the Tock kernel on the micro:bit using tockloader

```
$ tockloader flash microbit_v2.bin
[INFO   ] No device name specified. Using default name "tock".
[INFO   ] No serial port with device name "tock" found.
[INFO   ] Found 3 serial ports.
Multiple serial port options found. Which would you like to use?
[0]   /dev/cu.SOC - n/a
[1]   /dev/cu.MALS - n/a
[2]   /dev/cu.usbmodem1462302 - "BBC micro:bit CMSIS-DAP" - mbed
Serial Port

Which option? [0] 2
[INFO   ] Using "/dev/cu.usbmodem1462302 - "BBC micro:bit
CMSIS-DAP" - mbed Serial Port".
[STATUS ] Flashing binary to board...
[INFO   ] CRC check passed. Binaries successfully loaded.
[INFO   ] Finished in 43.729 seconds
```

For the Raspberry Pi Pico, the command is more complex (Listing 12-5). Besides the need to specify the board type and add OpenOCD as deployment means, we also have to add the --address followed by a hexadecimal value. This is the starting address where the kernel needs to be flashed. If we do not mention it, tockloader will try to flash the binary at address 0, which is not a valid flash address for the Raspberry Pi Pico.

Listing 12-5. Flash the Tock kernel on the Raspberry Pi Pico using tockloader

```
$ tockloader flash raspberry_pi_pico.bin --board raspberry_pi_
pico --openocd --address 0x10000000
```

Device Console

Tockloader can also be used to listen for messages coming from the devices over a serial connection. In this case, the command is `tockloader listen`. If we run this command, and then reset the device, we can notice some kernel messages displayed, as shown in Listing 12-6.

Listing 12-6. Print kernel information using tockloader listen

```
$ tockloader listen
...
[INFO   ] Listening for serial output.
Press any key to start the process console...
Initialization complete. Entering main loop.
```

Tip   `tockloader listen` is the only command that can to be run when using the micro:bit without bringing it into bootloader mode.

Install/Remove Applications

The next step, after flashing the kernel on the device, is to deploy applications. The advantage of the Tock architecture is that each application is a separate executable file and can be built and deployed independently from the kernel.

Note   Starting with Tock 2.0, the terminology refers to applications as a collection of one or more processes. Tockloader refers to an application as the executable file (TBF) used by Tock to run a process. By saying that we install an application, we mean that we upload a TBF file that contains the code and data.

To get started, we create two applications, one that makes the onboard LEDs blink and one that prints a message in the console using printf (Listing 12-7).

Listing 12-7. The hello application

```
#include <stdio.h>

int main(void){
  printf ("Hello Tock!\n");
}
```

We name the first application folder **blink** and the second **hello**, then we build each of them by using the make command in each application's folder (Listing 12-8).

Listing 12-8. Built the blink application

```
$ cd tock-project/applications/blink
$ make
```

```
...
Application size report for target cortex-m7:
   text    data    bss    dec    hex    filename
   3996    252    2400   6648   19f8   build/cortex-m7/
                                       cortex-m7.elf
```

Tockloader Install

Once we have obtained the tab files, we install them using the tockloader install command, as illustrated in Listing 12-9. By running tockloader listen, we can view the second process' output while the first application's LED is blinking.

Listing 12-9. Install two applications on the device

```
$ tockloader install build/blink.tab
[STATUS ] Installing app on the board...
[INFO   ] Flashing app blink binary to board.
[INFO   ] CRC check passed. Binaries successfully loaded.
[INFO   ] Finished in 5.651 seconds
$ tockloader install build/hello.tab
[STATUS ] Installing app on the board...
...
$ tockloader listen
... (we reset the device)
Hello Tock!
```

When running tockloader install without any TAB file, tockloader will search all the available tab files in the current folder and its subfolders and install all of them.

Tockloader Uninstall

To remove an application from the system, we run `tockloader uninstall` followed by its name. The example in Listing 12-10 removes the **hello** application.

Listing 12-10. Uninstall an application from the system

```
$ tockloader uninstall hello
[STATUS ] Removing app(s) hello from board...

[STATUS ] Attempting to uninstall:
[STATUS ]    - hello
[STATUS ] Uninstall complete.
[INFO   ] Finished in 2.137 seconds
```

Running tockloader uninstall without any application name will make tockloader present us the list of installed applications and ask us which one to delete.

Update an Application

When changing an application, we can redeploy it by using the `tockloader update` command. To test it, we can change the blink timing for the **blink** application and update it (Listing 12-11).

Listing 12-11. Update the blink application

```
$ make
. . .
$ tockloader update build/blink.tab
[STATUS ] Updating application on the board...
[INFO   ] Flashing app blink binary to board.
[INFO   ] CRC check passed. Binaries successfully loaded.
[INFO   ] Finished in 7.182 seconds
```

Inspect the Applications

So far, we have used tockloader to upload and delete the applications that run on the device. Besides these capabilities, tockloader can also be used to inspect the system and get details about its applications.

Among the operations supported are: list the installed applications or inspect the tab file associated with an app.

List Applications

Using tockloader list (Listing 12-12), we can print all the applications running on a device together with the following details about them:

- Name – the name of the displayed application;

- Enabled – if equals to True, the application will start automatically after the device boots; otherwise, the application needs to be enabled before it is started;

- Sticky – if equals to True, uninstalling the application requires the --force flag.

Listing 12-12. Tockloader list output

```
$tockloader list
[INFO   ] Using "/dev/cu.usbmodem1462402 - "BBC micro:bit
CMSIS-DAP" - mbed Serial Port".

┌─────────────────────────────────────────────────────────┐
│ App 0                                                     │
└─────────────────────────────────────────────────────────┘

  Name:                  blink
  Enabled:               True
  Sticky:                False
  Total Size in Flash:   8192 bytes
```

```
┌─────────────────────────────────────────────────────┐
│ App 1                                               │
└─────────────────────────────────────────────────────┘
  Name:                  hello
  Enabled:               True
  Sticky:                False
  Total Size in Flash:   2048 bytes
```

Inspect TAB Files

TAB files are specific to Tock. As their name states, Tock Application Bundle files contain the Tock application binaries for all supported architectures. By examining these, we can find details such as the included architectures or the date when it was built. We can also dig in and display information about a specific architecture TBF. Listing 12-13 illustrates the output of the tockloader inspect-tab command.

Listing 12-13. Inspect an example TAB file using tockloader

```
$ tockloader inspect-tab build/blink.tab
[STATUS ] Inspecting TABs...
TAB: blink
  build-date: 2021-08-10 12:11:25+00:00
  minimum-tock-kernel-version: 2.0
  only-for-boards:
  tab-version: 1
  included architectures: cortex-m0, cortex-m3, cortex-m4,
  cortex-m7

Which TBF to inspect further?
[0]     cortex-m0
[1]     cortex-m3
[2]     cortex-m4
```

```
[3]     cortex-m7
[4]     None

Which option? [0] 3

cortex-m7:
  version             : 2
  header_size         : 52           0x34
  total_size          : 8192         0x2000
  checksum            : 0x6e505e1f
  flags               : 1            0x1
    enabled           : Yes
    sticky            : No
  TLV: Main (1)
    init_fn_offset    : 41           0x29
    protected_size    : 0            0x0
    minimum_ram_size  : 4660         0x1234
  TLV: Package Name (3)
    package_name      : blink
  TLV: Kernel Version (8)
    kernel_major      : 2
    kernel_minor      : 0
    kernel version    : ^2.0
```

Application Configurations

When deploying a new application, we can specify some of the
characteristics analyzed above. To be more specific, tockloader
enables us to set if a process should start at boot or if it can be easily
uninstalled or not.

Enable/Disable an Application

By enabling or disabling an application, we specify if it should be loaded after the device boots or not. By default, the applications are deployed with the enabled flag set to True. However, by using the command tockloader disable-app [app_name], we can disable it. To enable back the application, we can use the tockloader enable-app [app_name] command.

Listing 12-14 illustrates how the two work using the *blink* application. To outline the result, we use tockloader list to print the application details. What is more, after disabling the app, we can reset the device and notice that the LED stops blinking.

Listing 12-14. Disable and enable an application using tockloader

```
$ tockloader disable-app blink
$ tockloader list
┌─────────────────────────────────────────────────────────────┐
│ App 1                                                       │
└─────────────────────────────────────────────────────────────┘
  Name:                 blink
  Enabled:              False
  Sticky:               False
  Total Size in Flash:  2048 bytes
$ tockloader enable-app blink
$ tockloader list
┌─────────────────────────────────────────────────────────────┐
│ App 1                                                       │
└─────────────────────────────────────────────────────────────┘
  Name:                 blink
  Enabled:              True
  Sticky:               False
  Total Size in Flash:  2048 bytes
```

Sticky Applications

Another important characteristic of the applications running on Tock systems is *stickiness*. This refers to how easily we can remove an application from the system. If the sticky flag is set to True, uninstalling that application requires the --force flag. By default, applications are not sticky.

Listing 12-15 illustrates the command required to set the sticky flag to True and the result if we try to uninstall that application.

Listing 12-15. Set an application's sticky flag to True

```
$ tockloader sticky-app example_app
$ tockloader uninstall example_app
[INFO] Not removing app "example_app" because it is sticky.
[INFO] To remove this you need to include the --force option.
```

To make a sticky app non-sticky, we need to run the tockloader unsticky-app [app_name] command.

Fault Policies

The Tock architecture is designed to allow for multiple concurrent processes run independently. The main advantage is that if one process fails, the others continue to run. However, to ensure this behavior, we need to pay attention to the system's *fault policy*.

Tock defines several policies based on which the system's behavior changes when a process crashes:

- PanicFaultPolicy – If a process faults, the entire system panics;

- StopFaultPolicy – If a process faults, the system stops it and continues executing the rest of the processes;

- StopWithDebugFaultPolicy – If a process faults, the system stops it and prints a debug message. It then continues to execute the rest of the processes;

- RestartFaultPolicy – If a process faults, the system will restart it;

- TresholdRestartFaultPolicy – It is a custom ProcessFaultPolicy implementation that uses a threshold based on which the process will be restarted or not. If the process has been restarted more times than the threshold, the system will stop trying to restart it.

Note   The fault policies are defined and documented in the **tock/ kernel/src/process_policies.rs** file.

By default, most of the board implementations set the fault policy to *PanicFaultPolicy*. To exemplify it, we first create a simple application that crashes with a NULL pointer exception (Listing 12-16).

Listing 12-16. Sample application that crashes

```
#include <stdio.h>

int main(void){
  int *array;
  printf ("%d", array[0]);
}
```

We build the application and deploy it on the device. To monitor how other processes behave, we also deploy the blink application. After the two apps are deployed, we run tockloader listen, reset the device and notice the error message (Listing 12-17). What is more, we can notice that the panic LED is blinking. This is because the kernel is configured to fault if any of the processes crashes.

Listing 12-17. Listen for serial output when a process crashes and the kernel is using the PanicFaultPolicy

```
$ tockloader listen
[INFO   ] Using "/dev/cu.usbmodem1462402 - "BBC micro:bit
CMSIS-DAP" - mbed Serial Port".
[INFO   ] Listening for serial output.
Initialization complete. Entering main loop.

panicked at 'Process example_app2 had a fault', kernel/src/
process_standard.rs:322:17
        Kernel version release-2.0
```

To set a more relaxed fault policy, which will make the system continue running even when a process crashes, we have to change a line in the board's implementation **main.rs** file to set FAULT_RESPONSE to StopFaultPolicy. For the micro:bit, the file is **tock/boards/microbit_v2/main.rs,** and the line we need to change is 63 (Listing 12-18). For the Raspberry Pi Pico, we need to change line 54 in the **tock/boards/raspberry_pi_pico/main.rs** file.

Listing 12-18. Set the fault response to StopFaultPolicy

```
const FAULT_RESPONSE: kernel::process::StopFaultPolicy =
    kernel::process::StopFaultPolicy {};
```

Once the policy is changed, we need to recompile the kernel and reflash it on the device. Then, we can notice that even though one of the processes crashes, the other keeps running.

Write a Custom FaultPolicy

The fault policies defined in the Tock kernel have a simple behavior. They mainly print the information about the fault encountered and stop or restart the process. However, if we aim to have a more complex fault policy that does something else than the default ones, we can implement a custom fault policy.

Similarly to the existing policies, the custom one has to implement the ProcessFaultPolicy trait. This is done in the **main.rs** file in the device folder of the tock kernel. In the case of the Raspberry Pi Pico, the path is **project/kernel/raspberry_pi_pico/src/main.rs**, while for the micro:bit the path is **project/kernel/microbit_v2/src/main.rs**.

The example we present further on can be implemented for both devices. The aim is to create a fault policy, called CountFaultPolicy that sums up the faults of a process and prints the total number each time the process faults. After a fault is encountered, the process will restart.

The first step in building the CustomFaultPolicy is to import the ProcessFaultPolicy trait and other adjacent traits and modules necessary: use kernel::process::{self, Process, ProcessFaultPolicy};.

Further on, we create the CustomFaultPolicy structure that stores the faults count in the count variable. We use a container to store the value, as it has to be mutable while the trait provides an immutable reference to it (&self). This is done with the help of the Cell wrapper. The definition and implementation of the structure are presented in Listing 12-19.

Listing 12-19. The definition and implementation of the CustomFaultPolicy structure

```
use kernel::process::{
    self, Process, ProcessFaultPolicy
};
```

```
use core::cell::Cell;

struct CountFaultPolicy {
    count: Cell<u32>
}

impl CountFaultPolicy {
    pub const fn new() -> CountFaultPolicy {
        CountFaultPolicy {
            count: Cell::new(0)
        }
    }
}
```

Further on, we implement the ProcessFaultPolicy trait for the newly defined structure (Listing 12-20). This requires implementing the action function, where the count variable is incremented and printed. Finally, we return Restart as the action for handling the fault. According to tock's definition in the **process.rs** file, Restart will lead to a reset in the process' memory and rescheduling the process from its init function.

Listing 12-20. The ProcessFaultPolicy implementation of CountFaultPolicy

```
impl ProcessFaultPolicy for MyFaultPolicy {
    fn action (&self, _: &dyn Process) ->
                        process::FaultAction {
        self.count.set (self.count.get() + 1);
        debug!(
            "Process has crashed {} times.",
            self.count.get()
        );
        process::FaultAction::Restart
    }
}
```

Finally, we need to initialize the structure and add it to the processes loaded by the kernel. Here, we first need to remove the old initialization that can be found around line 60 in the main.rs file for either devices:

```
const FAULT_RESPONSE: kernel::procs::PanicFaultPolicy
        = kernel::procs::PanicFaultPolicy {};
```

We comment this line and navigate to the line where kernel::process::load_processes() is called (towards the end of the file). There, we instantiate the fault_response variable and add it to the processes list instead of &FAULT_RESPONSE (Listing 12-21).

Listing 12-21. Registering the new fault response

```
let fault_response = static_init!(
    CountFaultPolicy, CountFaultPolicy::new()
);

kernel::process::load_processes(
    board_kernel,
    /* ... */
    fault_response,
    &process_management_capability,
)
```

Now we can reflash the kernel and upload the same faulty process as in the previous example. After we run tockloader listen, we can notice the debug messages in the console.

Override the Fault Handler

Another way of customizing the fault handling system, different from implementing a custom FaultPolicy structure is to register a custom fault handler. While the first approach helps us customize how faults are handled, this can prevent the process from faulting. In this case, we catch the generated fault and handle it instead of the kernel. However, there are few cases when overriding the fault handler is necessary (ex. handle faults related to running instructions that are not implemented for the current processor).

Note   Overriding the fault handler is recommended only in exceptional cases. In general, we recommend sticking to the default implementation and allowing the process to fault.

To exemplify this process, we create a new handler that prints a debug message when a process crashes. For this, we first need to restore the **main.rs** file

Once we have the original file, we first have to implement the ProcessFault structure for our device in the device's **main.rs** file. Listing 12-22 illustrates the lines we need to add for the micro:bit device. In the case of the Raspberry Pi Pico, we have to replace **MicroBit** with **RaspberryPiPico**.

Listing 12-22. Implement the ProcessFault structure

```
use kernel::process
impl ProcessFault for MicroBit {
    fn process_fault_hook(
        &self, process: &dyn process::Process
    ) -> Result<(), ()> {
        debug!(
```

```
    "Our awesome process called {} faulted!",
    process.get_process_name()
    );
    Err(())
    }
}
```

To implement the ProcessFault trait, we need to create a process_
fault_hook function that is called when a process crashes. In our case,
we print the debug message, then return an empty error. The details on
how the trait needs to be implemented are found in the **tock/kernel/src/
platform/platform.rs** file.

The value returned by the process_fault_hook function determines
the kernel's actions when a process faults. If the function returns an error,
the kernel will apply the default configured policy. If the function returns
Ok, the kernel will allow the process to continue. If the process still faults,
the process_fault_hook function is called again. This function is mostly
used to implement custom MCU instructions that are not available in
hardware. Think of it more like the segmentation fault signal (SIGSEGV)
handler from Linux, just that it is implemented in the kernel instead of the
application.

The next step requires to register the new structure as part of the
device resource. This is done in the kernelResource implementation,
where type ProcessFault = () is replaced by ProcessFault = Self and
fn process_fault(&self) -> &Self::ProcessFault {&()} is replaced
by fn process_fault (&self) -> &Self::ProcessFault { &self }

Finally, we compile and reflash the kernel, upload the applications,
then run tockloader listen. When we restart the device, we can notice
the debug message we set previously.

Note   More details on implementing a custom fault handler can be found in the **tock/kernel/src/platform/platform.rs** file on lines 130-160.

System Information

When deploying an embedded system in production, monitoring it is an important aspect. Tockloader can be used to print information about a device. The printed details include applications' information, but also device attributes. Listing 12-23 outlines an example of the output obtained when running tockloader info.

Listing 12-23. Tockloader info output

```
$ tockloader info
[STATUS ] Showing all properties of the board...
Apps:
```

```
┌─────────────────────────────────────────────────┐
│                                                 ┐
│ App 0                                           │
│                                                 ┘
└─────────────────────────────────────────────────┘
```

```
  Name:                  example_app
  Enabled:               True
  Sticky:                True
  Total Size in Flash:   2048 bytes
  Address in Flash:      0x40000
     version             : 2
     header_size         : 48         0x30
     total_size          : 2048       0x800
     checksum            : 0x3243745e
     flags               : 3          0x3
```

```
        enabled              : Yes
        sticky               : Yes
     TLV: Main (1)
        init_fn_offset       : 41          0x29
        protected_size       : 0           0x0
        minimum_ram_size     : 6144        0x1800
     TLV: Package Name (3)
        package_name         : example_app
Attributes:
00:     board = microbit_v2
01:      arch = cortex-m4
02:   appaddr = 0x40000
03: boothash = d07821e78b75d811de62f997de51808a50c38395
```

We can also print only the board attributes by running the tockloader
list-attributes command.

Inspecting Processes

So far, we have used tockloader to inspect the system and the application
executable TBF and TAB files. Finally, we have a way of inspecting the
processes while they are running on the system. For this, we use the
process console, which is a capsule designed to interact with the Tock
kernel. The capsule reads the keyboard input and executes the commands
that are typed.

Caution   If the process console capsule is enabled, all the other
processes cannot reliably read keyboard input.

To interact with the process console, we first run `tockloader listen`, as seen in 12-24. The list of accepted commands is printed when the process console starts.

Note   After running `tockloader listen`, reset the device to see the process console output.

Listing 12-24. Print system information using tockloader listen

```
$ tockloader listen
...
[INFO   ] Listening for serial output.
Initialization complete. Entering main loop.
Press any key to start the process console...
Kernel version: 2.0 (build 686d8d3)
Welcome to the process console.
Valid commands are: help status list stop start fault
process kernel
```

System Status

By running the `status` command in the process console, we can view basic information about the system: the total number of processes installed, the total number of processes that are running on the system, and how many times the processes have been preempted because the allocated timeslice expired (Listing 12-25).

Listing 12-25. The output of the status command in the process console

```
[INFO   ] Listening for serial output.
Initialization complete. Entering main loop.
```

```
Press any key to start the process console...
Kernel version: 2.0 (build 686d8d3)
Welcome to the process console.
Valid commands are: help status list stop start fault
process kernel
```
status

```
Total processes: 3
Active processes: 3
Timeslice expirations: 301
```

List Processes

The process console also enables us to view a detailed list of all the processes running on the device. This is done by running the list command, which prints a table containing all the processes with the following characteristics:

- PID – the process identifier;

- Name – the process name;

- Quanta – the number of times the process was preempted because its timeslice expired;

- Syscalls – the number of system calls the process has made;

- Dropped Callbacks – the number of upcalls that capsules have tried schedule and were dropped because the task queue was full;

- Restarts – the number of times the process crashed and was restarted by the kernel;

- State – the process' state;

- Grants – the number of grants that were allocated
  for the process; this is out of the total number of
  defined grants.

Listing 12-26 illustrates the output of the command when three processes are running on the device. We can notice that one of the processes (*blink2*) makes a lot of system calls, and another (*blink*) does a lot of processing and has exceeded its allotted time quanta frequently.

Listing 12-26. The output of the list command

```
list

PID Name Qu.. Sys Dropped.. Restart State Grants
0   c_hello 0  8     0       0       Yielded 1/14
1   blink2  0  9823  0       0       Yielded 1/14
 2 blink    68730 3   0              0 Running 0/14
```

Control the System Processes

The start and stop commands receive as parameters the name of a process and, as their name suggests, they start or stop the specified process. The example in Listing 12-27 stops, then starts the blink process.

Listing 12-27. Stop and start a process using the process console

```
stop blink

Process blink stopped
start blink

Process blink resumed.
```

Another command that controls the processes' behavior is fault. This forces the specified process to enter a fault state, and the kernel to apply to fault policy.

Finally, by running the process [process_name] command
(Listing 12-28), we can print memory information about the specified process.

Listing 12-28. The output of the process command

```
process blink
```

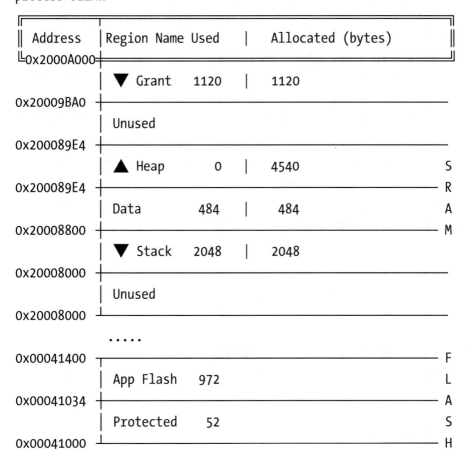

Kernel Memory

The last command the process console supports is meant to print the details about the kernel's memory, as shown in Listing 12-29.

Listing 12-29. The output of the kernel command

```
kernel
Kernel version: 2.0 (build 686d8d3)
```

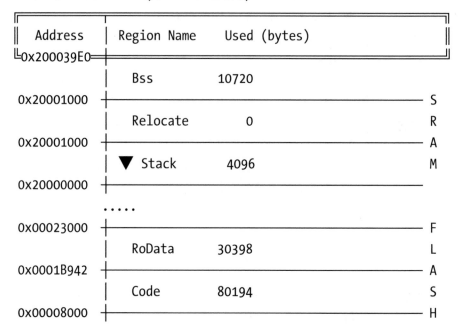

Summary

In this chapter, we focused on the means to configure and prepare our Tock-based systems for production release. By leveraging the tockloader tool and the process console capsule, we can flash the kernel, install/ uninstall applications, list applications and system details, and configure the running processes.

What is more, Tock allows us to configure system behavior related to fault handling by changing some parameters in the board's implementation file.

Tockloader has a large number of parameters and options that we can use to monitor and configure our systems, some of which were mentioned above. Further on, we recommend you read the official tockloader documentation[2] for the complete list of supported commands.

---

[2] https://github.com/tock/tockloader

Index

A

ADC library, 242
Advanced High-performance
        Bus (AHB), 15
Advanced Peripheral Bus (APB), 15
Advanced RISC Machine (ARM), 25
allocate_grant function, 336, 358
allow system call, 336
allow_readonly function, 362, 363
Apollo Guidance
        Computer (AGC), 2–5
Application Binary
        Interface (ABI), 50
Application Programming
        Interface (API), 50
app_state library, 257
Asynchronous system calls
    callback function, 72
    callback function returns, 71
    environment sensor, 69
    GPIO ports, 72
    process calls, 69
    read command, 70
    schedule, 71
    schedule/subscribe, 70
    system call pattern, 72
    yield system, 71

B

boards directory, 217
Bootloader software, 87

C

Capsule (Asynchronous)
    allow system call, 337–340
    buffer/share, 362–366
    command system call, 336
    command system, 366–370
    DigitLetterDisplay, 334, 335
    hardware components, 333, 334
    subscribe system call, 336
    TextDisplay driver, 341–343
    text displays
        character, 374
        hardware implementation,
            377, 378
        kernel structure, 375
        LED matrix, 371, 372
        signal application, 378, 380
    Tock drivers, 343–345
    writing capsule
        alarm field, 348, 349
        capsule's state, 360
        code, 345

© Alexandru Radovici and Ioana Culic 2022
A. Radovici and I. Culic, *Getting Started with Secure Embedded Systems*,
https://doi.org/10.1007/978-1-4842-7789-8

Printed in the United States
by Baker & Taylor Publisher Services